Cover: Teenaged OTC cadets at St Dunstan's College carrying out a practice assault on the eve of war. (*St Dunstan's College archive*)

Fonthill Media Language Policy

Fonthill Media publishes in the international English language market. One language edition is published worldwide. As there are minor differences in spelling and presentation, especially with regard to American English and British English, a policy is necessary to define which form of English to use. The Fonthill Policy is to use the form of English native to the author. Mike Osborne was born and educated in England; therefore British English has been adopted in this publication.

Fonthill Media Limited
Fonthill Media LLC
www.fonthill.media
books@fonthill.media

First published in the United Kingdom and the United States of America 2023

British Library Cataloguing in Publication Data:
A catalogue record for this book is available from the British Library

ISBN 978-1-78155-881-2

Typeset in 10pt on 13pt Sabon
Printed and bound in England

Acknowledgements

Grateful thanks are due to the following for permission to use images from their several school archive collections: Liz Larby at Greshams School; Elspeth Langsdale at Oundle School; Iain Macdowall at St Dunstan's College; Rachel Hassall at Sherborne Boys' School for images from the Old Shirburnian Society archive; Dorothy Goldsack at Sherborne Girls' School; and Beverley Matthews at Tonbridge School. Also, thanks go to Mick Wilks for his Auxiliary Unit operational base reconstruction; to Alan Beales of Bures; and to Mike Bardell for support and information. As ever, my wife, Pam, has supplied valuable advice and encouragement, and Alan, Jay, Josh, and Jamie at Fonthill Media have provided their customary high standard of professional expertise.

Contents

Glossary of Terms

AA	Anti-aircraft
AAA	Anti-aircraft Artillery (US Army)
AAOR	Anti-aircraft Operations Room
ACF	Army Cadet Force (from 1940, previously TCF)
ADCC	Air Defence Cadet Corps
ADEE	Air Defence Experimental Establishment
ADRDE	Air Defence Research & Development Establishment
AFS	Auxiliary Fire Service (amalgamated with NFS, 1941)
AFV	Armoured Fighting Vehicle
AI	Airborne Interception (radar)
AMES	Air Ministry Experimental Establishment (radar station)
ARP	Air Raid Precautions
ASDIC	Underwater sonar method of submarine detection
ASE	Admiralty Signals Establishment (research and development)
A/T	Anti-tank (gun, obstacle, etc.)
ATA	Air Transport Auxiliary (delivering new aircraft to airfields)
ATC	Air Training Corps (from 1941)
ATS	Auxiliary Territorial Service (later Women's Royal Army Corps)
BB	Boys' Brigade
BCF	British Concrete Federation (prefabricator of concrete buildings)
BEF	British Expeditionary Force (in France and Flanders 1939–40)
BD	Bomb Disposal (RE units)
BNCA	British National Cadet Association (managing body of cadets, 1923–42)
CBA	Council for British Archaeology
CCF	Combined Cadet Force, from 1948 (former Junior Officers' Training Corps)
CD	Civil Defence
CLB	Church Lads' Brigade

CTA	County Territorial Association (administrators of volunteer forces)
CO	Commanding Officer
CORB	Children's Overseas Reception Board (evacuation administration)
COSSAC	Chiefs of Staff Supreme Allied Commander
CV	*Curriculum Vitae*
DAS	Department of Agriculture for Scotland
DHS	Department of Health for Scotland
DORA	Defence of the Realm Act (legislation to expand government powers)
EA	Embarkation Area (pre-D-Day)
EMS	Emergency Medical Service (military hospitals)
FA	Field Artillery (US Army)
FANY	First Aid Nursing Yeomanry (catchall for women's paramilitary roles)
GC&CS	Government Code & Cipher School (Bletchley Park *Enigma* operation)
GCHQ	Government Communications Headquarters (successor to GC&CS)
GHQ	General Headquarters (national supreme Army command)
GL	Gun-laying (radar)
GLB	Girls' Life Brigade
GNTC	Girls' Nautical Training Corps
GOR	Gun Operations Room (AA direction and co-ordination)
GPO	General Post Office (national mail, telegraph and telephone systems)
GS	Grammar School
GWR	Great Western Railway
HAA	Heavy Anti-aircraft (gun, battery, regiment, etc.)
HE	High Explosive (shell, bomb, etc.)
HF/DF	High Frequency/Direction Finding (colloquially 'Huff-Duff')
HG	Home Guard
HMS	His Majesty's Ship (Royal Navy warship)
HO	Hostilities Only (RN personnel for only the duration of the war)
HS	High School (often a girls' grammar school)
ICI	Imperial Chemical Industries from 1926
IS	Infants' School
JS	Junior School
KRRC	King's Royal Rifle Corps (British Army infantry regiment)
LAA	Light Anti-aircraft (gun, battery, regiment, etc.)
LCC	London County Council (overall administration of London boroughs)
LDV	Local Defence Volunteers (forerunner of Home Guard)
LEA	Local Education Authority (local council responsible for schools)
MA	Marshalling Area (for pre-D-Day assembly of troops, vehicles, etc.)
MAP	Ministry of Aircraft Production
MI	Military Intelligence (MI5, MI6, MI19, MD1 departments etc.)
MoI	Ministry of Information (responsible for propaganda, disinformation, etc.)
MoS	Ministry of Supply

MT	Motor Transport
NAAFI	Navy, Army and Air Force Institute (canteens, welfare, etc.)
NATCG	National Association of Training Corps for Girls (umbrella organisation)
NCO	Non-commissioned officer (lance corporal, corporal, sergeant, etc.)
NFS	National Fire Service (amalgamated with AFS, 1941)
NHS	National Health Service (from 1948)
NUT	National Union of Teachers
OB	Operational Base (hideout for Auxiliary Unit patrol)
OCTU	Officer Cadet Training Unit (school for Hostilities Only prospective officers)
OSS	Office of Strategic Services (US equivalent of SOE)
OTC	Officers' Training Corps (Junior in schools, Senior in Higher Education)
PLUTO	Pipeline Under the Ocean (Bambi and Dumbo fuel pipelines into France)
PMC	Public Morality Council (social watchdog formed by LCC in 1899)
POW	Prisoner of War
PS	Primary School
PTSD	Post-Traumatic Stress Disorder (previously known as 'shell shock')
RAC	Royal Armoured Corps (tank regiments)
RAF	Royal Air Force (from 1918)
RAuxAF	Royal Auxiliary Air Force (from 1924)
RAFVR	Royal Air Force Volunteer Reserve (from 1936)
RAMC	Royal Army Medical Corps
RASC	Royal Army Service Corps (in the Second World War: catering, MT & logistics)
RDF	Radio Direction-Finding (later 'radar')
RE	Royal Engineers
REME	Royal Electrical & Mechanical Engineers (from 1942)
RMS	Royal Mail Ship (merchant marine)
RN	Royal Navy
RNAS	Royal Naval Air Station (Fleet Air Arm airfield)
RNR	Royal Naval Reserve (professional civilian seamen drafted into wartime RN)
RNVR	Royal Naval Volunteer Reserve (mainly HO officers, the 'Wavy Navy')
ROC	Royal Observer Corps (volunteer organisation reporting aircraft movements)
ROF	Royal Ordnance Factory (state-owned, often contractor-run, munitions plant)
RRDE	Radar Research & Development Establishment
RTR	Royal Tank Regiment
SCC	Sea Cadet Corps
SED	Scottish Education Department
SHAEF	Supreme Headquarters Allied Expeditionary Force (European theatre, 1943)

SIP	Self-igniting Phosphorus (No. 76 Grenade aka Albright & Wilson bomb)
SIS	Special Intelligence Service (aka MI6, UK foreign intelligence service)
SOAS	School of Oriental & African Studies (London University)
SOE	Special Operations Executive (from 1940, supporting resistance organisations)
SS	Steam Ship (merchant marine)
STS	Special Training School (for SOE personnel)
TA	Territorial Army (1920–39, resumed 1947, since 2014, Army Reserve)
TB	Tuberculosis
TCF	Territorial Cadet Force (1908–23, forerunner of ACF)
TRE	Telecommunications Research Establishment
TS	Training Ship (merchant marine)
ULTRA	The top-secret product of Bletchley Park's *Enigma* operation
USAF	United States Air Force (post-Second World War)
USAAF	United States Army Air Force (Second World War)
VAD	Voluntary Aid Detachment (volunteer nurses and medical auxiliaries)
VE	Victory in Europe (Day: 8 May 1945, commemorated annually)
VJ	Victory in Japan (Day: 15 August 1945, commemorated annually)
VTC	Volunteer Training Corps (First World War equivalent of Home Guard)
WAAF	Women's Auxiliary Air Force
WAC	Women's Army Corps (US Army from 1943)
WAEC	War Agricultural Executive Committee (co-ordinators of food production)
WJAC	Women's Junior Air Corps (from 1939)
WLA	Women's Land Army (volunteers in agriculture and forestry)
WRNS	Women's Royal Naval Service (colloquially 'Wrens')
W/T	Wireless Telegraphy (radio communication; originated by Marconi)
WVS	Women's Voluntary Service (from 1936; 'Royal' from 1966; now RVS)
YM/WCA	Young Men's/Women's Christian Association (welfare organisations)
ZAA	Anti-aircraft rocket batteries firing unrotated projectiles (UP)

Introduction

Britain fought the Second World War (referred to throughout this book as 'the war') as much on the Home Front as in the several foreign theatres of war. This inevitably meant that children and young people could not avoid involvement in the war effort or, tragically in many cases, becoming victims. In 1941, around 45 per cent of Britain's population was aged under thirty, making youth a much more significant, if—as teenagers (as a term) had as yet not been invented—largely unacknowledged segment of society. It would therefore prove of enormous value to involve youngsters in as many aspects of the war on the Home Front as was practicable. In 1942, all young people in the sixteen to eighteen age group were required to register with the government so that they might be channelled into an appropriate wartime activity. The school-leaving age stood at fourteen until the implementation of the 1944 Education Act raised it to fifteen, and the age of majority remained at twenty-one until 1968 when it was lowered to eighteen. Since only a small percentage of schoolchildren continued in any sort of education beyond the age of fourteen, the majority of the fourteen to eighteen cohorts was therefore available to serve the country in one way or another. For most of them, this meant through their employment as well as (at first voluntarily, and later as a requirement) through their involvement as members of, generally uniformed, pre-service training organisations.

It had all happened before. The Second World War witnessed a reprise of some aspects of the First World War (referred to throughout this book as the 'Great War') when schools, such as Newcastle's Royal GS, had been used as a base for the local Volunteer Training Corps (VTC) or, as at Portsmouth's Priory School, as hospitals; schoolchildren were mobilised as messengers for the police and the ARP service; underage schoolboys enlisted in the armed forces; Boy Scouts, Girl Guides, along with members of other uniformed youth organisations, took part in patriotic ceremonial, and carried out salvage collections and fundraising, activities for the war effort; Boy Scouts and others also guarded vulnerable points, monitored traffic movements, and took part in coast-watching duties; cadet units based in schools, factories, or VTC prepared youngsters for service in the armed forces; and youngsters worked in the Voluntary Aid Detachments (VAD) of the Red Cross and the St John's Ambulance. All these activities and circumstances would occur, once again, in the war under examination here, but to a far greater and more intense extent.

This book explores those ways in which young people, broadly in the twelve to eighteen age bracket, contributed to the war effort, and how the war affected their lives, taking the Home Front as its focus. Obviously, many young people went on to see active service as they reached the age for conscription, but this book confines itself to their contributions at home. Similarly, modern languages teachers such as Harry Ree, future professor of education at the University of York, who served in SOE with the French Resistance, or William Golding, the English teacher and Nobel Prize-winning novelist, who served as a naval officer from 1940–45, were only two of the thousands of teachers who saw active service, but whose exploits fall outside the scope of this present study. Large numbers of school buildings across the country were commandeered to serve a wide variety of functions and large numbers of them were damaged or destroyed by enemy action.

I have used a wide range of sources, the most important of which are referenced in the Bibliography or, sparingly, in the text. Recorded oral history and compilations of memoirs, along with the accounts recorded in the BBC's *People's War*, together provide some of the personal details that complement and illuminate the official version of events. Keith Strange's comprehensive and fascinating analysis of Cardiff schools' logbooks for the duration of the war provides the source for a short case study, which illustrates the main threads of the earlier part of Chapter 1, taking as its principal focus the disruption to schooling caused by the war. Many of the issues raised are also addressed in later chapters. Chapter 2 explores the extent to which school buildings were requisitioned by a range of different users, placing many of them on the front line in one way or another. Chapter 3 examines the contribution of youngsters to the defence of the nation: in the Home Guard based in schools or the wider community, and in their associated, highly secret Auxiliary Units; in ARP and the fire service; in the Royal Observer Corps; and in the armed services and the Merchant Marine. Young people had always, since the 1860s, enjoyed opportunities to become prepared for military service on a voluntary basis, but from 1942, such activity became more directed as, from the age of sixteen, participation in the Home Guard, cadet units, or other uniformed organisations became effectively obligatory for boys and girls alike. Chapter 4 examines the impact on schools of the enemy's continual bombing campaigns from the early hit-and-run tactics; through the various Blitz events of 1940–1, which devastated so many British cities; the Baedeker raids on cultural centres; the isolated and unexpected nuisance raids that came out of the blue; to the onslaughts of the V-1 'Doodlebug' flying bombs and the

V-2 ballistic missiles. Chapter 5 records the areas of the country's economic, social, and cultural life to which youngsters contributed either as employees or voluntarily through school or youth organisations. Appendices record some significant background facts. Throughout, I have sought to highlight the many ways in which young people contributed to the successful outcomes of the war, sacrificing their childhoods, their futures, and, sometimes, their lives.

Mike Osborne
Market Deeping
October 2021

1

The Context of Schooling during the Second World War

The dominant theme running through the school experience of the Second World War is one of disruption. This is reflected in the personal accounts of children who lived through the times and regretted their lack of education, expressing a genuinely felt sense of deprivation, not only of schooling, but of childhood itself. Not everyone was affected in the same way or to the same extent, but the overarching impression of wartime schooling is one of struggle, chaos, improvisation, adaptation, and, at times, frustrated aspirations. Many children's stories of the war contain serial evacuations, each involving either a change of school or a complete absence of schooling altogether. These interruptions, particularly for teenagers, meant that they could enjoy little coherence in their education and were lucky to access the same subject consistently let alone the same syllabus. Some, however, often as a result of where they lived, or of their families' situation, saw little change to normal life, while others were able to pursue an otherwise normal regime but in changed or changing locations. As early as 1938, children in the Medway towns in Kent got a foretaste of what was to come when they were given a half-day holiday so their schools could carry out a test run as First Aid Centres under the new ARP arrangements. The seriousness of the situation by 1942 was summed up in a Commons debate (see Chapter 5) where Mr Kenneth Lindsay MP voiced his concerns that 'The future of Britain is between the ages of 14 and 18, or else at school. There is no doubt that the generation growing up is going to suffer from the dislocation of the educational system'.

A further factor which is often overlooked is allied in part, as is education itself, to the social divide. This relates to the clear physiological differences in young people which can be attributed to the influence of health and nutrition. Various research carried out in the early 1940s reveal some disturbing facts. In 1942, a quarter of Merseyside's children were living below the poverty line, and 72 per cent of elementary schoolchildren in West Sussex failed to reach the recommended nutritional levels. By contrast, a study of pupils at Christ's Hospital, the 'Bluecoat' public school outside Horsham, found that the thirteen-year-olds were, on average, 2.4 inches (6.1 cm) taller than their elementary school contemporaries, and this disparity had increased by half as much again by the time they had reached seventeen. Such differences were carried over into occupational life in both the forces and civilian employment.

Hodgson cites examples of the effects on children and young people of the mental strain on them caused by bombing. It was suggested that children who remained in Bristol during the air raids were more than eight times more likely to be psychologically disturbed than those who were evacuated. However, in the north-west, it was Liverpool's under-twenty-year-olds who were seen by Home Intelligence as being the most obviously cheerful, an attitude that was contrasted with Manchester's corresponding gloom. These apparent differences would prove only temporary as increased bombing hit much of the industrial north. One quantifiable manifestation of the effect on youth of the uncertainties occasioned by the war was the flouting of authority and the undermining of moral values. The rise in cases of looting and pilferage coming before the courts, involving unrepentant youths sometimes taking their lead from adults, was but one symptom of societal dislocation. At the same time, much youthful activity was characterised by altruistic and selfless behaviour, as the war provided youth with more than the normal range of opportunities to experience disaster or personal achievement.

The Education System during the Second World War

In 1938, the school leaving age was still fourteen, only raised from twelve by the Fisher Act of 1918 which provided for compulsory education for all children from the age of five, but only implemented in 1921. Over four-fifths of children left full-time education at the age of fourteen and were welcomed at the Labour Exchange. Most children spent their school lives in public elementary schools, while, on average, around only 15 per cent might go on to secondary education, which took place in grammar or high schools, and local education authority (LEA) secondary schools. Most LEAs operated a selection system at age eleven. This consisted of competitive examinations largely centred on arithmetic, English grammar, and essay writing, but between a half and three-quarters of the 146 LEAs also used a variety of tests that purported to assess intelligence. However, only four of the seventy-five tests in use had formally been standardised. The criticism was levelled—as it would continue to be up until the eleven-plus exam was widely abandoned after 1965—that preparation for the selection examination exerted an unnatural dominance over teaching in the junior years of the elementary schools. Some of the grammar and high schools were direct-grant schools that, in return for an element of public funding, were required to draw 25 per cent of their intake from elementary schools, offering free education up to age sixteen. In some LEAs, between 1913 and 1937, this proportion might rise to 33 per cent or even half of the intake. In 1938, there were around 400,000 pupils in 1,400 secondary schools, around one-third of whom were receiving a free education. The majority of these pupils, slightly over 60 per cent, were from managerial or professional classes with only 10 per cent from the semi- or unskilled social groups. Thus from 1920 onwards, most secondary school pupils were from the middle classes with only a small number representing the ablest working-class children. In the Essex borough of West Ham in 1939, boys and girls had a 14:1 chance of winning a scholarship to secondary school, a ratio that would decline as more children aspired to a secondary education and were entered for the scholarship examination. Many LEAs paid for extra places at grammar and high schools over and above those schools' standing commitments and their own provision. The London County Council (LCC) operated on a principle of a minimum of one secondary school place per hundred of the population. West Ham's scholarships had increased threefold by 1938 from eighty-seven to 250. Only a tiny proportion of the nation's children attended schools in the private sector. These were predominantly fee-paying, but some offered scholarships using funds, often dating back centuries, set up for that specific purpose. They ranged from small preparatory schools taking in small numbers of pupils to the large public schools with several hundred pupils, and nearly all of them provided boarding education. The Common Entrance Examination was taken at age thirteen to determine where children from preparatory schools might continue their privileged education. This examination was competitive to an extent but other factors such as birth, wealth, status, and parental connections also came into play.

Those pupils who made it to secondary schools might be streamed after two years and would then work towards the School Certificate public examination, which had been established in 1918 by the Secondary Schools Examination Council. Candidates needed six passes including mathematics and English to matriculate. Exemption would be granted for candidates who managed credits in five subjects including mathematics, English, a science subject, and a foreign language. At this stage, many pupils left school at sixteen. Those who stayed on into the sixth form would take the Higher School Certificate at age eighteen. Some would apply for a bursary as an intending teacher, but the suspension of the planned raising of the school-leaving age to fifteen, which would be postponed until 1947 with the implementation of the 1944 Education Act, meant that fewer extra teachers were needed. Nevertheless, LEAs continued to fund university scholarships for prospective teachers as well as operating teacher training colleges. According to the figures in the Robbins Report into Higher Education (1963), in 1938 only 4 per cent of seventeen-year-olds and 2 per cent of eighteen-year-olds were in full-time education. Just 1.7 per cent of secondary pupils went to university, many of them treading the well-worn path from public school to Oxford and Cambridge; 0.7 per cent were at teacher training colleges; and 0.3 per cent at further education (technical) colleges—a total complement of 69,000 full-time students that year out of an eligible age group of more than 2 million, representing just 3.45 per cent of the cohort.

Alongside the public and private sectors, there were also schools that took boys to be sailors in either the Royal Navy or the Merchant Marine. HMS *Ganges* in Harwich and HMS *St Vincent* in Gosport both had their origins in floating hulks acting as boys' training ships. From 1905, a shore-based training establishment opened at Shotley near Harwich to train fifteen- to seventeen-year-old boys for the Royal Navy. HMS *St Vincent* opened in 1927 in the old Forton Royal Marines Barracks in Gosport. HMS *St George* and Ballakermeen High School in Douglas on the Isle of Man provided a secondary school curriculum to boy entrants to the Royal Navy. It opened in 1939, replacing HMSs *Ganges* and *St Vincent*, for the duration, in a converted holiday camp taking boys at sixteen, to be taught by qualified naval schoolmasters. It offered a fifteen-month-long course, training intakes of 600 boys at a time in specialisms such as visual signals or wireless telegraphy. The approach was largely practical, but time was also devoted to English, mathematics, science topics particularly relevant to seamanship, including navigation, as well as naval history. The stone frigate HMS *Impregnable* at Devonport trained boys, officially fifteen-year-olds but some younger, for service aboard warships. The Royal Marines' boy buglers at Eastney Barracks in Southsea were meant to be recruited at fourteen, but thirteen-year-olds could slip through.

Other training establishments prepared boys for the Merchant Navy. The Thames Nautical Training College occupied a succession of hulks, each named HMS *Worcester*, at Greenhithe from 1876, funded by shipowners, maritime insurance underwriters, and merchants, training boys for careers in the Merchant Navy. The school was evacuated to Foots Cray Place in Sidcup for the duration of the war. Liverpool had a similar establishment based in HMS *Conway*, launched in 1839. She was relocated to Anglesey in 1941 to avoid the bombing. Cadets at both schools automatically became Royal Naval Reserve cadets in wartime. While the official age for joining the Merchant Navy was sixteen, it was quite common for fourteen- and fifteen-year-olds to sign on with a shipping line and immediately be sent to sea. Even when a youngster received training at somewhere like the Prince of Wales Sea Training School in Limehouse, evacuated to Ingham Old Hall in Norfolk for the duration, it would last no more than six months. Training ships such as TS *Exmouth*, used as a Poor Law training school and moored on the Thames at Grays, took boys as young as twelve to prepare them for a life at sea. Another such training ship was the TS *Vindicatrix*, which was moored up to serve the Gravesend Sea School and evacuated to the mouth of the Sharpness Canal near Gloucester in 1939. Parts of the hutted camp remain along with a memorial to the 70,000 boys trained there during its lifetime. Between them, all these sea training schools prepared thousands of boys for service at sea each year.

The RAF ran an apprentice scheme from 1920 at RAF Halton. Boys, still legally minors, were recruited aged eighteen but must have passed a qualifying examination. They were then expected to complete their rigorous apprenticeship in only three years, qualifying as aircraft fitters to National Certificate standard. This course was further reduced to two years' duration in 1939 with the working day extended to cover the ground. A second course opened briefly at RAF Cosford but soon reverted to RAF Halton.

The Army Technical School (Boys) opened at Chepstow in 1929 and apprenticeships were offered by a number of other establishments, including Woolwich for the Royal Artillery and Arborfield for the Royal Engineers (RE), and, later in the war, for the Royal Electrical and Mechanical Engineers (REME). The Military Training Act 1939 implemented the call-up of males aged twenty and twenty-one for six months' full-time military training in a new militia. This was the first ever peacetime conscription scheme and was planned to run for three years. Once the six months was up, militiamen would join an active reserve and be liable for top-up training and annual camps. Militia training camps were constructed across the country, but only the first cohort began training in them, in June, as war broke out a few months later. The RE at Chatham continued to recruit fourteen-year-old apprentices in 1939 to complete a three-year apprenticeship followed by a six-month course on field engineering, and then eight years' service as a regular. After Dunkirk, these boys were sent to Chepstow and on completion of their greatly truncated training, this last peacetime intake became the nucleus of the innovative RE Assault Regiments. Still barely nineteen by 1944, they trained alongside RN commando divers on the beach at Brancaster in Norfolk, using armoured assault vehicles—'the Funnies' of the 79th Armoured Division under General Hobart, which would smooth the way for the troops landing on the Normandy beaches on D-Day.

Youngsters Joining the Labour Market

The Depression and the early years of the 1930s had witnessed adult unemployment rates of 14 per cent, but for juveniles, defined as fourteen- to seventeen-year-olds, the average across the interwar period was only 5 per cent. This might be explained by the existence of large areas of employment that, for various reasons—ranging from level of pay to industrial practices or to relative levels of skill requirement—welcomed unskilled young workers. Formal apprenticeships commenced at sixteen for boys and fifteen and a half for girls—though fourteen-year-old school-leavers were usually able to obtain interim employment, even if of a casual or seasonal nature; in 1931, almost a quarter of employed fourteen-year-old lads were working as delivery boys for retail or the GPO. Apprenticeships, however, were in decline, permitting employers to take on trainees, or 'learners', in less rigidly formalised ways and with looser commitments. Juvenile instruction centres, administered by the Ministry of Labour but delivered by local authorities, provided training in handicrafts and physical education for unemployed juveniles. Under the terms of the 1918 Education Act, all juveniles not in full-time education were required to attend continuation schools for part-time vocational training, some of it in the form of evening classes, but this was wholly dependent on employers releasing them and the circumstances and motivation of the students themselves. Full- and part-time vocational courses were provided by junior technical schools and technical colleges to prepare students for careers in professions such as architecture, engineering, and pharmacy, or in trades such as food and drink, automobile engineering, and textiles. Training schemes set up by the Unemployment Assistance Board, government agencies, and the Trades Union Congress were all aimed mainly at young men rather than juveniles. Even in 1938, the Ministry of Labour maintained twenty-nine camps containing nearly 25,000 young men carrying out heavy manual labour in an exercise intended to teach them skills, but also to harden them up. The need for this approach derived either from their experience of overwork prior to being let go at age sixteen when requirements for employers to increase wages and pay insurance contributions kicked in, or from the ensuing long periods of unemployment which might have induced ill health or a deterioration in physical fitness. One very clear aspect of employment was how small a part schools played in enabling children into work. In Lancashire in 1934, only around 2 per cent of both boys and girls reported getting their first jobs through school.

Training opportunities for girls, meanwhile, were generally harder to come by. Most girls working in domestic service or retail, therefore, learnt their trade by the 'standing next to Nellie' method. While the numbers of domestic servants had fallen during the decade following the Great War, the number had risen once more through the 1930s and domestic service remained the single largest category of employment for women and girls with 1.6 million, or 24 per cent of the female workforce, in such employment by 1931, with almost half of those in the fourteen to twenty-four age group. The domestic science curriculum for girls of twelve and thirteen in the elementary schools included cookery, laundry, and general housekeeping skills, but the provision of domestic service training schools that had begun in 1914 only accommodated fewer than 400 girls. However, according to Hansard, between 1928 and 1930, the number of juveniles who had completed courses of training in home-craft centres set up by the Ministry of Labour had jumped from under 250 to over 1,600. One such centre was the Auchinraith Domestic Centre in Blantyre on the outskirts of Glasgow, which trained unemployed girls as maidservants. Initiatives such as that of the Domestic Workers' Union seeking to increase the pay, living standards, and security of domestic servants were hampered by the scattered nature of their potential membership making organisation and recruitment difficult. Various efforts were made to introduce legislation to improve the lot of the domestic servant but, even when passed, proved difficult to implement. Some girls received proper training, were valued and well treated, while others remained put-upon skivvies. Between 1926 and 1930, in an attempt to raise the status of domestic service, one centre was operated in Market Harborough, followed by others and they were initially intended to train young women prior to emigration to Australia. Despite changing their focus to home employment, the centres, nevertheless, closed down once assisted migration had been brought to an abrupt halt by the Depression. As light industry developed, young girls gained more opportunities for unskilled and semi-skilled factory work in manufacturing or the rag trade, often gaining some training in the process. However, employers continued to enforce the marriage bar, thereby turning over their workforce and avoiding having to implement costly incremental pay scales.

Nursing was one of the vocations that offered training courses. Typically, aged eighteen, a girl would join a twelve-week introductory course in a hospital and, on satisfactorily passing an examination, would then begin work on the wards as a probationer nurse. The successful navigation of three or four years of service, and the accompanying examinations, would lead to state registered nurse (SRN) status. Many of those SRNs had attended schools up until the age of eighteen but a two-year training leading to state enrolled nurse (SEN) status was also on offer to less well-qualified candidates. Commercial courses that taught book-keeping, typewriting, shorthand, and commercial arithmetic were available for those seeking clerical work. Examinations set by the Royal Society of Arts (RSA) and the Chambers of Commerce could be taken, while some students would progress to take professional bodies' own qualifications. Clark's College was opened in London in 1880 to provide a commercial education initially for older students, but from the early 1900s, for pupils from the age of eleven. Clark's Colleges continued to open across the country as a franchise operation: Walthamstow and Ilford in 1913; Southampton in 1936, to an eventual total of twenty or more. An alternative source of clerical training was another franchised organisation, Pitman's, which had begun in 1837 and continued to provide courses for both face-to-face and distance learning.

In the 1930s, there was ongoing debate regarding the suitability of an academic education for girls. The 100,000 or so girls in public and LEA secondary schools, only some of whom would stay to complete their Higher School Certificate courses, were all receiving an education whose logical outcome was a place at university, but few would get that far. In theory, more occupations had become available for women, but circumstances often went against them. While women had become eligible for entry into the administrative class of the Civil Service in 1925, it was noted that few could afford the unpaid downtime needed to undertake the necessary coaching for the competitive examination. Between 1925 and 1935, only eleven women were successful in gaining entry to this higher grade. Only gradually would hitherto segregated departments such as the factory inspectorate, become integrated, thereby opening up more career opportunities to women. In 1938, there were 80,000 women in the Civil Service performing mainly clerical tasks and a lone female principal had been retained in post following marriage.

Wartime Disruptions and Distractions from Schooling

However piecemeal and disjointed the process of schooling might have appeared, it was soon to get much worse. The disruption caused by the war can be put down to a number of different factors relating to the availability and condition of premises; the security of pupils and staff; the course of the war; the impact of constant reorganisations on teaching and learning environments; the channelling of resources into structural modifications; issues relating to health and safety; population mobility; staffing fluctuations; levels of mental and physical resilience in the school and the community; parental expectations and preferences; and political decisions. It should be noted that in order to cut schoolchildren's travelling, thus enabling them to get home quickly in the event of an air-raid alarm, many authorities reverted to providing all-age schools. Although efforts were made by officialdom to minimise all these disruptive elements, events could remain subject to serendipity and might result in extreme and unforeseen circumstances. One boy whose own school had been evacuated went to stay with his grandparents at Lingfield and enrolled in the local school. When that school was itself evacuated far away to Cornwall, his parents were not informed, and he was left behind. As a result, he found himself sailing for the USA on the SS *City of Benares* and was one of the few children to survive its sinking.

Requisitioning of Premises

During the run up to war, properties to be commandeered were identified by government departments, the armed services and the health authorities for a range of purposes. While it is the large country houses such as Hardwick Hall, Woburn Abbey, or Beaulieu that tend to be remembered in this context, any building with more than four rooms on the ground floor and preferably provided with a reliable electricity supply was considered. Public buildings were often at the top of the list, and among them, schools were particularly targeted, especially in urban areas. A certain amount of confusion was caused when requisitioning authorities changed their minds and properties earmarked for one purpose ended up being used for something else, often to the extreme inconvenience of the original occupants. Informed when the war was still on the far distant horizon that his school would be required by the Admiralty, the headmaster of Malvern Boys' School hurriedly started to look around for an alternative home that might accommodate 500 boys, a large staff, and all the paraphernalia of a large residential establishment. Unexpectedly, the 10th duke of Marlborough, possibly seeking to pre-empt a dreaded occupation by the army, came to the rescue, offering to move his family into the east wing, thereby freeing up the rest of the cavernous Blenheim Palace for use by the school. On the outbreak of war, the school duly put its carefully worked-out relocation plans into operation and removed lock, stock, and barrel to Oxfordshire. In the meantime, a greatly expanded MI5 had moved from its cramped Mayfair home in Curzon Street into Wormwood Scrubbs Prison in west London. When the prison was bombed during the London Blitz in the autumn of 1940, it was decided to move out of danger, resulting in Blenheim being selected as its new base. Meanwhile, back in Malvern, the Admiralty had chosen to erect a clutch of temporary office buildings (TOB) as an alternative to using the college buildings. Thus, after a single year at Blenheim, the college was free to make the reverse journey home. Two short years later, it was found necessary (see Chapter 3) to move the Telecommunications Research Establishment (TRE) somewhere safer than the Dorset coast. Its planned destination was Marlborough, but intervention by R. A. Butler, protecting his former school, headed off the invasion. The TRE settled on Malvern, already home to HMS *Duke*, and the college was required to move once again. This time, it being reckoned that the worst of London's bombing was over, the school negotiated an arrangement to share the buildings of Harrow School. Space was conveniently available here as anxious parents had removed their children during the London Blitz, but it was a move not wholly welcomed by some Malvern parents who had regarded Worcestershire as a safer berth for their children. King's School, Rochester, was evacuated to Scotney Castle in Kent, with staff and pupils lodging in 'Finchcocks', a large Georgian mansion in Goudhurst until they were evicted by the army, which commandeered the house. The school was then forced into a further move to Taunton. Pinewood Preparatory School found itself in a similar predicament when it evacuated to Melchet Court near Romsey and was promptly evicted by the army.

As the war neared its conclusion, many of those establishments that had been displaced, often for the complete school life of whole cohorts, began to wonder when they might return home. A question asked in parliament in early December 1945 as to how many schools had been released from requisition in England, Scotland, and Wales elicited the figure of 709 having already been released up to that date from the total of 1,225. Data on the occupation of Scottish schools during 1940 and 1941 reveal that over eighty schools had been wholly occupied by HM forces and a further thirty-one partially. Meanwhile, the Civil Defence Authorities had wholly occupied nineteen Scottish schools but had also retained a foothold in 172 more. Throughout the course of the war, a total of more than 300 Scottish schools, representing 10 per cent of the total stock, were either wholly or partially given over to non-educational purposes for at least the first four years of the war, only reducing from 1943 onwards. Two-thirds of Aberdeen's forty schools had been wholly or partially occupied, thereby displacing a fifth of the school population.

Evacuation

There were three elements to the evacuation project designed to remove children and some of their mothers from the bombing to which it was assumed cities would quickly be subjected once war broke out. Families acted unilaterally to send or accompany their children to relatives or prearranged billets; local authorities organised large parties usually on the basis of school-based groups which would travel to a predetermined locality where children, teachers, helpers and mothers would be allocated on the basis of either prearranged billets or their hosts' on-the-spot selections; or schools negotiated individual lodging arrangements to move wholesale to a new location, sharing their hosts' facilities. Unaccountably, some of the localities chosen, particularly in the first two categories, proved to be just as dangerous, and sometimes more so, than the areas from which the evacuees originated. Towns on the east and south coasts would prove just as subject to air raids as London or Birmingham. Two Croydon schools, evacuated to Brighton's Whitehawk School, were forced to relocate several times before, being unable to anticipate the coming V-2 assault, deciding they were better off back home. Brentwood County HS for girls became a reception centre for evacuees who might well be jumping from the frying pan into the fire, as the town would receive over 1,000 bombs, nineteen V-1s, thirty-two V-2s, and suffer forty-three deaths and the partial destruction of over 5,000 homes.

Under the aegis of the Ministry of Health, schemes under the designation of Operation Pied Piper had been initiated in 1938, designed to evacuate up to 3.5 million people. In the event, this proved to be a gross overestimate as figures ranged from 8 per cent take-up in Rotherham to 76 per cent in Wallasey (see Appendix I). By the end of 1939, across the country, 827,000 schoolchildren, 624,000 mothers and young children under school age, 13,000 pregnant women, and 113,000 teachers and helpers had been evacuated. Parties from Gravesend and Dagenham were taken by paddle-steamer to Great Yarmouth, Lowestoft, and Felixstowe—incidentally, three of the first places to be bombed from the air, or bombarded from the sea, in the Great War. Greater Manchester clearly demonstrates the potential size of the operation with 190,000 children and priority adults eligible for evacuation. By April 1940, 71,000 schoolchildren, 58,000 pre-school children, and 4,000 expectant mothers had registered, and nearly 180,000 billets had been allocated in rural areas of the surrounding counties and as far away as Shropshire. An *Evacuation Handbook* was issued to schools detailing administrative arrangements. Preston took in 5,000 children from Manchester and 4,000 from Salford, as well as children from London. Fleetwood became home to 1,200 evacuees from Widnes.

Secondary Schools, evacuated *in toto*, would often share facilities with a host school. Portsmouth's Northern Secondary School, evacuated to Winchester's Peter Symond's School and Winton House, shared extra classrooms in corrugated-iron huts. Until Portsmouth's ARP organisation made its mortuary van available to transport their salvaged books, these, too, had been shared, but classes for each school had been kept separate. In contrast, in Zeals, the tiny Somerset village school integrated the evacuees, with forty-plus five- to fourteen-year-olds engaging in group work in the school's one and only classroom. Meanwhile in Headley, the equally small Surrey village school absorbed older pupils from Sydenham Secondary School and chose the pragmatic approach of adopting half-day teaching. In some places, the arrival of refugees from abroad and home-grown evacuees facilitated the reopening of under-subscribed village schools, with teachers redeployed from the cities. Many schools in vulnerable areas were evacuated to somewhere that appeared safer at the time. Hymers College in Hull went to Pocklington and Market Weighton, reasonably remote from enemy activity, but although Emmanuel School, Battersea, did well to get out of London, Petersfield's Churcher's College may not have provided the safest haven. Sometimes the decision to evacuate was taken only once the danger of staying put had been proven. The Moorside Primary School on Bromley's Downham Estate and the Bickley and Widmore School were among several schools bombed in the Borough in 1941, but it was only after the V-1s appeared in 1944 that Bromley schools were evacuated to Loughborough. When a whole school, or at least a large proportion of it, transferred, teachers would go as well, but where small parties of unaccompanied children were evacuated, there would be no extra teachers available to spread the teaching load. Village schools might be swamped by evacuees, forced to appeal for books, paper, and writing materials. Children could find themselves in classes of up to eighty children, often sharing teaching spaces with a second class just as large. One school in Coxwold, North Yorkshire, was the result of two schools, their buildings requisitioned by the military, coming together for the duration when Pannal Ash College from nearby Harrogate and Lindisfarne College from faraway Westcliff-on-Sea in Essex united as Newburgh Priory School. Additionally, a network of national camps, each accommodating 200 children and teachers, was set up to provide outdoor learning opportunities as another alternative.

In Scotland, the evacuation plans were in the hands of the Department of Health for Scotland (DHS). The country was divided into three areas. 'Sending' areas were those with a high expectation of sustained bombing and initially included Dundee, Edinburgh, and Glasgow, with the settlements along the estuaries of the Clyde and Forth—Greenock, Rosyth, Clydebank, Dumbarton, etc. being added after raids on them had begun. 'Receiving' areas would take in evacuees, and 'Neutral' areas would remain as they were. Much of the remote Highlands and Islands would lie outside these arrangements, designated 'Reserve' areas but open for private arrangements. The ceiling was estimated at 500,000 children, some mothers and sufficient teachers. In Glasgow, some 130,000 opted for evacuation with half the city's teachers, prompting the possibility of compulsory evacuation duty. In the event, less than 40 per cent of children in 'Sending' areas were evacuated.

While the war at sea was fought from day one, the anticipated aerial onslaught failed to materialise, and people began to talk about the 'Phoney War', the 'Great Bore War', or the 'Sitzkrieg'. Inevitably, a combination of homesick children, disgruntled mothers, frustrated and bewildered host families, and parents missing their children brought about a return home for many evacuees. On the outbreak of war, 8,500 children and teachers had been evacuated from Liverpool, but four months later, some 40 per cent of them had already returned home. Only 34 per cent of London parents and 14 per cent of Birmingham's had assented to their children's evacuation, with one million of them either refusing to register at all or failing to respond. In the end, although provision had been made for 73,000 of Birmingham's to be evacuated, only a third of that number presented themselves on the day, some being sent as far away as Ross-on-Wye. Many of these children would drift back as did pupils from West Bromwich Municipal Secondary School, evacuated to Tamworth, who returned home for Christmas 1939. Not much later, the children of Saltley GS returned from their billets in Hinckley in February 1940. However, the raids of November 1940 prompted over 20,000 children to leave the city in organised parties and the same number again in private arrangements. Some 23,000 children were eligible for evacuation from Nottingham, but only 5,000 took up the offer. Many were taken to towns around the city, but some travelled to Oakham and the Mundella School went to Stamford. The impact on reception areas could be significant. Retford was sent 6,000 children from Leeds, the West Midlands and Great Yarmouth, and Mansfield received 1,600 evacuees from Southend. Throughout the country, however, of those who had gone, by May 1940, barely a quarter of a million children remained in their assigned billets. In March 1941, the MOI reported that of the 8,708 children evacuated from Belfast, 4,952 had returned home. However, numbers overall were inflated by refugees from the continent and significant contingents of children and their teachers from the Channel Islands, escaping the German occupation of June 1940. Some of these constituted discrete groupings, which were enabled to re-establish their own schools in empty buildings.

The summer of 1940 saw a step-change in the course of the war on the Home Front. Many children who had returned home were re-evacuated and up to 100,000 others went away for the first time. If Eastbourne, Cromer, and Bournemouth had appeared safe havens in 1939, they now sat firmly astride the invasion beaches. Evacuation from these south and east coast towns added a further 100,000 evacuees to the total. On 2 June, 1,200 children and their teachers from Harwich, Parkeston, and Dovercourt boarded trains taking them to the relative safety of Gloucestershire and Herefordshire. Over the course of the war, it has been estimated that 2.5 million children experienced evacuation in one form or another. Westminster City School and Westminster School had been evacuated to, respectively, Tonbridge and Lancing, but both were forced to move on into the supposedly safer south-west: the first, to Exmouth, and the second, to Exeter. Both had fetched up in an area which was no less dangerous than that whence they had come. Westminster finally moved to Bromyard in Herefordshire, occupying three large houses. The March 1942 issue of *The Elizabethan*, Westminster's school magazine, is split into sections recording the school's parallel activities in London, where the rump of the school remained open for business, and Herefordshire. Even when an evacuated school had settled in, it could face further challenges. The 600 pupils of Taunton's School in Southampton had moved to Bournemouth, becoming the first occupants of Bournemouth School's brand-new buildings. A complicated regime had been worked out whereby, working a six-day week and by renting nearby public halls, classrooms were used by one school and practical areas by the other on a half-day basis. These arrangements would be reversed weekly and then be alternated over time, so that all pupils were treated equally. After the Dunkirk evacuation, however, this routine was disrupted when the army temporarily requisitioned the school for the whole of June 1940 to accommodate first French troops and then the remnants of the British Expeditionary Force.

Although evacuation to camps proved generally unsatisfactory in Scotland, due to several factors including remoteness and dual control, one experiment was seen as being particularly successful. About 200 girls and boys from Glasgow schools, aged fourteen in 1939, were placed in a residential setting at Cally House near Gatehouse of Fleet in the Stewartry of Kirkcudbrightshire. The school was organised in mixed classes and was run on democratic principles by a dedicated, and mainly residential, staff. Many of the pupils came from grammar schools such as Hillhead, which had been requisitioned by the military, and covered a wide range of academic subjects, scoring well in public examinations and benefiting from the character training possible in such a setting. Sadly, when evacuation came to an end in 1944, Scottish law, as it then stood, could not permit this type of residential school to be maintained by the state, and to everyone's great disappointment, Cally House was closed. In 1941, after the Clydebank raids (see Chapter 4) attempts made to replicate the success of Cally House elsewhere were not deemed totally successful.

Days before the outbreak of war, some of those able to afford it were sending their children abroad to escape whatever nastiness was planned for Britain as, in Baldwin's words, the bomber would always get through. Responding to the criticism that children from poorer backgrounds were missing out, the government decided to sponsor the subsidised overseas evacuation of schoolchildren. It set up the Children's Overseas Reception Board (CORB) to organise this programme in conjunction with Thomas Cook, the travel agent based in London's Berkeley Street, together employing over 600 staff. Teachers and others could volunteer to accompany the children as guides and chaperones. Local authorities, young people's organisations, and churches were invited to nominate children who, for whatever reason, might benefit from the programme. A means-test determined how much parents would be charged, and most groups also included children whose parents paid full price outside the CORB scheme. The programme's illustrious thirty-two-strong advisory council contained ministers representing their relevant departments—health, education, pensions etc.; representatives of the Girl Guides and Boy Scouts, the YMCA, the WVS, the teaching unions, charities and churches, as well as acknowledged experts such as Laurence Cadbury the philanthropist, and Sir Ronald Lindsay, a former ambassador to the USA. A parallel eight-strong Scottish council met in Edinburgh.

Having passed a medical examination, the selected children would be carried across the Atlantic to Canada or the USA, or further afield to South Africa, Australia, or New Zealand by merchant ship. Some 211,000 children, including 27,000 from Scotland, were initially registered with the scheme, with more to follow. The first ship carrying evacuees as part of the official CORB programme was the SS *Anselm*, which delivered eighty-two children to Halifax, Nova Scotia, in July 1940. This was followed by fifteen further voyages taking a total of over 2,600 children to various, mainly Commonwealth, destinations. The first CORB transport to sail in a convoy was SS *Volendam* carrying 320 children, travelling from Liverpool to Halifax, in Convoy OB205. Another of the thirty-two ships in the convoy was the RMS *Rangitata* carrying 113 evacuee children and bound for New Zealand. Just one day into the voyage on 30 August 1940, SS *Volendam* was torpedoed by *U60*. Miraculously, all the children were rescued by other merchant ships or escort vessels and returned safely to Greenock. Two weeks later, SS *City of Benares*, as flagship of OB213, embarked ninety children, including two survivors from the *Volendam*, bound for Canada. It was struck by torpedoes fired by *U48* and sank inside half an hour. Of the 365 passengers and crew, only 105 were rescued, including only thirteen of the children, but not the two survivors of the previous trip. Despite the large numbers of children on the waiting list, this disaster brought the official CORB programme to an abrupt end, although the organisation remained in being until 1944. A number of private initiatives continued the scheme, an example being RMS *Scythia*, which was sponsored by readers of the *Boston Evening Transcript* and carried forty-eight children from Liverpool to Boston in late September 1940, less than a week after the sinking of the *City of Benares*. A small group of staff and pupils from Sherborne Girls' School went to lodge with a school in Toronto, but such arrangements were rare, and the neighbouring boys' school elected to stay put on financial grounds if nothing else.

Measures to Counter Aerial Bombardment

From 1938, planning for Air Raid Precautions (ARP) at both national and local levels was gaining momentum. From the beginning, there was a preoccupation with countering the effects of poison gas, and much ARP training took this as its focus. The official policy on the provision of shelters required local authorities to provide sufficient public shelters for 10 per cent of the population on the basis that these would be for those people caught out on the street during a raid. It was assumed that the remaining 90 per cent of people would be either at home, at school or at their place of work. Employers were therefore directed to provide suitable shelters for their workforce. Some local authorities were quicker off the mark than others. In Luton, the borough council decided to make elaborate and costly provision, and from May 1939, deep tunnel systems were dug in four locations. The 6-foot 6-inch-wide (2-metre-wide) brick-vaulted tunnels reach a depth of 80 feet (25 metres) and extend for 250 yards (230 metres). Both entrances are accessed by several flights of concrete stairs, but an emergency exit uses fixed vertical ladders to reach street-level manholes. Incorporated in the tunnels are doglegs designed to minimise the effects of blast, a lesson learned in the trenches of the Great War. Nottingham was another city where an ARP network was an early development with nearly 300 communal shelters dug into the rock under the castle, more on the surface, thousands of domestic shelters and a fire-fighting training centre. Stockport boasts the largest purpose-built civilian air-raid shelter in the country, capable of accommodating nearly 4,000 people in 1939 and extended a year later to provide space for 6,500. The official advice issued by the Home Office from 1936 onwards suggested three types of shelter. Depending on the circumstances these could be sunken, covered trench shelters; strengthened basements of mills or similar factory buildings; or surface brick-built shelters. Householders would be issued with family-size Anderson shelters, designed by William Paterson and Oscar Carl Kerrison, but named for Sir John Anderson, the home secretary, who was responsible for their widespread promotion and distribution.

As places of work, schools would be expected to provide appropriate shelters for their staff and pupils, either in the form of strengthened basements or surface shelters, although it is apparent that, in the early days, at least most primary schools sought to get their children home when the sirens sounded. The provision of school shelters was an enormous operation which would take an appreciable time to complete at great cost. In the West Riding of Yorkshire, which included cities like Leeds and Bradford, over 201 schools were provided with shelters that afforded a very precise 67,594 places. Many local authorities and individual schools opted for the cut-and-cover trench system. This involved cutting trenches to a depth of 7 feet (2.1 metres) with narrow passages widening out to areas with either seating or bunks. Trenches, which could be linked as inter-connecting, zig-zag systems, were meant to be 20 feet (6.1 metres) apart; roofed with rafters, resting on wall-plates; covered in corrugated-iron sheeting topped with 2 feet (61 cm) of earth; and reinforced with an additional layer of rubble on top of all that. However, Guildford Education Committee rejected a plan for concrete-lined trenches that would shelter 2,400 children at a cost of £5,700 (£285,000). They would contemplate nothing short of deep bomb-proof shelters and made the decision to postpone the reopening of schools after their initial closure until such shelters might be constructed.

Across the country, the most common surface shelter was for fifty persons, with an entrance and a chemical toilet cubicle at each end. In Newcastle upon Tyne, the shelters at Throckley Middle School were of a similar pattern but with a smaller footprint and capacity, being 20 feet (6 metres) long and 11 feet 6 inches (3.5 metres) wide. The problem with the surface shelters was that blast could push the brick walls outwards dropping the concrete roof onto those sheltering underneath. Schools in particularly densely populated areas, such as Glasgow or inner London, might suffer from further problems relating to accommodating shelters. Such schools were usually several storeys high within small concrete or asphalt playgrounds and heavily subscribed, which could mean there was nowhere to put shelters to hold even half a school's roll with the result either that some children would have to go further to shelter, or fewer children could attend school at the same time. In September 1940, Sandfield School's shelters in Guildford were completely obliterated after receiving a direct hit, probably from a parachute mine. Fortunately, this happened during the night when they were unoccupied. Ironically, this may have come as a relief to many of the school's parents as they considered the shelters to have been located too far from the school and across a busy road and may also have vindicated the Education Committee's preference for going deep. The Foxenden Quarry Deep Shelter under a carpark in York Road, one of eighteen deep shelters provided for the town, was dug in 1941 with space for 1,000 people including one whole bay reserved for Sandfield School.

After Dunkirk, Sussex could expect to be bombed and an official shelter policy was developed. At Hastings GS, cut-and-cover trenches were dug with overhead protection provided by railway sleepers covered in earth and with piled sandbags covering the entrances. Similar shelters were constructed for schools in Seaford and in Brighton where an accessible example survives at Whitehawk PS. It lies within a grassy bank and extends 100 metres with bench seating. The former East Grinstead GS was provided with five trench shelters, each 65 feet (20 metres) long, which can also still be seen. Three were linked together in an E-shape, while the other two were separate structures. In Worthing, although it was initially determined that schools would not be given shelters, with trench shelters being provided in nearby recreation grounds, surface shelters were eventually provided in schools. In Lewes, the construction of school shelters was delayed and then rushed so that waterproofing was necessary, as a range of alternative untried construction methods and materials had been used. At Malling School, curved steel and sandbag shelters were constructed, but within a year, the sandbags had rotted, and a layer of concrete was substituted. The boys' school in Mountfield Road had shelters made of large diameter, sunken, spun concrete pipes, while the girls' school had brick-built surface shelters. The Western Road School was one of several that had ten semi-sunken, pre-cast concrete slab shelters, which became so wet that pupils were forced to stay inside the school during alarms. Another type of shelter generally supplied across the county was designed by the British Concrete Federation (BCF). This was constructed of precast concrete sections with reinforced interlocking side and roof beams, was semi-sunken and held fifty people. At Chichester Boys' HS, four brick-built, turf-covered, surface shelters survive. Not all schools were provided with purpose-built shelters if an equally safe alternative was available. At Ardingly, the primary school's shelter was in the basement of the rectory. Many schools, especially those perceived as being in out of the way locations, had no designated shelter provision at all. One boy in rural Essex remembers cracking his head as he dived under the billiards table in his form room when the local airfield was attacked during daylight hours. Only at night might the school's cellars become available to provide some protection.

In September 1938, the headmaster of Sherborne School wrote to parents explaining the measures being taken to protect the school in the event of it being bombed. Boys would shelter in their own boarding houses, but trenches would be dug on the field and the cloisters would be sandbagged. Over the next eighteen months, additional measures included the removal of the outdoor swimming pool's entrance to improve access to a water supply for fire engines; further work to the undercroft and cloisters to establish the school's central shelter; and the construction of blast walls to shield entrances into the buildings. The boarding houses each contrived their own individual shelters. One house used a stone passage with walls 2 feet (61 cm) thick with a warm drying room on one side. The passage was provided with long benches and boys were asked to provide airbeds for sleeping on if it became necessary. Another house dug a trench in the garden, 150 feet (46 metres) long, divided by traverses into four sections, and roofed with rafters and oak planks, galvanised iron sheets, densely woven hurdles to contain an earth covering, and 1,000 sandbags. In August 1940, the headmaster again wrote to parents to relate how he had carried out an inspection of these shelters to ensure that they could stand up to any 'unlikely contingencies'. A third house had identified two refuge rooms on the ground floor surrounded by substantial walls and earth banks to minimise blast. A fourth house used its deep cellar, fitted out with triple tiers of bunks as its shelter. At Oundle, deep shelters containing five-tier bunks were dug, but a warning system which should have rung bells in all the boarding houses proved impractical owing to a design fault that triggered too many false alarms, leading to it being scrapped. Tonbridge School's first shelters were built after the Munich Crisis in 1938. By the time that war had broken out, the school's works staff had been instructed to build enough shelters for the whole school community. There had been 400 boys in 1939, but this number soon dropped by a quarter, only increasing once it became clear that the school would not, after all, constitute a primary target for the *Luftwaffe*. These shelters were of brick and corrugated iron, to specifications provided to schools by the appropriate government agency. Each school house had its own shelters and an ARP post serving the school and the northern parts of town was established in one of the houses.

On 20 July 1939, Farnham Girls' GS moved into brand-new premises in Menin Way, but by the end of the summer recess, the school was facing the threat of bombing. Permission to shelter, initially forty, pupils in the semi-underground boiler room was obtained and the new term began, a few days late, and then only for part-time schooling supplemented by home study. By half-term, shelters had been constructed with provision for 100 girls in the basement, and only then could a normal routine be reinstituted. Within a year, pupil numbers had doubled with the arrival of the Greycoat Hospital School from Westminster, rendering the shelter provision inadequate at a stroke, and the spacious new school buildings cramped. The lack of shelter accommodation necessitated alternate morning and afternoon working.

Whitgift School in Croydon was not evacuated in the war but was protected by several cut-and-cover shelters, described in a commentary on Croydon in the Second World War, and dug in the school playing fields. These were originally known as 'Munich Shelters' and each seated around thirty persons. The Subterranea Britannica website has a description of one of these surviving trench shelters which, unusually, is entered via a sloping step ladder at each end, accessed by manhole covers. This must have made getting a class of schoolboys into it a time-consuming operation whatever the perceived urgency.

In council schools, children were issued with gas masks and drilled regularly in their use, along with the accompanying India rubber stitched into a handkerchief which attempted to protect the teeth against the effects of blast, and earplugs tied together with a yard of string. Crocodiles of children practised the walk to the shelter, which might be in the playground or just outside the school gates. Not all schools, particularly those in rural areas, enjoyed such proximity to shelter. At Limpsfield, children had to run over the village cricket field and then across a further field laced with barbed wire before they could reach safety. If they were still out in the open when aircraft were overhead, they were instructed to lie down on the ground. During the Battle of Britain, as dogfights raged above them, many whole days were spent in the shelter and, as the village lay under the bombers' flightpath to London, whole families moved into the shelter at night-time. Contemporary press photographs show, generally older, boys and their teachers building air-raid shelters at their schools. In Sheffield, large shelters were constructed in school grounds which would later be used as general teaching spaces, their use carefully controlled by staff and senior pupils.

Large city elementary schools often consisted of three storeys with a basement, reached by a staircase, under which would be a cloakroom that could be given a concrete roof to form a secure shelter. Alternative exits were provided, or else lightly blocked hatches that could be pushed through allowing those sheltering to escape. However, there would be many casualties when thick concrete roofs in such shelters collapsed on their occupants under the weight of the two or three floors above. Given the potential for casualties, including fatalities, caused by flying glass, windows were to be criss-crossed by strips of brown adhesive tape, 1.5 inches (4 cm) wide, a task often delegated to pupils designated 'sticky-tape monitors'. Some schools were simply too difficult to be made safe. In Heaton, Newcastle upon Tyne, the infant department at Chillingham Road School had a glass roof, so the children were transferred to North Heaton School, later returning to the less vulnerable junior department. No such risks existed at Nottingham's Bluecoat School, an ancient foundation recently established as a grammar school on Mansfield Road, as a 20-foot-deep (6-metre-deep) cave shelter in the underlying sandstone, capable of accommodating 100 people was created there.

Birkenhead High School on the opposite side of the Mersey from Liverpool was evacuated to Shrewsbury but shelters, funded by parents and staff, were built in

1940 to enable girls to return home to continue their education in relative safety. Accessed via a corridor from a cloakroom, the shelters consisted of two long tunnels, each seating 100 girls and staff. Rediscovered in 2011 during building work, the shelters have been opened and, with the help of a Heritage Lottery Fund grant in 2015, will be restored and made available as a learning resource. Similar circumstances obtained with Withington Girls' School which had been evacuated to Uttoxeter in September 1939 but had returned to Manchester the next spring. Two large shelters were dug, supplemented by the building's cellars. Though cramped, efforts were made to brighten up the walls and girls remembered being taught in them as a generally pleasant experience. The school, its grounds, and the area around suffered heavy incendiary attacks throughout the latter part of 1940. In Ipswich, the shelter under the playground of Clifford Road Primary School operates as a museum visited by school parties and the general public. It was dug in 1939 with 200 places for school and community use. Heap Bridge Primary School, Heywood, has excavated the 100-person air-raid shelter in its grounds and has plans to make it available for school and community groups to visit. The surface shelter at West Ewell Infants' School in Epsom has been demolished to make way for the school's expansion, but a section of brickwork bearing children's drawings of V-1 Doodlebugs has been salvaged to be kept by the school and exhibited. Essex County Council provided its schools with standard surface shelters, of brick with concrete roofs, many of which survive. To enable people to make use of the public shelter provision, it was necessary to have an efficient warning system. Sirens were mounted on prominent buildings and very often these were schools. In Nottingham, the Crane School, the John Player's School in Bilborough, and the Boys' Home in Cranmer Street were chosen for three of the city's thirteen sirens. In Scarborough, sirens were mounted in Falsgrave, Hinderwell, Friarage, and Central Schools.

Staffing

Both men and women teachers were called up for either military service or to fulfil specific tasks identified by the government in the areas of physical education, nutrition, or research in the munitions industries. In June 1943, the cookery teacher at Farmor's School, Fairford, was 'temporarily removed' to run the RAF canteen at Cheltenham Technical College, thus removing domestic science from the school's curriculum. The chemistry teacher at Bury GS was co-opted to double as the borough's gas officer. Fortunately, his duties would be undemanding, but the detectors scattered around the borough still required regular checking. Some LEAs continued to dismiss women teachers when they got married, but others actively encouraged them back into school to make up for staffing shortages. Local teacher union branches lobbied education committees, often in vain, to have these rules abolished, suspended, or relaxed. Eventually the Board of Education drew attention to the wasted resource represented by unemployed married women teachers and directed LEAs with an Act of Parliament in 1944, to suspend any local arrangements which exacerbated the shortages. Schools might find themselves staffed by a majority of women teachers, a circumstance many older male staff in boys' schools found uncomfortable. Most children in the junior and senior classes at elementary schools, and in all types of secondary schools, experienced exclusively single-sex education, so the influx of women teachers into masculine environments brought about predictable culture shock. To many boys, though, being taught by women teachers with energy and enthusiasm was infinitely preferable to being taught by the superannuated dugouts of the Great War who stocked many, particularly preparatory school, staffrooms. There also exists anecdotal evidence for men who, invalided out of the services and clearly suffering from PTSD, were not up to the demands of teaching, spending their time gazing out of the window. However, the two over-sixty-year-old retired male teachers recalled by Nottingham HS managed to maintain the school cricket team's excellent results. In Scotland, a quarter of male teachers were, by 1942, serving in the forces or in the munitions industry, but their numbers had largely been made up by the employment of female teachers, many of them married women.

Given the scarcity of women science and mathematics graduates, one of the disadvantages of losing so many young male teachers to the forces and the munitions industry was a shortfall of expertise in those subjects. Universities continued to function through the war but with much reduced numbers of both staff and students. New graduates, particularly in science-related subjects or mathematics, were sometimes directed into teaching as they could prepare sixth formers for their Higher Certificate examinations and thus themselves be fed into the war effort. There was also a need for graduates in foreign languages to train linguists, particularly for intelligence work. Attempts were made to support non-specialist teachers working outside their comfort zones by producing educational films with accompanying teaching materials. Additionally, radio programmes enabled teachers to keep children informed of the war's progress and to stimulate discussion of current events.

Teachers were under a wide range of pressures. They were encouraged to enrol as ARP workers; they were posted away from home with evacuees which often entailed negotiating local working arrangements and liaising with their children's host families; they were often expected to provide social entertainment for their evacuated charges outside normal school hours; if children returned from evacuation they might have to improvise facilities for individual and group-work while covering for colleagues who had remained with the evacuees; as colleagues were called up they might be required to undertake unfamiliar tasks with minimal preparation; *in extremis*, they might have to extinguish incendiary bombs, clear away bomb damage, salvage books and equipment, and effect temporary building repairs. Entirely new duties such as salvage collection, fundraising for war funds and soliciting National Savings contributions, along with new activities arising from the provision of free milk and school meals could all be regarded as interfering with teachers' primary roles. Together, such additional administrative tasks were calculated as consuming four hours a week of teacher time, and it was suggested that the three Rs had been supplanted by the three Ms: milk, meals, and money. Although encouraged to belong to organisations such as the Home Guard, their employers often saw this as a source of conflict, particularly in the event of an emergency such as an invasion occurring. Was the teacher's duty to the children in his care more important than his duty to defend the country? (See Chapter 3)

There were also contractual issues since the employment of teachers was not the regulated business it would become after the war. Women teachers were still required to resign when they got married. Most, but not all teachers who were conscripted or volunteered for war work had their pay made up by their employers, so in 1944, the House of Lords ruled that pay must be made up for those on active service. In Lewes, however, the council declined to implement the national Burnham pay award causing resignations from councillors and teachers alike. Eventually, by a single vote, the council agreed to pay a war bonus to its employees including teachers, but not to those who had already left their employ.

Part-time Schooling

On the outbreak of war, most LEAs shut their schools immediately as they were unprepared to withstand bombing. Some were to reopen shortly, but many, including Croydon's, stayed closed for six months. Birmingham's schools offered voluntary attendance until sufficient shelters might be completed enabling a resumption of normal business. From late September 1939, the *Surrey Times* published progress reports on the construction of school shelters and when schools might be expected to reopen. Even those schools that did manage to remain open throughout the war were affected by the need to conserve fuel and light. Between each November and the end of January, the school day was shortened, and the Christmas holidays were extended. However, not everyone was lucky enough to enjoy stable schooling of any sort and some of those, who were schoolchildren at the time, have written of being out of school for a whole year or more, regardless of those complications caused by evacuation. A boy in Bromley was out of school for two years when his school was destroyed, and he had to wait for returning evacuees in 1942 to resume lessons. Schools in coastal areas such as Margate, which, under the requirements of DORA, had been cleared of much of their civilian populations for the duration, shut down completely.

It may have initially been seen as a cause for rejoicing as one watched one's school going up in flames, or as was recorded in New Southgate's Tottenhall Road, seeing all one's schoolbooks cascading down the street under the pressure of fire hoses, but it soon sank in that life's opportunities were also being washed away. Haberdashers' Aske's Boys' School at Cricklewood was evacuated to Mill Hill, not a great distance to commute, but schooling was only available on two days per week, and many pupils dropped out and secured employment. In early

1940, only fifteen of the LCC's 900 schools were open, as were only nineteen of Nottingham's 120. Even after significant time had elapsed, many schools around the cities had insufficient shelters in which to accommodate everyone during the frequent daylight raids, so they were forced to timetable their pupils in two groups on alternate days. In areas where there were evacuees, schools often worked a shift system with their own children working mornings and the evacuees, afternoons, changing around every couple of weeks. Berkhamsted HS for girls had use of the classrooms in the mornings, and their lodgers, South Hampstead High had the afternoons. The two schools managed quite separate existences except for concerts and sports. King's College Taunton became host to both Eltham College and King's School, Rochester, and used every possible structure on its campus to accommodate the influx. One such building was a timber aircraft hangar of Great War vintage, which only relatively recently succumbed to 'two fires and general neglect' (*pers. com.* from CCF CO, January 2003).

In early 1943 when it appeared that the Blitz was over, schools were beginning to return to London. Although Dulwich College remained open and Alleyn's and Prendergast's Girls' had returned, the LCC realised that the emergency school established at Colfe's, established as the South East London Emergency GS for boys, was under pressure. They wanted to see St Dunstan's returning to Catford to take in those of their own boys who were temporarily lodging in other schools, along with boys from Haberdashers' Aske's at New Cross and Brockley County, formerly the West Kent GS. This, for several reasons, did not happen, but by the end of the year, of the seventy-eight London secondary schools, twenty-nine had fully returned, thirty-one had reopened in part, split between home and reception area, and only eighteen remained entirely evacuated, operating only away in their reception areas. When Colfe's was hit by a V-1 one night in 1944, all its pupils moved to Aske's, staying there until Brockley County was able to reopen.

One of the factors that had put an enormous strain on schools was an unexpected result of evacuation, in particular the situation in which large numbers of children had been evacuated *en bloc* with their teachers and then, perhaps within a few weeks, a significant number of them had returned home. Many children had been evacuated from cities where most of the school buildings had been requisitioned by ARP and had ceased to function as schools. In the summer of 1940, it was reckoned that up to one million children had no school to attend. In January 1940, Dundee, Edinburgh, and Glasgow were back to having 90 per cent of their children resident, but many of their teaching force marooned out in the glens. Those city authorities, nevertheless, lobbied to have their schools reopened as soon as possible, even if they had to cobble together programmes of group work, postal tuition, and individual assignments. In time, numbers of teachers were recalled from their reception areas to re-establish their schools back home. The problem of premises was never wholly resolved but by using church and village halls, chapels, and other community buildings, it proved possible to provide a few hours of schooling for most children each day. Teachers taught small groups of children in their own homes, at least one teacher finding a use for her Morrison shelter as a worktable. Alongside the youth clubs provided by the National Society of Boys' and Girls' Clubs, churches and social clubs ran out-of-school activities for children who had little opportunity for study or recreation, but there were plenty of children who ran wild or played football all day. Glasgow's pre-war special school population of 4,614 children had halved by September 1941, and half of those missing could not be traced, although it was recorded that forty-three of them were described as 'roaming the streets'.

Schools that were fortunate enough not to be occupied by third parties were able to organise themselves more quickly. Haberdashers' Aske's Girls' School in Acton was evacuated to Dorchester where lesson time was shared with a local school. About half the girls had stayed behind in London with some of them enrolling in Ashford County School, but so many children and teachers had returned home that it soon became a viable option to reopen. Only towards the end of 1943 had schools returned in significant numbers. Not all children were lucky enough to have the luxury of premises and spent time in open air lessons in the park, or long walks in the countryside until makeshift accommodation might be made available. Despite many schools having robust air-raid shelters, teaching was suspended after the Sheffield Blitz of December 1940, as the council decided it was too much of a risk to have large numbers of children together in one place. One boy remembers classes being held for ten or so children in his front room on two half-days each week. At Petworth where the boys' school was bombed with great loss of life, the London evacuees escaped the devastation as they attended their own school in the Iron Room Congregational Chapel.

At least one school was set up specifically for evacuees and refugees. The school at Yealand Conyers in Cumbria catered for children aged from three to twelve and was staffed almost entirely by volunteers. It had been established by Manchester's Quaker community in 1939 as a safe refuge for children. The principal was Elfrida Vipont, a prominent Quaker who was a teacher and a children's author. Some schools were forced to expand owing to an influx, not of evacuees, but of war workers. At Stonehouse near Stroud, the children of workers at the Sperry Gyroscope and Hoffman's shadow factory making ball- and roller-bearings doubled the existing school population, and a church hall had to be leased to provide additional teaching spaces. The school, moreover, remained open throughout the summer holidays as parents were unable to arrange alternative childcare.

Typical of the experience of many children was that of some of the pupils of Highfield Infants' School in Southampton. When most of the children, along with children from many of Southampton's schools, were evacuated to the Andover area, some stayed behind. These, who had received no schooling for two months, finally had an hour a day, topped up with home visits by the remaining teachers. Three months later, two oversize Anderson-type air-raid shelters had been built with a total capacity of 135 children and eight adults. The adjacent church vestry could accommodate a further seventy children and two adults, but it would be over a year before the shelters were supplied with electricity. When the church was bombed in March 1941, the school's drains were damaged, limiting the use of the toilets, so after a few days of being closed, the school was permitted to reopen with small groups of children being allowed on the premises only for an hour at a time. Following the bombing, many of the parents of those who had returned from previous reception areas elected to send their children away again, this time to Blandford in Dorset. As we have seen, one way around the problem of damaged school buildings and scarcity of staff was for teachers to work for an hour at a time with groups of ten or twelve children in people's front rooms. When Stoughton Junior School was requisitioned for use by the Canadian Army, the school moved into neighbouring public halls and private houses. As the local paper reported: '... householders are lending rooms in which small groups can be given instruction, with the result that almost any house in Stoughton may be a school...'

The Scottish Education Department (SED) was among those promoting double shift working for transplanted schools but sought to make optimal use of available resources by suggesting that 'the judicious use of local accommodation might permit full-time education for both "native" and "incoming" children'. The SED also envisaged the operation of 'more homogenous classes' comprising both local children and evacuees being taught together. This particular notion was proven optimistic when some Catholic parents objected to their children's integration into Protestant classes.

Curriculum

The normal classroom routine was disturbed from the very beginning by attempts to prepare schoolchildren for aerial assault. Gas mask drill and getting to the air-raid shelters in a speedy and orderly manner were constantly practised in the hope that frequent alerts would reduce the time taken to a minimum. All this, before any actual threats had materialised, ate into lesson time, especially for the younger children. Mobile gas vans toured schools and children were made to walk through tear gas with their masks on to check that they had been put on properly. Brutally, many were made to repeat the exercise without their masks, in order that by experiencing the effects they might better appreciate the need for wearing them. Some schools built their own on-site gas chambers, more efficiently to carry out this training. The widespread expectation of air-launched gas attacks saw the installation of markers painted with gas-sensitive paint, which would change colour if gas were present. Children of all ages, even in infants' schools, were appointed as gas monitors to look out for the warning signs and to alert their classmates. A memoir from Winchester records the children in a junior school receiving training in how to deal with incendiaries using stirrup pumps and buckets of sand and water. However, it would not be long before, in many towns such as Hull, Cardiff, or Liverpool, children would be directly involved in those scenarios which had featured in their training. In 1941, a series of essays in the form of letters were written by ten- to fourteen-year-old schoolchildren in Hull describing 'What happened to me and what I did in the air-raid'. Around 2,000 children in a dozen Hull schools, as well as two Birmingham schools, took part in this exercise, apparently designed to evaluate the response of schoolchildren to their experience of the horrors of aerial bombardment. There remains, however, controversy over the use to which these writings were eventually put. Although many of them demonstrate the resilience of the children concerned who were surviving some of the worst bombing of the war it would appear that when the analysis was presented to Churchill by his scientific adviser Frederick Lindemann, positive factors were heavily downplayed. This was possibly done to strengthen the notion that similar treatment of German cities would destroy civilian morale. Children record copying the war diary off the blackboard every week and listening to radio reports of the war's progress, but few contemporary accounts mention anything approaching any attempt to have war aims explained to them. Many children would have met Jewish refugee children and may have gained insights into their situation, and several have mentioned being taken off school by a parent to see the film about the discovery of the camp at Belsen, but not until the war's end and then only as individual initiatives.

For older pupils, lessons often centred around the progress of the war with maps on the classroom walls and visits from former pupils who were between postings or convalescing from wounds. Pupils at Portway School in Shirehampton were let out to wave goodbye to US troops leaving Avonmouth Docks prior to their final D-Day training in Devon and Cornwall.

Children benefited from *ad hoc* events such as when the local ARP warden wheeled a Spitfire engine into Brinsley School in Nottingham for the boys to look at, but it would take a more concerted approach to stimulate youthful interest in science and technology.

The realisation that an effective technical education would contribute to a successful end to involvement in war had been voiced since Lloyd George's speeches in 1918 and echoed by Haldane and Churchill. It was fortunate, then, that many boys developed a sudden and urgent interest in mathematics and science subjects as it began to dawn on them that to have a realistic chance of being accepted by the RAF, especially as aircrew, they would need to get some relevant qualifications on their CVs. Those who had already left school often decided to enrol in night school so that when they were called up, they might demonstrate a willingness to learn that had hitherto been decidedly lacking in their school careers. Ironically, it was just those science-based and technical courses, requiring specialist teaching facilities, which were hit hardest by evacuation. Some efforts at positive discrimination were attempted. In order that a constant flow of students might be provided to science courses at Glasgow's Royal Technical College and Heriot-Watt College, Edinburgh, the Ministry of Labour directed that those teachers in the thirty- to thirty-five-year-old age group with degrees in physics, chemistry, mathematics, or engineering should not be called up or transferred to industry. Even where a school offered a well-established tradition of science teaching, things could go wrong. Roundhay Boys' HS in Leeds was strong on science but was evacuated to share teaching spaces with a school in Lincoln, which lacked the requisite facilities, giving prominence to classical studies. While a select group of boys at Dulwich College were learning Japanese (see Chapter 3), many schools, in a move presented as being patriotic, took German off the curriculum, one school offering horticulture as an alternative. One boy, at school in Stoke Newington, records that all he was ever taught at school was how to keep rabbits.

Schools were visited by what one memoir describes as the 'Tanks and Guns Circus', hoping to attract recruits into the army. Officers from fashionable regiments such as the Rifle Brigade and the King's Royal Rifle Corps confined their recruiting visits to schools such as Eton, Charterhouse, Winchester, and Rugby. The commandos aimed their recruiting efforts at boys who were, or had been, Boy Scouts, a much wider demographic. Westminster School's OTC based in Herefordshire received a visit from an officer, an old boy of the school, on the HQ staff of the Royal Armoured Corps' 1st Armoured Group, bringing along with him a Covenanter tank. The motion picture industry was mobilised to produce films intended to attract mainly boys into the armed forces and the pre-service organisations. These included commissions from the Ministry of Information and the War Office promoting membership of the ACF, the ATC, and the Sea Cadet Corps. Magazines also presented the various cadet organisations as providing exciting and challenging activities as a prelude to the armed forces with their continuations of past military glory. Some boys took their preparation for war a bit too far by manufacturing bombs and even rockets, only letting up when neighbours' lives began to be seriously endangered. In the East Midlands, when, prior to D-Day, large quantities of bombs and ammunition were stored by the roadside on country lanes, pilfering was widespread. A group of boys at Trent College found this treasure trove of explosives irresistible but failed to appreciate the differing strengths of British and US Army cordite. Their experiments resulted in a large explosion during a cricket match against Worksop College. In the interests of all, the headmaster declared an amnesty, collecting the munitions and returning them to the ordnance stores. At Oundle, however, when boys experimented with explosives, the headmaster's objection centred on the fact that as a chemistry graduate who had run one of ICI's explosives factories in the Great War, they ought really to have invited him to participate.

Where schools were sharing buildings and only receiving part-time schooling, efforts were made to provide useful activities outside of the classroom. One of these was foraging for medicinal ingredients such as foxgloves (*digitalis*) or rosehips. Schools made use of the countryside for everything from nature rambles to spy hunts. Evacuees from cities, mystified by the very existence of a life divorced from cinemas and chip shops, might be expected to benefit from gaining an understanding of an unfamiliar countryside. It was also thought that the war would motivate children to spend their leisure time in sewing, knitting, and mending, both to supplement their own wardrobes and to produce comforts for the troops. All one girl from Wiltshire remembers of her time in school was endlessly knitting. Fortunately, she loved doing complicated patterns for socks and scarves, and ceaselessly turning out gloves in air force blue, black for the navy, and khaki. Schools in towns were expected to maintain allotments, and in more rural areas, market gardens, however modest. Boys evacuated from Portsmouth's Priory School to Bishop Wordsworth's GS in Salisbury found digging the allotments, which had taken over part of the school's playing fields, timetabled as an official part of the curriculum. Similarly, the boys of St Clement Danes mucked in with their Southfields School hosts to dig the school allotments in Headington. All too often, however, the sparse activities provided in overcrowded classrooms consisted of repetitive low-level and tedious exercises offering minimal stimulation and negligible progression. One child in Liverpool reported that his education, in a class of just four stay-behinds, barely approached anything meaningful in an educational sense, consisting of four hours a week spent playing board games.

While younger children might have received some benefit from the range of learning experiences occasioned by evacuation, older pupils, studying for public examinations, perhaps with a view to going to university, suffered the interruptions to their studies that educational dislocation clearly brought. One boy whose Bath school closed in the Blitz never to reopen, despite managing to secure a place in the City of Bath Boys' School, itself heavily damaged in the same raid, took two or three years to regain his correct level in a system based on streaming. Once removed from the routine, many never returned. Even if they made the examination room, as prepared as they could possibly be, the distractions of Doodlebugs and rockets might totally derail them. Invigilators might apply peacetime rules of not leaving the examination room even as the bombs were falling. City of London School, next to Blackfriars Bridge near the City's bullseye, had returned from a stay at Marlborough. A request for their candidates to sit their examinations in the peace and calm of the Wiltshire countryside was refused and examinations were sat in the Guildhall's basement, sharing the space with ARP Control. At Chigwell, boys sitting external examinations, which were interrupted by air raids, were instructed to descend, in silence, of course, to the shelters, and then, on resumption, record the duration of the interruption on their answer papers. It is not recorded whether more marks were awarded for parachute mines or incendiaries. Such disconcerting experiences were certainly responsible for students abandoning their studies.

One girl was sitting her Scottish Senior Leaving Certificate in mathematics, physics, Latin, chemistry, French, and English at the time of the Clydebank Blitz, with a view to going to Glasgow University. Evacuated to Helensburgh, she decided to go straight into employment, securing a job at the Marine Aircraft Experimental Establishment at RAF Rhu. In such unpredictable times, swanning around in Sunderland flying boats to film and analyse the performance of anti-submarine rockets, and working on the development of the bombs that would be delivered by the Dambusters, beat the periodic table and Latin verbs hands down. There were, however, attempts to keep students on course, particularly if their chosen areas of study coincided with national priorities. By the selective use of scholarships, the government was enabled to direct those boys who showed outstanding linguistic ability, toward particularly those oriental languages whose study would benefit the war effort. Girls would get their turn to shine when domestic science also became important due to concerns over rationing and nutrition. In 1942, some 20,000 Scottish schoolgirls took part in a competition to cook oat and potato products, seeking innovative and transferable recipes. Those seventeen-year-old boys who had already secured their School Certificate and wanted to become aircrew in the RAF could join a University Air Squadron for six months and learn to fly at public expense. They would study mathematics, mechanics, and physics with a specialist course in magnetism and electricity, engineering, meteorology, or navigation. Once the war neared its conclusion, however, these opportunities quickly evaporated.

Unsurprisingly, there was evidence to suggest that educational achievement was declining. Data from Scotland showed that infants who started school in Glasgow in 1940 were a year behind in their reading ability. Inspectors opined that clever and eager pupils suffered not much at all, but the less able missed out on the reinforcement that repetitive practice might bring in those topics or skills, which would benefit from rote learning. In Fife, there appeared to have been no drop in standards, but this was an area little troubled by the war. In England, a ten-year-old girl changing schools was asked by her new head teacher if she could read. Once she had got over the shock of this inexplicable question, she was put to reading aloud to her non-reading classmates. In England and Wales, the local examinations boards found it easier to maintain an effective administration of their systems even if many of their clients had been disadvantaged by discontinuities in their preparation. In Scotland, however, the centralised examination system was effectively abandoned with teachers being asked to make their own assessments of their students' attainments, a system often found unsatisfactory and a situation that has gained echoes in the strange circumstances of 2020 and 2021.

When proficiency tests were incorporated into pre-service training, the results were mixed. The RAF was understandably keen to capitalise on youngsters' enthusiasm for what they saw as a romantic and glamorous service. They were able, therefore, to be picky about selecting only the best candidates. In order that a common standard might be set throughout the ATC, proficiency examinations were set by RAF Training Command. Only school-based ATC units had the capacity to teach the second level of this test, but the basic level was open to all; however, out of the 156,000 members of the ATC in 1944, only 14,000 (or 11 per cent) attained a pass in this basic RAF proficiency examination.

In contrast to many of the negative or pessimistic accounts of a dislocated curriculum, an account in the *Wiltshire & Gloucestershire Standard* of 25 May

1940 reports in a rather gushing style on the work done by pupils from Bifrons School evacuated to Cirencester from Barking in east London. The pupils, working out of a church hall, had produced work of an exceptionally high standard, which involved land survey using technical instruments some of which they had themselves constructed; drawing up the resultant maps in a variety of media including needlework; a production of Punch and Judy; work resulting from a visit to Chedworth Roman villa; and other drama and craft activities carried out in evening clubs organised by the school. All this was shown in a successful public exhibition. One local correspondent, however, requested that potato printing be removed from art classes to preserve a valuable food resource.

In preparation for the publication of the 1944 Education Act, the Norwood Report of 1943—prefaced by a quotation from Plato (naturally in its original classical Greek)—examined the secondary curriculum in detail. This exploration led to the proposed tripartite organisation (grammar, technical, and modern) predicated on a recognition of the differing needs of secondary-age pupils characterised by a move toward the adoption of the principle of a more 'child-centred approach'. In its summation of the current state of secondary education, while admitting that improvements were always possible, the report's authors made the positive assertion:

> If further evidence were needed to prove the qualities of the Secondary Schools, the history of the last three years would provide it. If we said that their boys and girls have shown themselves ready to undertake whatever tasks came their way, to stand up to hardship and discomfort, and worse, with courage and cheerfulness, and in the things that matter have shown themselves capable and steadfast, we should be saying what is true, but claiming no more than can be claimed for all the youth of the country. But the pupils of the secondary schools have also shown themselves enterprising, adaptable and capable of meeting in quantity and quality the very special demands made in new developments of applied Science and of linguistic study. It is not too much to say that, if a demand of similar range had been made in the last [First World] war, it could not have been met: in this war it has been met. That is one very real measure of the achievement of the Secondary Schools...
>
> Norwood Report, p. 11, HMSO, 1943

Aspects of Child Health and Safety

Even were a school to be available, many children would have been unable to obtain much benefit from the teaching owing to emotional, physical, and psychological factors. Apart from all the universal childhood worries and teenage angst, they could be suffering from specific anxieties about fathers and brothers away on active service; about being able to survive the bombing; about losing contact with parents and siblings through evacuation; all exacerbated by basic concerns over food on the table and roofs over heads. Those youngsters who, night after night, tried to sleep on the platforms of underground stations or in freezing cold and damp Anderson shelters; or carried out fire-watching duties; or had patrol duties with the Home Guard could not be expected to be at their liveliest in class or in the workplace. Some schools instituted a half-hour snooze each morning. One way of dealing with children who suffered problems as evacuees was to label them as 'difficult, maladjusted, neurotic or delinquent' and gather them together in hostels, each holding twenty or so (generally) boys. By 1943, 224 such hostels housed 3,500 children, so labelled. Child Guidance Clinics, where they existed, and counselling services were overwhelmed by the largely unsatisfied demand.

As well as physical injuries sustained by children in bombing raids, their general level of health was deemed to be impaired by the circumstance of living cheek by jowl in cramped conditions in shelters, rest centres, and overcrowded or primitive homes. Children from a school for the deaf evacuated to Surrey suffered an outbreak of diphtheria in 1940, directly attributable to the excessive time they were spending crowded into airless shelters. In fact, while 8,000 children died in air raids, over a thousand more than that died from diphtheria alone, a figure to which must be added those dying from other diseases such as tuberculosis (TB), polio, tetanus, whooping cough, scarlet fever, measles, mumps and rubella, or complications arising from all these and other conditions which thrive in close human contact. Increases in infant mortality were attributed to the especially cold winter of 1940–41 and the disorganisation of evacuation. The disruption of domestic life and lack of fuel were exacerbated by families having to camp out in situations which lacked the basic amenities of electricity, heating and cooking facilities, leading to steep increases in pneumonia and bronchitis. Incidence of TB had been falling through the 1930s but showed a resurgence in the war years, peaking in 1941. Between 1939 and 1943, over 7,000 under-fives and nearly 5,000 children in the five to fifteen age group died from respiratory or other forms of TB. Evacuation is thought to have caused diseases such as scarlet fever, diphtheria, and polio to migrate from urban to rural areas which enjoyed lower levels of immunity, and it was found that disease would radiate out from small market towns to the surrounding villages.

Apart from injuries inflicted by enemy action or illness arising from insanitary living conditions, significant numbers of children were killed in road traffic accidents. In September 1939, there were over 1,100 deaths on the roads, and in the worst year, 1941, over 9,000 people, many of them children, were killed. These were generally the result of the blackout when vehicles and pedestrians were mutually invisible but, in the eyes of many magistrates, cyclists were responsible for their own misfortunes by failing to spot vehicles approaching from behind. Street lighting had been switched off permanently, and vehicles' headlights were masked, with light shining only through small, residual slits. During the course of the war, there were 50,000 road deaths—more than died in the London Blitz—and the annual toll of 1,000 deaths of children under ten was accepted well into the 1950s.

Beyond these dangers, however, children and young people often managed to inflict significant injury on themselves through their own ill-considered actions. Children were injured playing in bombed buildings and picking up souvenirs. Incendiaries or butterfly bombs, while attractive to the souvenir hunter, could be live and unstable, and unexploded anti-aircraft shells could cause unexpected injuries when struck with bricks or hammers. Children were warned about playing around water storage tanks, placed on school sites to serve the fire services. In Highclere, schoolchildren cleared out the contents of a crashed German bomber, carrying away instruments, machine guns, ammunition, and other souvenirs. Sadly for them, the police promptly called round at their school and they were forced to hand it all in. Day boys in Oundle's Laxton School greatly enjoyed the bedlam that throwing blank cartridges onto the common-room fire and then running away would unfailingly produce. Although most beaches were out of bounds for very good reasons, they might still prove enticing. In Bournemouth in 1942, two evacuees from Southampton climbed through the barbed wire defences and, after detonating a mine, were lucky to escape with only injuries. Small boys in Port Talbot watched transfixed and waited for the inevitable explosion as dogs ran over the mined beach. Boys from the Duke of York's Royal Military School, evacuated from Dover to a hotel in north Devon, had access to a beach previously used for commando training. Coming from army families, they could see the potential in the small arms rounds, grenades, and small quantities of gelignite they found. Deciding that grenades were, perhaps, a little too noisy, they nevertheless amused themselves by putting small amounts of explosives in the coke stoves and manufacturing little booby traps using rifle cartridges. It appears that they were aware enough to avoid causing themselves or their victims any injury beyond shattered nerves. On the Isle of Man, two lads would cycle home from the firing range with unexploded mortar bombs dangling from their handlebars. Having hammered off the fins and unscrewed the nose cones, they emptied the cordite into lead pipes into which had been inserted fuses. Once the blue touch paper had been lit, they must have stood back sufficiently to avoid serious injury. Other children, however, were less lucky. In appropriately named Chard, two lads came across a cache of self-igniting phosphorous (SIP) grenades and sustained severe burns. Where children were living in close proximity to training areas, there were many more accidents. Around Lewes, where the Canadian Army spent much of the war carrying out battle training, there were numerous incidents involving children picking up live ordnance. One boy hit a live shell with a chopper, losing his eye, and others were injured when phosphorous bombs exploded. Court proceedings were instigated by Sussex Police against another fifteen-year-old boy in Lewes for illegal possession of ordnance when he was found to have a 3.7-inch AA shell and parts of 25-pounder shells at his home. In Cheltenham during Easter 1941, a fourteen-year-old scoured an army training area for ordnance curiosities. He had found what he took to be a practice mortar bomb and, unable to penetrate the casing, he took it home to have another go. His persistence in breaking open the bomb with a hammer resulted in his own death and that of his playmates in the resultant explosion.

As well as the instigator, two girls and three boys aged between six and ten were killed and a third girl lost an arm. Widespread roadside storage of explosives prior to D-Day presented children with both dangers and challenges. A similar tragedy befell an Essex family in Twinstead near Sudbury. As reported in the *Essex Newsman Herald* (8 September 1944), four sons aged between ten and eighteen were killed when it was supposed that they were playing with detonators, possibly originating in the Bures Forward Ammunition Depot. The hammer and other tools which were the agents of their deaths were found to have been blown sixty yards away into neighbours' gardens. Despite frequent newspaper reports of such incidents, youngsters persisted in dicing with death. Having been warned only the previous day, a twelve-year-old boy was killed when he threw the nose cap of a 25-pounder shell against a concrete wall and was killed by the resultant splinters. One lad from Burnage HS was killed by a live round he had been playing with, and two ten-year-olds evacuated from Birmingham died at Bestwood, Nottingham, when they threw the detonator from a hand grenade into the kitchen stove. Engaged in legitimate activity, a pupil of Cranleigh School was killed when a Sten gun, a weapon notoriously dangerous to its users, discharged accidentally during a Home Guard exercise. Other incidents saw the deaths of at least a dozen children on firing ranges across the country, but the great majority of those inquisitive youngsters who, knowingly or unknowingly, risked injury or death must have got away with it. Five boys who broke into a military store stole Verey lights (flares) and smoke grenades, and then used cordite to make fireworks, which they let off on a train. No injuries resulted, but they were summonsed to juvenile court and placed on probation.

Employment

On their return to the city from an unpleasant or apparently unnecessary experience as an evacuee, some children found their schools had been closed. One solution, for any child over fourteen, was to be enticed by the plentiful jobs to be had, some of them paying good money and all it took was a trip to the local Labour Exchange. As there were no public examinations to hang around for, children could leave school the day after their fourteenth birthday. Factories of all sorts were recruiting unskilled or semi-skilled operatives, and young girls could also go into telephonist/receptionist or clerical jobs with little training, thereby releasing adults for more demanding work. Boys could work in factories, offices, mines and quarries, transport and communications, or on the land (see Chapter 5).

The Experience of One City's Schools: Cardiff

Keith Strange's fascinating and exhaustive synthesis of the logbooks of 120 schools in Cardiff and the County of Glamorgan neatly illustrates how all these factors affected children's education in one heavily bombed city over the course of the war.

In 1939, the City of Cardiff had 125 elementary schools educating over 30,000 children up to the school-leaving age of fourteen. Just under 4,000 children, aged eleven to sixteen attended ten high schools and were expected to sit public examinations. A tiny number of those stayed on for a further two years, and even fewer went on to university or teacher training colleges.

Despite its perceptions of being out of range of Germany-based bombers, Cardiff, with its extensive docks, was one of those British cities most closely targeted by the *Luftwaffe*. In September 1938, the director of education called a conference at which he explained to head teachers the urgency of putting evacuation procedures in place for getting children out of the school and into their homes in the event of an air raid. At many schools, older pupils were paired with younger ones to gather at designated assembly points to ensure an orderly and speedy evacuation. During the Munich Crisis, ARP activities were recorded as being disruptive of schools' normal functioning; teachers were quizzed by the police about their emergency planning; and courses for head teachers were being run at the law courts. By January 1939, evacuees were beginning to trickle into Cardiff to be enrolled in local schools, and in March, teachers who were members of the Territorial Army or the other reserve forces were allowed a fortnight's leave for military training. Arrangements were made in April to accommodate up to 9,000 evacuees from Birmingham were it to become necessary. Jewish refugees also arrived in the city from Nazi Germany and were taken into schools there. In June, schools received a circular regarding the provision of shelters, and at the end of August, schools received Circular 39, which laid out the details of the Education Department's ARP regulations. These explained how children living within five minutes from their school should be sent home immediately when the warnings were heard. Others would remain in the school buildings, which would therefore need to receive structural reinforcement internally, and in external shelters. Male teaching staff should undertake training as ARP wardens, and female staff should train in first aid; children should practise their gas mask drills and those of an appropriate age should learn to administer first aid; schools should install blackout and tape over windows; and the programme to provide them with shelters would commence. Eight Cardiff schools were designated first aid party and ambulance depots with a further four identified as reserve first aid posts, and all those dozen schools would have telephones installed. At the same time, two schools—Crwys Road and Maindy Senior—were allocated entirely for military purposes and their pupils would be transferred to neighbouring schools, effectively from 1 September. The military authorities also requisitioned the uncompleted Lady Margaret High School.

Once war had broken out, all schools closed for two weeks, but even when the older children returned, curriculum was immediately affected as no children would be allowed to attend swimming pools or other specialist teaching centres if located further than five minutes away from their homes. As shelters had not yet been provided, parents were asked to transfer their children to schools within five minutes from home as necessary, and some schools amalgamated and reorganised to accommodate the new circumstances. The planned raising of the school-leaving age to fifteen was suspended, no child under five years of age would be admitted and, in any case, all infants' schools remained closed, not to reopen until after Christmas. Ten days into the war, the city engineer had begun the process of providing either playground shelters or implementing structural alterations to reinforce classrooms. Boys at Cathays High filled sandbags for the protection of entrances. The school day was being increasingly interrupted by evacuation rehearsals, gas mask drills, and the installation of blackout. Fifteen teachers were called up by the TA including six from one school, and a further dozen male and female teachers were permitted to enlist in the forces, all being guaranteed to be paid the difference between their teachers' pay and their forces' pay. Despite these losses to the teaching force, women teachers would still have to resign on getting married, but as a concession, they might expect their applications for supply work to be looked on favourably.

By the end of September, the number of evacuees from London and Birmingham was slowly increasing, a further pressure on schools already involved in consolidation exercises. Schools were urged to convert any spare ground into gardens for the growing of food, and the school day was compressed to recognise lighting restrictions. On 10 November, the first stage of the shelter programme was approved by the Board of Education, the first shelters being built in those schools nearest to the docks and other vulnerable industrial areas. On 2 January 1940, tenders were invited for the construction of 199 shelters. The cost of these, added to shelters already under construction and sandbagging operations, came to a little less than £30,000 (around £15 million at today's values). Most of the shelters were the standard, brick-built, fifty-person surface model. Where there was no suitable space in school playgrounds, shelters had to be erected in the street and must therefore be available to the general public, but with an understanding that the school had first call during school hours. Whether this would prove a reasonable expectation, in the unpredictable circumstances of an air raid, was not apparently discussed.

In March 1940, of the nearly 10,000 householders circularised regarding the taking in of evacuees, only 247 of them offered to take 382 children between them and at the same time, some of the earlier evacuees decided to return home. Efforts by the WVS secured further offers of billets for 908 children, and in May, 500 evacuees from London and Birmingham plus over 200 from the Medway towns arrived. Where possible, groups of evacuees were taught in discrete groups merely sharing the premises of Cardiff schools, but many were admitted in small numbers to, particularly, infants' schools. By June, there were 1,207 child evacuees, seventy-nine teachers, and twenty-five helpers in Cardiff, with more to follow.

Cardiff received its first air raid on 20 June 1940 followed up on seven successive nights, and these interruptions affected attendance at schools which put their starting time back to 11 a.m. Anxiety over the continuing raids halved attendance in many schools and sank even lower in others. The decision was taken to split the summer holidays into two separate breaks in August and October. Schools would remain open for recreational activities throughout the holidays, particularly aimed at helping the host families of evacuees. Air raids began to claim the lives of schoolchildren, increasing in intensity until on 4 September a particularly heavy one caused severe damage to school buildings and more deaths and injuries. Thus far, Cardiff was the most heavily bombed place in Britain and damage to a dozen schools had been reported. Unsurprisingly, some evacuees decided that Cardiff was less safe than most other places and returned home. While those embarked on SS *Volendam* were all saved, the five Cardiff children on SS *City of Benares* were among those lost. More evacuees from London arrived and were taken into Whitchurch High School where classrooms had been converted into dormitories. Schools were issued with galvanised buckets and stirrup pumps for dealing with incendiaries, but storms flooded many of the school shelters rendering them unusable. The city engineer reported that of the 280 shelters built at schools, half of them were wet owing to rain driving through the entrances and the porous nature of the bricks. He recommended raising the height of the blast walls protecting the entrances, damp-proofing the walls, and installing seating.

In late November 1940, more evacuees from Birmingham had brought the total in the city to nearly 2,500. More raids in January 1941 caused damage to schools, which were showered with incendiaries, and some were put out of action entirely. Others were assigned as emergency centres and more closed owing to nearby unexploded HE bombs awaiting disposal. In this spate of raids, the heaviest so far, two dozen schools were severely damaged when 111 aircraft deposited well over 100 tons of HE bombs, parachute mines, oil bombs, and 5,000 incendiaries on the city, killing 156 inhabitants and severely injuring nearly 500. As a result, a meeting of head teachers discussed canvassing parents to gauge the level of support for evacuating Cardiff's own children to somewhere safer. An added complication was the outbreak among schoolchildren of epidemics of mumps, measles, and chicken pox. A year later, soap shortages and limited bathing facilities led to outbreaks of scabies and head lice. In June 1942, Lever Brothers of Port Sunlight would offer a mobile bath unit to the city that would visit selected schools on a fortnightly rota.

In the wake of the most severe bombing, attendances fell to 40 per cent in many schools and as low as 35 per cent at others as heavy snow fell and children were moved out of uninhabitable homes. Conditions in the shelters were no better as boilers failed and temperatures failed to rise above 40F (4C). Parents' meetings were held in schools to explore the possibility of evacuation, but enthusiasm was tepid with only around a quarter of parents of Cardiff's 32,000 schoolchildren in favour. A survey of Cardiff's 1,300 teaching staff found 60 per cent of male teachers involved in voluntary ARP duties and 38 per cent of female teachers carrying out some form of Civil Defence work as volunteers.

Early in March 1941, further heavy raids hit Cardiff destroying schools and houses and causing over fifty deaths with sixty HE bombs and 7,000 incendiaries.

More schools were taken out of use as they were needed as rest centres for those made homeless. Schools organised fire-watching vigils with staff, older pupils, and neighbours, but more fire-fighting equipment was needed. March, April, and May showed one unending catalogue of damage to schools; attempts to make do and mend; the salvaging of books and equipment; and concerns over the continuous strain on all concerned. On 30 May, the official evacuation of children from Cardiff schools began, and 4,256 children, around 13 per cent of the school population, as well as other individuals evacuated privately, were moved to safer rural locations. However, problems arose as schools in the city remained open in unsatisfactory conditions; some evacuees returned home; there were still evacuees from elsewhere in the city; teaching staff were split between their schools and the reception centres in the country; and the aerial onslaught showed little sign of letting up. One consolation might have been the Education Committee's decision to have lighting and heating installed in the schools' shelters. After Whitsun 1941, some school rolls had halved owing to resettlement; deaths and injuries; evacuation; exchanges between schools; and evacuee visitors returning home. But Cardiff's own evacuees returning home could not compensate for falling numbers.

All through these terrifying times children had been knitting comforts for troops; raising money for National Savings, war bonds, Warship Week, and the Lord Mayor's Spitfire Fund; foraging for wild fruit; writing letters to adopted merchant ships or HMS *Cardiff*; raising specific sums for everything from a single parachute to an ambulance or for charities such as Dr Barnardo's or the local hospital; and collecting rags and metal salvage. A woman teacher was impressed by the government as a PT instructor and senior girls gave cookery demonstrations to help the general public cope with rationing. Steel helmets and blankets were delivered to schools for the use of fire watchers, supplementing the items previously delivered, with torches and spare batteries, bunks, and mattresses quickly following. Although air raids continued, the examination for high school entrance went ahead, but in one school, half of those who passed either refused a place or had, in the meantime, been evacuated.

So many teachers had been called up that, although falling rolls had allowed for classes to be amalgamated, boys' schools were forced to take on women teachers. Despite the teacher shortage, the director of education reminded head teachers that he would not approve the appointment of married women nor allow male teachers to be retained beyond the normal retirement age. This matter would be raised many times over the next two years, but the Education Committee was unable to agree to a recommendation to rescind this policy. What they could agree on, though, in March 1942, was the dismissal of several teachers who had registered as conscientious objectors. In June 1942, the committee agreed in principle to offer posts to married women whose husbands were serving in HM forces and, failing anyone in that category being available, then any suitable, available person could be appointed, but only temporarily. The Board of Education in London directed that LEAs should suspend local regulations for the duration in the light of serious teacher shortages, but the committee's compromise measure was to set up a list of approved reserve teachers. Not until October 1943 would the decision be taken by the committee to allow suitable and capable superannuated teachers to continue teaching on six-month contracts. Finally, in December, a married woman was employed at Gladstone Infants' School as a temporary supply teacher, a first, thought worthy of record in the school log. At Cathays High School, the previously all-male staff by the end of 1943 consisted of four male and three female teachers. However, in defiance of the Board of Education's directive, the general principle of terminating the contracts of female teachers on their marriage had not been abandoned, and in January 1944, the Glamorgan Higher Education Association (NUT) submitted a resolution: 'That this Association deplores the regulation of the Glamorgan Education Committee which compels female teachers to resign upon marriage during the present emergency'.

The committee voted to disregard this resolution. Only in November 1944 did the committee finally take note of the representations of the unions representing head teachers and teachers and obey the Board of Education's instruction to suspend local regulations affecting the employment of married women. As the board had pointed out, all available teachers were required in order to maintain 'educational services in England [*sic*]'. From henceforth, marriage on its own would cease to become a sole reason for dismissing a woman teacher.

Following concern over the number of malnourished children in the city's schools, the City Education Committee approved an increase in the provision of free milk to all children, and of midday meals in public elementary schools charged to parents at cost, and the army was asked to release one of its requisitioned infants' schools to be converted into a central kitchen. The committee was, however, unable to agree to use the schools as a channel for promoting the Blood Transfusion Service. Schools, many of them with a dwindling stock of bomb-damaged classrooms, were still having to juggle their own day-to-day requirements with the competing needs of the ARP's rest centres and the canteens required by the school feeding organisation with its depot at Wenvoe. Public halls were hired in many cases as there was simply no room to spare in the schools themselves, although washing up facilities were contrived in fifteen of them. The children of at least one school were catered for in the Celtic Corridor British Restaurant and three schools were designated shadow kitchens in July 1942.

Possibly timed to coincide with the establishment of the Royal Ordnance Factory at Llanishen, three wartime nurseries, in Splott, Ely, and Grangetown, were established with four more to follow and, additionally, nursery classes were started at six infants' schools. At Grangetown Continuation School, new classes were started in mathematics and English, and seven of the eight students enrolling were members of the ATC. Those boys who had left school at fourteen and wanted careers in the RAF realised that they needed to make up some lost ground. Senior girls, approaching their exams in the summer of 1942, attended recruitment sessions for the WAAF. So acute were the pressures limiting children's education that the twelve Co-operative Women's Guilds of Cardiff felt it incumbent on them to protest about the government's proposal to make farm work for children over twelve compulsory. They were adamant that such a move would not only be detrimental to the children's health but would also be a serious handicap to their education, given its already limited nature.

By September 1942, Cardiff's schools appeared to be regaining some sense of normality. While they still had to be regularly serviced, the requirement for gas masks to be carried at all times was dropped. School meals were being served in most schools; the nurseries were opening on Saturdays; the mobile shower units were well used; much of the ARP equipment was being cleared away; the majority of evacuees had returned home; but women teachers' contracts were still terminated on marriage and conscientious objectors were still being dismissed.

The poor state of their homes and the low levels of nutrition, however, were causing medical problems. Five cases of dysentery were reported at one of the nursery schools and cases of scabies, impetigo, and head lice were still around. More worryingly, cases of diphtheria, pneumonia, scarlet fever, and meningitis were also recorded. In ARP terms, no chances were being taken. Some 247 shelters, some of which had been constructed with lime mortar, were strengthened and internal shelters were beefed up with Portal frames, strengthening the joints of vertical supports and roof trusses. The sirens were tested periodically triggering full-scale air-raid drills right into the spring of 1943.

All this was warranted as the raids were not yet over. Metal Street School was severely damaged on the night of 18 May, with relatively minor damage at others of the city's schools and many of the surrounding houses damaged or destroyed. Fifty aircraft had dropped bombs and landmines destroying or damaging 4,000 homes and killing forty-five people including six schoolchildren. This was to be Cardiff's last air raid. During the aerial assault, the city had suffered altogether 355 deaths and 502 seriously injured. A total 600 homes had been completely destroyed and 30,000 more damaged.

Despite earlier concerns over children's well-being, in June 1943, girls from Heathfield House were taken by lorry to work on farms and forestry nurseries, being paid 1*s* 10*d* each for eight hours work (working out, in today's terms, at £4.58p or about £0.57p an hour). Towards the end of 1943, even though most of Cardiff's evacuees had returned, the city continued to host children from other areas notably London, the Thames and Medway estuaries, and Birmingham. Problems of bedwetting and impetigo continued to arise, along with scabies and head lice ('dirty heads') caused by people having to live among ruins or in less-than-ideal communal conditions. Concerns over diphtheria remained and medical officers visited schools to carry out the Schick test on younger pupils and a programme of immunisation significantly reduced the number of cases.

Despite a relaxation in some restrictions, it remained necessary to avoid complacency. The headmaster of Cardiff High School applied for permission, apparently successfully, to install a miniature rifle range in a school workshop as a contribution to preparing boys for military service. The school's ACF contingent was inspected on 28 June 1944. It had over forty members who trained on Wednesday evenings and shot on the school's new miniature range on Saturday afternoons. In February 1944, a large Civil Defence exercise took place, with shadow kitchens being staffed in schools. As part of the build-up for the Normandy landings, the US Army was granted permission to use the bombed-out Marlborough Road School for training in house-to-house fighting, at a rent of £5 (£250) *per annum* set by the War Office and undercutting the £15 *p.a.* (£750) requested by the town clerk. At the end of March, an air-raid alert was sounded, and this would turn out to be the very last of the city's 585 alerts over the four years. A few months earlier, the ringing of school bells, previously the signal that an invasion was taking place, had recommenced. However, it was not yet all over. In June, evacuees from London, under attack by flying bombs, the V-1 'Doodlebugs', began to arrive. Nearly 600 mothers and children had arrived by the middle of July and Whitchurch Mixed School was again closed to pupils for processing and feeding the evacuees. Within a few weeks, the number of evacuees, mainly from London and the Home Counties where V-2 rockets had also begun to land, had risen to over 1,150 children, all being admitted to Cardiff's schools. The LEA suggested, not unreasonably, that then might have been a good time to return the Birmingham children, their homes no longer being under threat of bombing.

At last, the LEA could look to the future. An enquiry aimed at identifying promising thirteen-year-olds in elementary schools who might continue their education up to age eighteen with a view to becoming teachers, found 107 children whose parents might be amenable. In January 1946, the military camp on the Heath Estate would be leased to the Ministry of Education for four years as an emergency (teacher) training college for Wales. In October 1944, the Lady Margaret High School for Girls, requisitioned by the military back in 1939 while still under construction, was handed back. The cost of repairing the damage and dilapidation caused during its occupation was assessed at almost £4,000 (£200,000). In October, the police resumed responsibility for school crossing patrols on the termination of the existing ARP arrangements and in January 1945, blackout material was removed from schools and the next month, the emergency water tanks in school playgrounds were emptied by the fire service. Heating and lighting appliances were removed from school shelters in April; protective netting was taken down from schools' windows; and stores of blankets and other items held in schools used as rest centres were collected.

In December 1944, over 200 evacuees from Maidstone had gathered at Whitchurch Mixed School prior to returning home, followed by most of the London children, while only five children from Birmingham and eight from Maidstone remained in Cardiff. Children from London were still being admitted at the beginning of March 1945 as it would be a further month before the last of the V-1s and V-2s landed. Cardiff's schools celebrated VE Day with services of thanksgiving and attendance over the following days was recorded as sparse owing to children attending street parties. The last evacuees, apart from those very few whose parents could not be traced, would only leave Cardiff at the end of July. Over the next few months following VJ Day, men and women teachers who had served in the armed forces, or in government-sponsored work as scientists or instructors, slowly drifted back to their former posts, and married women teachers relinquished theirs, at least one of them as a GI bride. In April 1946, the schools' 290 air-raid shelters were scheduled for demolition, and on 7 June, Cardiff's schools participated in a Victory Celebration Day with religious services, fancy dress parades, singing and special teas, grateful to have survived.

2

The Repurposing of School Premises

From the very beginning of the war, much of Britain assumed the appearance of an armed camp. A register of premises available for requisition by the civil and military authorities had been prepared in 1938 and contained 30,000 entries reflecting the anticipated requirements of the armed services; government ministries and departments; and ARP. Theoretically, local authority establishments were exempt, but the Emergency Powers (Defence) Act of 1939 cut across all previous arrangements. In the event, the War Office alone requisitioned half a million acres of land including whole settlements. These included six entire villages in the Stanta Training Area in Norfolk (commandeered in 1942), Tyneham in Dorset, and Imber in Wiltshire (both taken over a year later). Eighty years on, all remain in MOD occupation, but their churches are protected and maintained while most other buildings are ruinous. At Tyneham, however, the schoolroom, which had closed in 1932, has been rebuilt and refurbished to its original state. The village of Stanmer near Lewes was also taken into the Canadians' training area and their inhabitants evacuated. The Stanmer Estate was used for both artillery practice and house-to-house fighting, and extensive repairs, undertaken by Brighton Council, were necessary after the war. In all, 113,350 non-industrial premises were requisitioned for defence purposes during the war. Even in remote Caithness, the six largest schools were commandeered by the military. School buildings were also, on occasion, commandeered for industrial purposes. In Gloucestershire, Berkeley Primary (formerly Secondary) School's science laboratories, wood and metal workshops were taken over by Listers of Dursley for the manufacture of diesel engines.

Prior to the outbreak of war, the Rae Committee had formulated evacuation plans for government departments. These would be implemented as a series of separate operations with some being assigned colours as code-names. Black Move would see 60,000 personnel in essential war-related jobs relocated into an area between Bath and Birmingham with its epicentre in Worcester. Yellow Move would take 30,000 non-essential staff into an arc in the north-west stretching from Llandudno and Rhyl in North Wales, through Buxton and Matlock in Derbyshire to Morecambe and Blackpool in Lancashire. The prime minister and his cabinet would have gone to Spetchley Court and the royal family to Madresfield, both in Worcestershire. Under the command of a major in the Coldstream Guards, the eponymous Coats Mission, named for its leader Major James Coats (often rendered as Coates), was an army unit on permanent standby to escort the royal family from Windsor Castle or Buckingham Palace were the Rocking Horse Move to be activated. It was composed of armoured cars of the 2nd Northamptonshire Yeomanry and the 12th Lancers with a company of Coldstream Guards. While elements were stationed at Windsor and Wellington Barracks, their main base was the Coldstream Guards' Holding Battalion's depot at Elstree School, which had been evacuated to Woolhampton House in Berkshire. The Coldstream Guards element consisted of five officers and 124 guardsmen of impeccable reputation. The Northwest Suburban Plan would see specifically Air Ministry personnel moved into schools in the Harrow area.

When, still in the Phoney War period, Scottish Command was asked to relinquish schools in the cities that had evacuated children but now needed them as many of the children had returned, the requests were turned down. A bigger problem were the 206 Glasgow schools wholly or partially requisitioned or earmarked as AFS or ARP centres, first aid posts or rest centres. Here the argument for retention was based on community safety not mere military convenience, and considerable sums of money had been spent on conversion or adaptation. The problem would only get worse as the 138 Scottish city schools occupied in the autumn of 1940 would increase to 293 a year later.

Evacuation of Government Departments to School Premises

Many of the planned provisions of the government's decentralisation plans were never implemented but significant numbers of civil servants were relocated. Black Move took many of the Admiralty's administrative departments to Bath where hutted complexes were built but existing buildings such as Kingswood School, evacuated to Uppingham, were also taken over. The Air Ministry identified around 1,400 key personnel it wanted moved out of London. They were the main component in the Northwest Suburban Plan, which would take over seven schools including Harrow County Boys' and Girls' Schools. The Ministry's War Group, designated as an 'Insurance Party', would occupy Belmont School in Harrow Weald. The Accounts Department was lodged in Stroud but may possibly have been intended for either Westonbirt School at Tetbury, or Wycliffe College, both also in Gloucestershire.

Wycliffe College at Stonehouse near Stroud ended up as the final destination for the Air Ministry Meteorological Branch. The headmaster had been notified of the intended requisitioning of his school on Boxing Day 1938 and the school was evacuated to Wiltshire during 1939. Very soon after the boys had left, stores, personnel, and equipment arrived from the Meteorological Office's HQ in Dunstable. Prior to May 1940, France had been the main supplier of weather data, but after Dunkirk, new sources had to be found. One of these originated at GC&CS at Bletchley Park, which had learnt to decode German weather transmissions and then to compare the product with the Enigma-encrypted messages forwarded to U-boats, helping to solve both codes through triangulation. According to the local newspaper, weather beacons, deposited in the Atlantic by U-boats, were recovered and brought to Wycliffe for dissection and evaluation. Other research carried out there, covered FIDO—the fog dispersal system used on a handful of emergency airfields; aspects of jet propulsion; and German V-2 rockets, particularly their gyroscopic guidance systems. Other Air Ministry departments went to Worcestershire: to King's School on College Green next to Worcester Cathedral; to preparatory schools in Barbourne; and to Aymestrey Preparatory School in Crown East.

The Air Ministry's planning, production, and research departments had been reorganised into the Ministry of Aircraft Production (MAP), and this new body under Lord Beaverbrook constituted the largest group of Air Ministry migrants. Nearly 2,000 of them were sent to Harrogate, occupying several hotels and schools. Queen Ethelburga's (Girls') College was evacuated to Studley Royal; Harrogate Ladies' College to Swinton Park; Pannal Ash (Boys') College to Coxwold; and Ashville (Boys') College to Bowness-on-Windermere. This left the way clear for MAP to take over these four boarding schools, along with New College, which had been previously subsumed into Ashville. Although Beaverbrook retained over 3,000 staff at Thames House on the Embankment opposite the Palace of Westminster, many of them would subsequently be despatched to the generally safer Harrogate. However, news of MAP's presence in Harrogate may have seeped out as the Majestic Hotel, one of its sites, was bombed in September 1940. Most government departments had evacuation plans, some of which were carried through. Bromsgrove GS was earmarked for staff of the Foreign and Colonial Office, and only some staff from the India Office were actually posted there.

The Newcastle upon Tyne Royal GS had been moved into new buildings in Jesmond in 1907. Throughout the Great War, it had served as the HQ of the Northumberland VTC, and in 1939, it was formally requisitioned, the pupils being evacuated to Penrith, only returning in October 1944. It became the regional war room and office of the regional commissioner for the North of England with the ARP reporting centre next door at Jesmond Dene House. The commissioner was the government's representative with plenipotentiary powers in his own region. He commanded ARP and made decisions regarding the deployment of CD resources including the mobile columns. He would liaise with the local military and with local authorities, effectively controlling the police, education, medical, and fire and rescue services. Several of the eleven commissioners were senior military figures: retired generals or admirals. The

War Office pay and records (infantry) department moved into the Welsh Girls' School in Ashford (Middlesex), which had been evacuated to Powis Castle not to return to Ashford until 1945. The Ministry of Food was relocated to Colwyn Bay on the North Wales coast from June 1940. As well as most of the town's hotels, Penrhos College, a girls' boarding school, evacuated to Chatsworth House, and Rydal (Mount) Boys' School, transferred to Conway, were both occupied. The LCC had moved into its new offices in county hall on the Lambeth side of the Thames from the Palace of Westminster in two stages in the 1920s and in the 1930s as the buildings were completed. In 1939, it redeployed many of its clerical staff from county hall's exposed position on the riverside out to the suburbs. Many of them occupied two floors of St Dunstan's College in Catford, only to return to their offices after a short stay during the Phoney War, the lull before the storm.

Admiralty Use of School Buildings

A brand-new leisure complex, consisting of a swimming bath and marina with a large underground carpark, was about to be opened in King's Parade, Hove, in 1939, but it was immediately requisitioned by the Admiralty as HMS *King Alfred*, to train naval officers. Initially, some 1,700 Royal Naval Volunteer (Supplementary) Reserve officers, many of them weekend yachtsmen, were trained at Hove, but once it became clear that many more officers would be needed by the Royal Navy, it was necessary to expand the operation into larger premises. Early in the war, Westminster School had been evacuated to Lancing but reckoned it had moved closer to danger and moved on to Exeter, even more dangerous as it turned out. After Dunkirk, Lancing itself then evacuated to Downton Castle in Herefordshire, and its preparatory feeder, Mowden School at 10–14 The Droveway, Hove, went to Oxenden Hall, Market Harborough. Both schools were then requisitioned by the Admiralty as, respectively, HMS *King Alfred II* and *III*. Over 20,000 RNVR officers were trained at HMS *King Alfred* during the war, coming from all walks of life with some of them applying while still at school. Mowden was also the new location for the Royal Navy's selection board, moving from Portsmouth and using the school's library for medical examinations. It was also the reception centre for each of the *King Alfred*'s new intakes for the first two weeks of their training, the cadets being billeted in small hotels and private houses. They then moved on to Lancing for a further six weeks of instruction, moving back to Hove for the final four weeks of their training, this time based in the leisure centre. In cohorts of up to 500, they slept in dormitories in the vast underground carpark. After graduating and being commissioned (only temporarily, of course) into the Royal Navy, the new officers would spend two weeks at Greenwich RN College learning how to behave like officers and acquiring the etiquette of the wardroom. Those officers who were posted to small craft might receive their training in mines and torpedoes at HMS *Vernon*'s annexe, along the coast from Hove, at Roedean School.

HMS *Vernon*, based at Portsmouth's Gunwharf, was the Royal Navy's specialist research and training facility for torpedoes, mines, and diving. As Portsmouth came under sustained aerial attack, one raid killing over 100 of the *Vernon*'s staff in the Dido Building, it was decided to relocate. The place chosen was Roedean School for Girls outside Brighton, which in May 1941 became the Admiralty Torpedo, Mining & Electrical Training Establishment along with the headquarters and administration sections of HMS *Vernon (R)*. There was a problem in that the army had already moved in when the girls were evacuated to Keswick. Despite arrangements for sharing having been negotiated, the army was effectively evicted (see below). The need for space rapidly accelerated and the St Dunstan's Home for the Blind in neighbouring Ovingdean, only opened in 1938 but evacuated to Shropshire and Dorset in 1940, was requisitioned for electrical training. By this time, there were 150 officers, 1,000 ratings, and 100 Wrens in residence. Wrens were being trained to maintain and arm torpedoes so that shore-based ratings might be released for service at sea. Such was the immediate pressure on space that the accounts department and main stores were moved into Mowden School, Hove, and the mine research department was transferred to Kimmerghame House on Carrington Road on the Fettes College campus in Edinburgh. After it had been requisitioned as part of the Admiralty's move to Bath, Kingswood School became home to research and development projects including work on the Mulberry Harbours, the artificial ports being built to resupply the D-Day landings.

When the destroyers of the Royal Canadian Navy came to Britain as convoy escorts, it became necessary to establish an office to deal with manning and pay arrangements. Rooms at Stoke Damerel School in Devonport were commandeered initially as HMS *Dominion*. Moves to a private house in Havelock Terrace and then to the Royal United Services Home for Girls in Albert Road followed. Once Greenock had become established as the home base for the Canadian escort vessels, their administrative centre moved to Scotland into a former workhouse as HMCS *Niobe*. The naval presence in Stoke Damerel School, however, continued in 1943 as an offshoot of the RN Barracks and was named HMS *Drake II*.

Weymouth College, a public school on Dorchester Road, decamped to Wellingborough School in Northamptonshire, where a new house was set up for the thirty-three boys and several staff who had elected to make the move. Their school, a grand Victorian pile with a chapel, was taken over by the Royal Navy in June 1940 as HMS *Kredemnon*, a degaussing station, the name coming from the Greek for 'Magic Circle'. The unexpected introduction of magnetic mines by the German armed forces wrought havoc on British shipping until a way of countering them was found. The ingenious solution was to pass ships over a sunken electric cable which neutralised their magnetic fields thus protecting them from the mines. Within a short time, degaussing techniques were perfected whereby current-carrying coils were installed in the ships themselves, reversing their natural magnetic field. After 1941, the underwater loops were abandoned but ships continued to be checked to ensure that they were protected. The building is now in residential use as apartments.

Opened in 1904 at Eastney and in Portsmouth's naval barracks, the Admiralty Signals Establishment (ASE) was the department concerned with telegraphy and telecommunications. As its importance, particularly in the development of radar increased, so did its vulnerability in bomb-ravaged Portsmouth, so in 1941, it moved into the Haslemere area. Partly due to its location near a railway station on the London to Portsmouth line, King Edward's School, Witley, was commandeered as HMS *Mercury II*, housing the laboratories and workshops of the experimental department of HM Signal School concerned, particularly, with the applications of radar in maritime warfare. Only after the approval of King George VI had been obtained was the school, with its royal charter and under the patronage of Queen Mary, reduced in size and relocated to the old workhouse at nearby Hambledon. This move to Witley facilitated the link-up of all the different experimental groups working in the field of radar, which had, hitherto, been scattered around in different venues and consisted of three equipment, and nine techniques divisions, employing upwards of a thousand scientists and technicians. Eminent scientists such as Fred Hoyle and Hermann Bondi, recently released from internment, and other Fellows of the Royal Society, most of them theoretical physicists, worked alongside established practitioners from the Watson-Watt operations of the 1930s, with many of the breakthroughs in anti-submarine and airborne interception (AI) radar taking place there. Throughout 1942, the focus was on getting the developments into use and the Royal Navy's ships were being fitted out with new radar equipment at the rate of one every day. These included long-range and gunnery radars and Type 271 sets, as well as upgrades to existing equipment. Type 271 radar enabled escort vessels to detect U-boats on the surface or even at periscope depth and airborne radar fitted to long-range aircraft of RAF Coastal Command achieved significant successes in detecting and sinking U-boats in the Atlantic. Additionally, periscope-fitted radar enabled Allied submarines to detect U-boats more effectively and together, all these developments began to turn the tide in the Battle of the Atlantic. Although a series of huts had been added to the school buildings, there remained a need to expand the available accommodation even more. In 1942–43, a large, four-storey block was built with a range of built-in features that met the specific needs of the occupants. These included a two-storey-high roller door for getting bulky equipment into the building; a cargo lift accessing the roof; rails on the roof for shifting large pieces of equipment; and the use of flexible partitions to create appropriate workspaces for specific tasks. From 1953 until 1995, this building was occupied by the National Institute of Oceanography. Soberton Towers School at Droxford was requisitioned by the Admiralty as part of HMS *Mercury* based in Petersfield. The building was used for training Wrens in wireless telegraphy, specifically to work in RN 'Y' Stations, intercepting enemy radio transmissions but some of the graduates from Soberton Towers were moved on to Haslemere to join ASE.

In 1939, Eastbourne College was prepared for war. The cloisters were bricked up and further protected by sandbags for use as an air-raid shelter by both the school and local inhabitants. In the event, in anticipation of an invasion, the school was evacuated to Radley in May 1940. Following brief use by the RAF, the college buildings were requisitioned by the Admiralty to provide alternative premises in the event of enemy bombing putting the torpedo schools at Devonport, HMS *Defiance*, or HMS *Vernon (R)* at Roedean, out of action. In June 1942, the college was announced as HMS *Marlborough* and opened three months later as a Royal Naval Torpedo Training Establishment and the Portsmouth and Chatham Electrical School, combining elements of HMS *Collingwood* from Portsmouth and HMS *Pembroke* from Chatham.

St Bede's Preparatory School in Dukes Drive, Eastbourne, was evacuated to St Edward's in Oxford, and the buildings were commandeered in 1943 by the Admiralty as a further outstation of HMS *Mercury*. Around 2,000 telegraphists were trained there, specialising in interceptions of enemy codes and ciphers. Following their initial three months' training as telegraphists in Brighton, ratings went on to St Bede's to learn German or Japanese Morse codes, or to learn the German language. Telegraphist ratings bound for service on convoy escorts were taught how to use HF/DF (Huff-Duff) high-frequency radio direction finding to be able to pick up German U-boat transmissions and thus to pinpoint their positions. Those who had learnt Japanese Morse might be posted to listening stations such as HMS *Highflyer* at Trincomalee in Ceylon (Sri Lanka). The school buildings at St Bede, dating from 1900, are still in use.

Felixstowe was a naval town handling large numbers of ratings being trained, primarily for the RN Auxiliary Patrol Service based at the Sparrows Nest, HMS *Europa*, so it was inevitable that local schools and hotels would be requisitioned. The Wrens moved into St Margaret's School releasing the Royal Hotel for the wardroom; the base hospital was established in the St Nicholas' nursery school; and cooks were trained in Church Road School.

Portsmouth GS had been established from 1879 on the site of a bastion of the town's seventeenth-century fortifications, close to the newly built Clarence, Victoria, and Cambridge Barracks. Cambridge Barracks was designed to accommodate an infantry battalion but by 1926 had become redundant. Portsmouth GS was able to restore the derelict officers' mess and to take over the rest of the barracks. In 1939, the school was evacuated to Bournemouth and the navy requisitioned the buildings. A history of the site includes a reference to a signals unit with responsibility for decoy lights on the seafront. The school had acquired the open area behind the Hilsea Lines as playing fields in 1931, but in 1939, the whole area was requisitioned by the Admiralty as an outstation of HMS *Excellent*, the navy's gunnery school, and HMS *Phoenix* which trained firefighters. Air-raid shelters were built and an LAA battery installed, while the Victorian casemates became magazines for AA shells.

Bay House in Stokes Bay was occupied by a private naval academy, destined to become Gosport County School after the war. Several buildings in the neighbourhood were requisitioned by the Admiralty as HMS *Porcupine* to be used for the co-ordination of the construction of the Mulberry Harbours, mainly the *Phoenix* caissons and attached pier-heads, fourteen of which were built in Stokes Bay. Bay House was then requisitioned by the War Department in 1943 as the officers' mess and living quarters for troops of the 79th Armoured Division who were testing their Duplex Drive amphibious tanks in the bay in preparation for the Normandy landings.

Many other naval functions were also accommodated in requisitioned school premises. A member of the WRNS reported attending for interview and medical at a recruiting office in a school in Manchester's Albert Square; Dover College served as the local RN HQ as HMS *Lynx*. It also provided accommodation for Wrens working in the tunnels of Dover Castle, Admiral Ramsay's control centre in the Admiralty Casemate, better known as 'Hellfire Corner'. Highgate School was home from 1941 to 1944 to HMS *President V* as a training establishment for accountant branch ratings; and Hodgson's House at Eton College became one of a number of administrative offices making up HMS *President III*. Campbeltown GS in Kintyre was commandeered as an anti-submarine training centre for ASDIC operators, HMS *Nimrod*, described as 'dreadfully depressing ... appallingly overcrowded ... and devoid of even the pretence of comfort'. Hammocks were slung three-deep from floor-to-ceiling iron stanchions allowing a width of just 14 inches (35 cm) of sleeping space. The present writer's father, who trained there as an ASDIC rating, however, admitted to only pleasant memories of his time in the town. In Dumbarton, Keil School in Helenslee House was evacuated to Kintyre after the Clydebank bombing and was subsequently taken over by the Free Norwegian Navy.

Use of School Buildings by the British Army

As the British Army expanded in the late 1930s, new premises were needed, particularly for the duplicates of TA regiments and other newly raised units. Clapham Girls HS became the HQ of 48th Royal Tank Regiment, the recently formed duplicate of 42RTR, itself a reorganised infantry battalion of the local East Surrey Regiment. Both tank regiments fought in North Africa and Italy in the 21st Armoured Brigade, 7th Armoured Division. St Bede's School in Bradford was due to open in new buildings in September 1939 but was occupied instead by a battalion of the Duke of Wellington's Regiment. As household troops, the three battalions of the Coldstream Guards had no TA element but raised 4th (Motorised) and 5th Infantry Battalions in 1940, adding a short-lived 6th Battalion in 1941, and establishing a depot and holding battalion at Elstree School. The Coldstreams' 4th Battalion was part of the 30th (Guards) Brigade within the London District Field Force, whose 'primary role is to deal with air and seaborne invasion'. In January 1942, its 6th Battalion was occupying part of Harrow School and was inspected on the school's parade ground. The next month, two of the battalion's companies attended a drill parade at Merchant Taylors' School. Rigorous training was interspersed with ceremonial, and in March, a rehearsal for the St Patrick's Day parade was held at Harrow School and an officer went to Merchant Taylors' to conduct a Certificate 'A' Examination for the OTC there. As part of 33rd Independent Infantry Brigade (Guards), the battalion took part in anti-invasion exercises with the local Home Guard. In May, the battalion left Harrow and moved to Devon, returning to Northwood a month later, by which time Malvern College had moved into Harrow School. The 4th Battalion, Gloucestershire Regiment, converted to become a searchlight regiment in 1938, tasked with the defence of Avonmouth and Bristol. In 1942, the regiment relinquished its drill hall in Old Market Street, Bristol, to American troops and moved into Badminton School in Westbury-on-Trym, where it remained until sent to London to defend against the V-1 offensive in the summer of 1944. Schools all over the country were used as billets. St Dunstan's College in Catford was occupied by REME after 1941, and even the fifteenth-century Wainfleet School on the Lincolnshire coast was taken over by military units on coast defence duties. The 1st Battalion, Queen's Royal West Surrey Regiment, part of the 2nd London Infantry Brigade, based on the south coast, moved into Southover Manor School in Lewes, later occupied by the Canadians and, later still, part of the D-Day marshalling area system. The Duke of York's Royal Military School, Dover, had been a military transit camp in the Great War and would be again this time round. The boys were evacuated to Saunton Sands Hotel at Braunton in north Devon.

The Pioneer Corps (Royal from 1946) was raised to carry out light engineering and labouring tasks for the army. It was permitted to recruit trusted enemy aliens but functioned as a combatant corps, so it did not generally attract conscientious objectors. From 1940, Dingle Vale School in Liverpool, housed its 12th (Holding) Battalion and the Corps Training Centre. Pioneers served with the BEF in France and at the D-Day landings, working on the Mulberry Harbours and PLUTO, the oil pipeline that pumped fuel to the Normandy bridgehead. Dingle Vale, now Shorefields School, appears to have escaped the bombing that damaged many neighbouring schools.

After Dunkirk, what remained of the British Army needed depots to rebuild itself, unit by unit, and training centres, particularly for officers, to expand the army's capabilities. St Lawrence College at Ramsgate became an Officer Cadet Training Unit (OCTU) for the RASC in 1940. Free French army cadets, initially aged from fourteen to seventeen, from the St Cyr military academy moved into No. 5 House at Malvern College. When Malvern was requisitioned by the TRE, they were moved to Ribbesford House near Bewdley. As preparations were made to defend the country against the expected invasion, bases and local HQs were needed. Barton Court GS in Canterbury became HQ of the Fortress Canterbury defence scheme. The 5th (TA) Battalion of the Norfolk Regiment took over Gresham's School, evacuated to hotels in Newquay, to defend the Norfolk coast. Roedean's No. 3 House had been requisitioned by the army and saw a succession of units including the Argyll & Sutherland Highlanders and the Queen's Royal West Surrey Regiment in residence, as well as Canadian regiments. When the Admiralty took over the rest of the school for HMS *Vernon*, the Senior Service politely and disingenuously enquired how many tents the War Office might need to accommodate the troops being dispossessed. The soldiers moved out smartly to Olde Place in Rottingdean. Prior to its occupation by HMS *King Alfred*, Lancing College provided billets for the Royal Ulster Rifles in July 1940. Troops, including battalions of the Queen's Royal West Surrey Regiment and the King's Own Scottish Borderers, were based in Sherborne School early in the war, drilling in the school's courts. Having returned from Dunkirk, the 4th Infantry Division was assigned to anti-invasion duties in the south of England establishing its HQ in West Downs School in Romsey Road, Winchester. The 65 (Norfolk Yeomanry) Anti-Tank Regiment was deployed to Dorset to crew the odd collection of obsolescent artillery, which would repulse the coming invasion. Its 258 Battery occupied a recently vacated prep school on the highest point above Swanage and was promptly bombed, an occurrence for which the gunners were held entirely responsible by the locals. This was probably Forres School, now Purbeck View School, which, once the Yeomanry had sailed for Egypt, was subsequently taken over by the TRE from Worth Matravers. In Essex, Felsted School, which had been evacuated to Ross-on-Wye, became the HQ of XI Corps, responsible for the defence of Essex and Suffolk.

By 1941, the army was gaining in every way with more men, more equipment, and better training facilities, but space was still at a premium. The 54th Infantry Division, one of XI Corps' constituent divisions between 1941 and 1943, served two stints based on the Suffolk coast. In the absence of alternatives, the division chose schools for their HQs. There were Brigade HQs at Dell Road School on Oulton Broad and at Summerhill School, Leiston; Battalion HQs at Felixstowe Girls' School and St Felix School, Southwold; and right down to Company HQ level, in schools at Yarmouth Road and Notley Road in Lowestoft, and at Pakefield.

Towards the middle of 1943, preparations for the invasion of France were well under way. Bernard Montgomery, commanding 21st Army Group for Operation Overlord, the invasion of continental Europe, established his HQ in St Paul's School, Hammersmith, in west London, which had previously been British Army Land Forces GHQ. He was a former pupil of the school and used to joke that the first time he made it into the headmaster's study was as commander of a large part of the British Army. Montgomery was an extremely meticulous planner, demanding a high level of staff work and a whole year of intricate planning had been overseen by General 'Freddie' Morgan. Montgomery was also a skilled communicator who relied on face-to-face contact with subordinates at all levels to ensure they knew what was expected of them and understood the means for achieving his goals. Thus, Overlord was preceded by an intense round of briefings. His penultimate briefing for Overlord, labelled Breaker IV, was held at Felsted School, and the final briefing, Breaker V, was held on 15 May 1944, back at St Paul's School, around three weeks before the planned date of D-Day on 5 June. Present in the school were HM King George VI, Churchill, Eisenhower, and the chiefs of staff; Admiral Ramsay, commanding Operation Neptune, the naval element of the invasion; dozens of staff officers; and the weathermen, on whose advice the invasion would go ahead as planned or be delayed. Once Southwick House, already requisitioned by the Admiralty as HMS *Dryad*, had been selected as the Advanced HQ for Overlord, the whole village was swamped by staff officers and planners. The village school became a venue for meetings, and the children were despatched to the air-raid shelters that had been built to serve the adjacent WRNS quarters in 'The Elms'. In 1929, Rookesbury Park, outside Wickham in Hampshire, was leased as a school for fifteen girls. Pupils were among those rejoicing at its requisitioning by the RASC in 1940 as the house had no electricity or running water. A former pupil remembers the water supply being pumped up from the river. Prior to D-Day, the Wickham parkland with Rookesbury itself became an Overlord camp for units which included the Reconnaissance Corps. Ramsgate's St Lawrence College also became billets for troops awaiting their D-Day call.

All over the country, Allied troops were gathering for the invasion. Airborne forces were concentrating in the East Midlands around Leicestershire, south-west Lincolnshire, and Rutland where Oakham School provided a parade area for 4th Parachute Brigade. The preparations for D-Day throughout the spring of 1944 had involved the complex organisation required to get the initial assault wave of 120,000 troops with all their equipment, transport, AFVs, fuel, and supplies in the right place, at the right time, and in conditions of comparative secrecy, to be closely followed up by a much larger body of reinforcements. Marshalling areas (MA) were identified for each unit to be near its embarkation port, and each MA was given a letter and a number, with most MA HQs located in requisitioned properties. These embarkation ports extended from Cornwall, along the south coast, to the Thames Estuary and up into Essex, Suffolk, and Norfolk, with more camps spreading across South Wales (MAs 'U-W'). Southover Manor School in Lewes had been evacuated to Firle Place earlier in the war to be occupied by Canadian troops. In 1944, it housed the HQ of MA 'J', assembling troops for embarkation from Newhaven, Embarkation Area (EA) J2. There were over 100,000 troops in the Eastern Command MAs including reinforcements as follow up to the initial assault. The Royal Wanstead School, with an emergency HQ at Fife Road School in Canning Town, became the HQ of MA 'T', where units slated to embark from Tilbury and London Docks were concentrated. The Sector HQ for Tilbury (EA 5/ MAs 'S' and 'T') was in St Chad's School. Most MAs had eight or more sub-areas each containing up to five 500-man tented camps, erected from March onwards, or else large open spaces for vehicle parking. Taunton's School, part of Southampton's enormous MA 'C' with twenty-four sub-areas, had previously been used as overnight billets for troops in transit, but by early 1944 was a permanent barracks for troops awaiting transportation to the Normandy beaches via Southampton Docks (EA C5). Much work was needed on infrastructure with bridges needing strengthening and vehicles being prepared for the landings. The tanks of 1st RTR of 7th Armoured Division were waterproofed by REME troops at Orwell Park School (MA 'R5') outside Ipswich. All these camps were completely sealed by the end of May for security reasons, although occupants' reminiscences cite numerous 'escapes'.

The Auxiliary Territorial Service (ATS), forerunner of the Women's Royal Army Corps (WRAC), had been formed in 1938 but underwent an enormous expansion in 1941 when unmarried women between the ages of twenty and thirty were called up under the National Service Act. By the end of 1943, the ATS had 200,000 members, and large training facilities such as Newbattle Abbey Adult Education College were required. Queen Ethelburga's College, a girls' boarding school in Harrogate, was requisitioned to accommodate two ATS Training Wings. The Army 'Y' Service had been set up to monitor German wireless transmissions and to send the product through as quickly as could be managed, generally by motorcycle courier, to the GC&CS at Bletchley Park for decryption. Many of the 'Y' Service personnel were ATS women who received their initial wireless training at working stations such as Douglas, Isle of Man, or Cheadle. Queen Ethelburga's changed its role from basic ATS training to 'Y' Service operations when No. 8 ATS Wing moved in as 1 Command Signals. The women lived in the school and were trucked out on twenty-four-hour shifts to the listening station at Forest Moor, off the A59 road at Blubberhouses, a 'Y' Station that still operates under its current name of Menwith Hill.

An additional and unforeseen problem had arisen from the intensification of the bombing campaign against Britain's towns and cities. This was the presence after raids of unexploded bombs. Some bombs were intended to have a delayed action, but some simply malfunctioned. This caused situations where residents were held in limbo while the authorities decided on the status of an apparently dormant but potentially lethal bomb. The Royal Engineers (RE) were responsible for the disposal of such bombs and stationed bomb disposal (BD) units around the country, many of them containing conscientious objectors who jumped at the chance to perform a humanitarian task. Between September 1940 and July 1941, nearly 25,000 bombs were dealt with and made safe. Some of these BD units were based, like the ARP services, in schools. The 21 BD Company, RE, was responsible for north London with one squad being co-located with the ARP reporting centre at Woodhouse School, Finchley; Cassland Road School in Hackney home to another detachment; and the company's MT workshops in St Aubyn's School, Woodford Green.

Just as the Normandy landings were taking place, a new threat emerged on the Home Front. Between June and October 1944, nearly 10,000 V-1 flying bombs were launched at south-east England. These were 'popularly' known as Doodlebugs and could be brought down by anti-aircraft fire or by fighter aircraft. An enormous concentration of AA artillery was deployed along the south and east coasts to intercept these projectiles before they could land, but many of them managed to penetrate these defences causing enormous damage and thousands of, mainly civilian, deaths and injuries. This AA deployment was code-named Operation Diver and each Diver site, of which there were hundreds, consisted of four or eight HAA gun emplacements; gun-laying radar; a command post; and accommodation in huts for the hundred or so gunners and their support services. Many sections of the defences had AA operations rooms (AAOR) or HQs in buildings, many of them schools, requisitioned for the purpose. The Diver deployment consisted of several sectors: the Kentish Gun Belt extended along the North Downs and was supported by a Coastal Gun Belt extending from Eastbourne to Dover. One of its four AAORs was in the 'Army Hut near the Cricket Pavilion' of Tonbridge School, and it controlled a quarter of the more than 1,000 guns in the Belt. The first reinforcement of the Kentish Gun Belt took place in late June and consisted of a large number of one- and two-gun LAA batteries. As reported in the Wartime West Sussex Project, Ardingly College was ringed by half a dozen of these deployments. The HQ of 5 AA Brigade in the Coastal Belt was in Westbourne House School in Folkestone, with two of its constituent regiments, 136 HAA Regiment in St John's School, and 124 LAA Regiment in Little St John's School, both in Seaford. A school, now Northbourne Park School, opened in Betteshanger House in 1936, and became the HQ of the Newhaven Section's 40 AA Brigade, with its 88 HAA Regiment at Tyttenhanger School in Seaford. The Gun Operations Room (GOR) for 102 AA Brigade, manning one of six sectors of the Coastal Belt, was at St Dominic's School in the St Leonards Section. The Duke of York's Royal Military School in Dover was the HQ of 173 HAA Regiment within 71 AA Brigade's Dover Section. The Thames Estuary was protected by the Diver Box, with the Diver Strip running up the coast into Suffolk and terminating at Great Yarmouth in Norfolk. One of eight GORs was in St Audrey's School, 64 The Broadway, Thorpe Bay in Essex. The final piece of the jigsaw was the Diver Fringe, north of The Wash extending from Skegness to Filey.

Use of School Buildings by the Canadian Army

The 1st Canadian Infantry Division had already arrived in Britain in December 1939, and in August 1940, in response to Churchill's request for help in the face of an anticipated enemy invasion, the 2nd Canadian Infantry Division joined it here, together forming the Canadian Corps, based in Aldershot and manning anti-invasion defences in Sussex. On the coast, Southover Manor School in Lewes had been evacuated, first to nearby Firle Place, and then to Holt Castle near Worcester. Mansfield College, a Jewish girls' boarding school at 47 Cromwell Road in Hove, evacuated to South Wales, and Ovingdean Hall School was evacuated to Devon. All three became Canadian Army unit HQs and billets. Following their requisitioning in 1939 as overflows for the barracks, Stoughton Juniors and Northmead Boys' School in Guildford, were allocated to the Canadians, and in Farnham, Barfield School at Runfold gave up its hockey field for the tents of the Cape Breton Highlanders. Four Canadian regiments passed through Roedean before the Admiralty took over the school and Newlands School in Seaford was home to the Seaforth Highlanders of Canada. Lancing College provided the location for the final planning for the disastrous Dieppe expedition, Operation Jubilee, pushed ahead by Mountbatten, heedless of justifiably strong opposition. This was carried out by mainly Canadian troops supported by British commandos and conveyed in naval landing craft. The Canadian 4th, 5th, and 6th Brigades of the 2nd Canadian Division took part and suffered crippling casualties.

Windlesham House School occupied Highden House in Washington near Pulborough in Sussex. At the beginning of the war, it was evacuated, first to Somerset and then to the Lake District. The 2nd Canadian Infantry Division took over a large area around Storrington and Washington as a training area centred on Parham House. Highden House had been extended for use by the school in 1934 and it became the Royal Canadian School of Infantry in 1942. Several concrete blockhouses, built for training purposes, stand both in the school grounds and on Highden Hill. These are constructed of concrete blocks strengthened with metal plates and are of unusual design, presumably being intended to simulate the German defences to be encountered in France. The HQ of the Department of Petroleum Warfare was also housed in the school. This was the body charged initially with developing defensive measures such as flame barrages on the seashore to impede invasion forces and flame traps and *fougasses* used as roadblocks on land, to seal enemy bridgeheads behind the beaches. Later came offensive, mobile flame-throwers, something the Canadian forces, particularly, adopted enthusiastically. The D-Day operations saw adapted Churchill tanks as flame-throwers, named Crocodiles, in the assault on the defences of the Atlantic Wall, and the PLUTO project, the two pipelines labelled BAMBI and DUMBO, conveying fuel to France.

Use of School Buildings by the Polish Army

St Margaret's School, Polmont, a girls' boarding school near Falkirk, was requisitioned for use by Polish troops as a signals training school. Instructors taught radiotelegraphy and international communications codes along with basic skills such as using small arms. Taking pity on the Polish troops preparing to spend the winter of 1940–1 in cattle pens, they were handed Forfar East School by the Angus education authorities. In 1944, the HQ of the Polish 1 Corps was in Falkirk where the Dawson Park Special School, a residential facility, had been requisitioned, possibly in connection with a move from Bridge of Earn.

Use of School Buildings by the US Army

Early in the war it had been assumed that despite the presence of aircraft factories and port facilities, as it lay out of range of aircraft flying from Germany, Bristol would escape being bombed. Following the fall of France and the establishment of German airfields in Brittany, this notion was soon dispelled as the Bristol Blitz began. Bombs fell uncomfortably close to shelters on their school field and, taking the advice of the Regional Commissioner, Clifton College's 300 pupils were evacuated early in 1941. The War Office had been prevailed upon to agree an exchange of some hotels in Bude for the college buildings which were instantly requisitioned for an Officer Cadet Training Unit (OCTU) of the Royal Army Service Corps (RASC). In January 1942, the US Army's V Corps was the first formation to deploy to the European Theatre of Operations USA (ETOUSA), first landing in Belfast before moving into mainly south-west England where Corps HQ was duly established in Clifton College. The divisions comprising V Corps were employed in the North African landings known as Operation Torch but had returned via Liverpool in November 1943, with the 1st US Infantry Division going to Blandford in Dorset. Round about this time General Omar Bradley, who had created the 82nd Airborne Division and had commanded several different corps as deputy to Eisenhower, was promoted and given command of the 1st US Army. This would spearhead the invasion of France under Montgomery's command. The HQ of V Corps had moved to Taunton, so he established his own HQ at Clifton, living at a house called The Holmes, now part of the University of Bristol and located in the Botanic Gardens, and commuting to Clifton College where his staff were in residence. Planning for D-Day was centred on the school's library and committee room. The topmost storey of the Wilson Tower became a wireless room in direct communication with Eisenhower's SHAEF HQ at Bushy Park, Teddington; Montgomery's 21st Army Group HQ at St Paul's School in Hammersmith; the Chiefs of Staff Supreme Allied Command (COSSAC) in underground railway stations off London's Tottenham Court Road; and with Bletchley Park. Two of the five D-Day beaches, Omaha and Utah, had been allocated to 1st US Army, which was mainly scattered around the south west, but with some of its formations based in the West Midlands. King Edward's School in Birmingham was in the midst of a move to new premises in Edgbaston when war broke out and evacuation to Repton took place. In 1944, as the US Army units arrived in Britain prior to D-Day, the 90th US Infantry Division established its HQ in the school.

The US Army used light aircraft for liaison and courier travel between far-flung units: the HQs of Bradley's three corps were located at Taunton (V), Tiverton (VII), and Warminster (XIX). Beggar's Bush Field, which had constituted Clifton College's playing fields, became an airfield for the light aircraft which provided these links. US Field Artillery (FA) units also used light aircraft as aerial observation posts and Canford Park School outside Bournemouth, with an airstrip on Turbary Common was used by a US Army FA unit for use by its Piper L-4 Grasshoppers.

The US Army maintained a strong presence in Northern Ireland from its arrival there in 1942 through to the Operation Torch landings in North Africa in 1943 and the Normandy operation, when many of its units moved to France. One reason for maintaining the US presence in Ulster was to mount Operation Fortitude North, which was a deception exercise to fool the German High Command into preparing for an invasion of Norway. Large numbers of civilian properties were requisitioned as billets including schools like Bessbrook Technical School in County Armagh, previously occupied by No. 511 Field Park RE.

Use of School Buildings by the RAF

The RAF used schools as billets, but also as HQs and as remote operations rooms. The King's School, Worcester, served as the HQ of No. 81 (Operational Training) Group, and Farnborough Secondary School was HQ of RAF Army Co-operation Command until 1943, when it was transformed into the 2nd Tactical Air Force, supporting ground operations, particularly during the invasion of France in 1944. Earls Hall School was the HQ of RAF Rochford at Southend. St James Road School, Chichester, housed the off-site operations room for RAF Tangmere 1940–44, which was moved to the nearby Bishop Otter Teacher Training College prior to D-Day. Outside Arundel, Tortington Park School was used as billets for WAAFs working at RAF Tangmere and RAF Ford. An Ursuline Convent at Westgate, Hatton House, with a 'school for young ladies', provided billets for WAAFs at RAF Manston, as did another convent on Elstree Road, Stanmore, for the WAAFs at the plotting tables of RAF Fighter Command's operations room and headquarters at Bentley Priory, which itself had been a girls' school until its acquisition by the Air Ministry in 1926. It was not necessary to be requisitioned to be affected by Air Ministry developments. The RAF Transport Command airfield at Down Ampney near Cirencester opened in June 1943. The village school's playing field was taken over and the children of some families were forced to change school as the airfield had sealed off the access by public road.

Use of School Buildings by the USAAF

In February 1942, Brigadier-General Eaker of the US Army Air Corps arrived in Britain to establish a bomber force. This would operate alongside RAF Bomber Command in carrying out strategic bombing raids against German targets in Occupied Europe. Owing to its proximity to RAF Bomber Command's HQ at Naphill, High Wycombe's Wycombe Abbey School for Girls, just 5 miles (8 km) away, was selected as Eaker's new HQ under the codename Pinetree. Despite opposition from the headmistress and unsuccessful appeals to the Board of Education, the school was given just three weeks to vacate its buildings and was effectively closed for the duration. The administrative offices of the 8th USAAF occupied the classrooms, but large numbers of huts and tents were erected to house the 12,000 male and female staff. A command centre had also been added for the use of RAF Bomber Command in 1941 and this was shared with the USAAF staff for a year before being handed over to Eaker, whose staff referred to it as the 'Mole's Hole'. It was buried underground under 10 feet (3 metres) of concrete, and 25 feet (8 metres) of soil. The bunker, on three floors, had a double skin of thick concrete walls, was equipped with air conditioning, an air filtration system, gastight doors, and was provided with emergency power and water supply. The war room was the venue every morning for the announcement of planned operations and orders, detailing targets for the day, would be despatched to all the 8th USAAF's constituent air divisions, combat wings, and bombardment groups across East Anglia, a force that together could put over 1,000 bombers and 1,200 fighters into the skies. The 200-acre (80-ha) site owned by the school included Daws Hill House which the school had purchased in 1928 to avoid the estate being developed. It became home to the Combined Operations Planning Committee where staff and intelligence officers from the USAAF and Bomber Command worked together to identify targets and to ensure raids were co-ordinated and duplication avoided. The school's houses became home to air force departments: engineering, public relations, and surgery, and the school hall was divided up into discrete offices. By the end of the war, the site resembled a town with a hutted camp housing the Photo-Reconnaissance Wing, and residential sites with hundreds of huts, including a compound for the several hundred WACs who worked on site. The photo-reconnaissance section included the damage assessment section of the RAF's Central Photographic Interpretation Unit at Medmenham in Oxfordshire. By this time, Pinetree had become Army Air Force Station 101 or Camp Lynn. The school's reoccupation was as drawn out as its exit had been sudden. After the Americans had gone, the Air Ministry was loath to relinquish its tenancy and homeless people had moved into the vacated huts. Agreement regarding compensation was eventually reached and the school moved back in at the end of 1946, while the underground facility remained the property of the Air Ministry. The USAF then returned in the 1950s and stayed on until after 1990.

The component parts of the 8th USAAF each had HQs in a variety of locations, often in requisitioned buildings. In the autumn of 1942, the King's Canadian Residential Open-Air School in Bushy Park, which had housed a military hospital in the Great War, was commandeered as billets when the 8th USAAF established its HQ, Camp Griffiss (Station 586), nearby. The enlisted men housed in the school hosted a Thanksgiving dinner for the children in the November. The 65th Fighter Wing's squadrons were spread across ten different airfields from Northamptonshire to Essex, in five fighter groups. Its HQ was based south of Cambridge, in Saffron Walden GS, later known as Dame Bradbury's School. The buildings, dating from the 1880s, although the school goes back to the sixteenth century, had initially been requisitioned by the RAF in 1940, and subsequently handed over to the USAAF as an operations centre. Its closest airfield was Debden and the farthest away was Horsham St Faith's outside Norwich.

Use of School Buildings by Home Guard Units

Right from the start of the Local Defence Volunteer (LDV) movement, when Far Forest School in Kidderminster was just one of dozens hosting early recruitment meetings, schools played a part in Home Guard activities. Given that from their beginnings, the LDV, later Home Guard, units were dispersed right across urban and rural areas, an enormous number and variety of premises were needed to house their HQs, stores, armouries, and training facilities. The Latymer Foundation School on Hammersmith Road became the HQ of Major-General Dalby, commanding Zone 'F', one of five such Home Guard Zones in London's south-west sub-area. It included the 3rd (Fulham) and the 6th and 7th (Hammersmith) Battalions, just three of the 135 Home Guard battalions drawn from the London and Middlesex District. Schools also served as battalion and company HQs. There were HQs at Wellingborough School for the 7th Battalion and at Walton Senior School in Peterborough for the 2nd (Soke of Peterborough) Battalion, Northamptonshire HG; at St Hilary House, 22 Sussex Square, Brighton, a boarding house of St Mary's Hall School, for 10th (East Brighton) Battalion, Sussex HG; at Paston GS, North Walsham, for the 5th Battalion, Norfolk HG; at Rose Hill Schools, Dudley for 3rd Battalion, Worcestershire HG, and at Toll Bar School, New Waltham, for 7th (Grimsby Rural) Battalion, Lincolnshire HG. On occasion, the original choice of HQ might prove unsuitable. The No. 2 Company of 12th Battalion, Northumberland HG initially chose Jesmond Dene House as its HQ, but it proved inadequate for the company's training needs, so a move was made to Heaton Secondary School, which proved a better choice even though it had been damaged in a bombing raid in July 1940. Larger schools clearly offered more extensive accommodation to meet the varied and extensive needs of developing units. Woking GS was used by Surrey HG for signals and radio training, and Redditch County HS ran a range of training courses including intelligence gathering. King's School, Peterborough, Wyggeston Girls' School, Leicester, and grammar schools at Appleby Magna, Northampton, Newport (Shropshire), Lamport, Lutterworth, and Cambridge, all housed HG Company HQs. In cities and large towns, the HG units could be quite large and so, where available, larger premises for company HQs were found as at Watt Close School, Bromsgrove, George Road School, Warley, or Aymestrey School, all in Worcestershire, and in Leeds, St Peters School on Dewsbury Road served as the Battle HQ for 'E' Coy. 8th West Riding (Leeds) Battalion. Large urban or suburban primary schools could do just as well as at Westcotes Church School and St Barnabas School, both in Leicester; Grafton Road PS in Gospel Oak and St Saviour's School in Maida Vale, both in north London; or the Central School, Hackbridge in Croydon. The larger platoons that could be raised in towns were often based in local primary schools as at Bushland and Victoria Road Schools in Northampton. In rural Leicestershire, The Schools, Woodhouse Eaves, provided a company HQ, as did Abberley Hall Preparatory School near Stourport in Worcestershire. In Carmarthen, two platoons of 'B' Company, 1st Battalion, Carmarthenshire HG were based at Pentrpoeth Schools and one platoon of 'D' Company at the girls' HS. Most rural villages, however, could raise only a platoon with anything from ten to fifty members, and many found their village schools suitable as bases. Those in Northamptonshire included

Kislingbury, Cottingham and Gretton; in Somerset, Brompton Regis, Claverton, Shepton Mallet, and Babcary; in Sussex, Bolney; and in Norfolk, Larling. By mid-1941, the Home Guard was engaging in extensive exercises across wide areas of land. Dean Close School, Cheltenham, was the temporary HQ for the umpires in one such exercise held around the Tewkesbury area and, inevitably, dubbed the Battle of Tewkesbury. It involved several local HG battalions as well as regulars from the RASC and RAF. As the Home Guard developed into an all-arms fighting force, specialist units were formed. Eastover School in Bridgwater was home to No. 2148 Independent MT Platoon attached to the Somerset HG. In Croydon, Whitgift Middle School provided a parade ground for the 60th Battalion, Surrey HG. The significant numbers of Home Guard casualties during the war included five officers and NCOs killed when the HQ of 'E' Company, 57th (Catford) Battalion, County of London HG, in Brockley Road School, Crofton Park, south-east London, was hit by a V-1 Flying Bomb in June 1944, when three of the victims, were decorated veterans of the Great War.

Use of Schools by ARP for Wardens' Posts, Rest Centres, AFS Fire Stations etc.

From 1938, local authorities were required to establish networks of ARP provision. Given that there was a strong expectation in official circles that schoolchildren would be evacuated out of urban centres, schools were the obvious choice in cities for wardens' posts, reporting or control centres, first aid posts, rescue party depots, ARP training centres, rest centres, decontamination centres, communal feeding stations and food stores, ambulance depots or AFS stations. Expenditure of the princely sum of £20 (£1,000) was allowed for each school's conversion, so this obviously precluded significant structural alterations. School buildings—especially those three-storey Victorian and Edwardian ones that dominated many housing neighbourhoods, regarded as invulnerable bastions of municipal solidity—would be supplemented by more modern buildings which might have steel frames and concrete floors. Scarborough's Central School was one of several such ARP Posts and in the Newcastle upon Tyne ARP organisation, thirteen ARP centres were in schools, as were five first aid posts, two emergency water supply points, four ARP canteens, and fully thirty emergency feeding centres. In Gateshead, schools accommodated sixteen emergency rest centres with ten more in neighbouring Blaydon. In some instances, only specified parts of the building might be taken over, in the same way that schools used to provide polling stations. However, schools designated as rest centres or emergency feeding stations, in the event of bomb damage to their surrounding areas, might expect an influx of several hundred families seeking shelter and sustenance. Such events would clearly make a significant impact on the schools' running and would preclude any meaningful teaching activities. Holy Trinity School in Gravesend opened as a British Restaurant in May 1941 and three further schools in the town hosted canteens for use as communal feeding stations.

The Ducane Road site of St Clement Danes GS in Hammersmith had already been commandeered by ARP so the headmaster's meeting to inform parents of his plans for evacuation had to take place in the nearby Burlington School. Across the country, schools were selected to fulfil the various ARP functions. The control room at Hassocks was in the Infants' School; the ARP reporting centre for Middlesex was in the Woodhouse School, Finchley; Lowestoft's was located at Church Road JS; Bristol's was at Badminton JS at Westbury-on-Trym; and Leytonstone's at Harrow Green School. ARP depots were set up at Bankhead School in Partick in Glasgow and Summerhill School in St George, Bristol. ARP wardens' posts were established in the Garrison Lane Secondary School, now Deben HS (District C5), and the Brantover School (District E7) in Felixstowe; in the Eastgate School near Lincoln Cathedral; and in Walthamstow Hall School in Sevenoaks. ARP heavy rescue squad depots were set up at West Square School in Southwark and at Glengall Grove School in Peckham. Redcar's six fire watch depots, storing equipment for the town's fire-watching parties each allocated specific streets to patrol, were housed in six local schools: Coatham, Warrenby, West Dyke, John E. Batty, Ennis Square, and Zetland. In Sandy, first the Baptist schoolroom was taken over as a CD rescue party depot, and then, in 1941, the Public Elementary (C of E) School became the mobile unit depot.

There was an ARP training centre in Liverpool's Melville Place School for the Deaf and classrooms at Sir Thomas Rich's School in Gloucester were used for anti-gas training courses. A first aid training centre was set up at St Mary's School Finchley. Two of Nottingham's first aid posts were in the Wells Road and Ronald Street Schools while both of Friern Barnet's were in schools: Holly Park Infants' and Oakleigh School in Oakleigh Road North. One of the reasons that St Dunstan's College could not return to Catford in 1943 was that Lewisham Borough Council needed the school as a first aid post. Ambulance depots were located in Magdalen College School in Oxford and Abbey Road School in West Ham. In Portsmouth, combined first aid posts and ARP depots were established in Kent Street Infants', in Portsea, and in Cottage Grove School, Southsea. There were mortuaries at St Aldhelm's school room in Bedminster, Bristol, and Clydebank HS. In Newark-upon-Trent, all the town's three cleansing or decontamination centres were in schools: Newark Girls' HS, Barnby Road Schools, and Warburton Street Infants'. Station Road Schools housed a communal feeding centre in Beeston, Nottingham as did Hele's GS in Exeter. Holden Crescent School, Lovers Lane School, and Mount Senior School in Newark-upon-Trent all held emergency food-stores and feeding centres. The emergency communal feeding organisation in Lewes was centred on the Girls' County School and the Mountfield Road Schools, which between them would take in two-thirds of the anticipated 650 refugees from coastal areas. In Redcar, the food control committee's HQ was in West Terrace School, and its base kitchen was in West Dyke School. Among the many schools designated as rest centres for housing bombed-out families were Clyde Street School in Helensburgh,

Stanley Street School in Deptford, Dorchester County Girls', and Hyndland School in Clydebank. In Tynemouth, empty classrooms in the Queen Victoria School were commandeered for the storage of furniture and other items salvaged from over twenty bombed-out houses. Air-raid shelters were fashioned in Bristol's Ilminster Avenue School in Knowle and in St Peter's School in Wapping. In many places, all the main ARP functions were brought together in a single building. At Benwell in Newcastle upon Tyne, Pendower Hall, housing a special school, was an ARP wardens' post, first aid post, a rest and feeding centre, and held an emergency water supply. It also took in children who had been brought back from evacuation for medical reasons and standard fifty-person surface shelters were built.

Despite fire services being independent and locally based, nevertheless, there existed some common patterns, with each permanent fire station having additional AFS sub-stations, many of which occupied council school buildings. In London, each fire station was allocated six sub-stations lettered U, V, W, X, Y, and Z. Fire Station 68, at Redcross Street in the City of London, had three of its six sub-stations in the LCC elementary schools in Baltic, Central, and Chequer Streets. Outside London, Matthew Arnold School in Liverpool and Ham Lane School in Shoreham were representative of the dozens of AFS sub-stations supplementing the regular fire brigade premises. In August 1941, these independent, locally administered brigades would all combine with the AFS to form the National Fire Service, leading to the standardisation of equipment, more efficient use of resources, and better coordination. Local difficulties had always brought forth reinforcements from neighbouring, and not so near, brigades. Devonport HS for Girls had been evacuated to Tiverton and its buildings were taken over by the fire service as billets for crews brought in from outside to tackle the Plymouth Blitz. With the advent of the NFS, planning to bring external help to emergency situations would be less piecemeal. Attempts were also made to provide respite for ARP personnel and Bradfield College in Berkshire was requisitioned by the Red Cross as a rest centre for Civil Defence workers. Schools would often assume the functions of bombed buildings, as when the Gatehouse School in Sewardstone Road, Bethnal Green served as a temporary church after the adjacent church of St James the Less had been destroyed.

Schools and the Management of Evacuees

Schools also fulfilled a number of organisational functions connected with evacuees. They provided convenient assembly points for children and their accompanying adults, gathering them together prior to travel, or receiving incomers and allocating them to their billets. In September 1939, Scarborough received 25,000 evacuees from Hartlepool, Middlesbrough, and Hull, with Falsgrave and Orleton Schools being pressed into service as reception centres. In reception areas with such large evacuee populations, it would prove necessary to organise dedicated medical centres for treatment and for monitoring the health of child evacuees. Scarborough, with its many thousands, a significant number of whom had brought inner-city medical conditions and hygiene issues with them, set up medical centres in Hinderwell and Northstead Schools, and a cleansing station at the Junior Instruction Centre. Although some 6,000 evacuees had trickled home from the town over the winter, many remained, gradually reducing over the war years, but boosted in 1943 by children from Brighton, and in 1944 by a further influx arriving from London's Kings Cross, fleeing the flying bombs.

Schools and the Secret War

On the outbreak of war, the primary centre for the RAF's research into radio direction finding (RDF), or more commonly 'radar', had been established since 1935 on an exposed stretch of Suffolk coast at Bawdsey Manor. Known as the Air Ministry Experimental Station (AMES), this installation was perceived as being rather too vulnerable to raiding parties and on the basis of personal connections, was precipitately shifted north to Dundee Training College. It was quickly established that this venue, even with its two overspill annexes was entirely unsuitable, and a further move back south to Worth Matravers in Dorset was effected in late 1940, renamed as the Telecommunications Research Establishment (TRE). Soon afterwards, the Army Cell that had joined the Air Defence Experimental Establishment (ADEE) quit the bomb-ravaged RAF Biggin Hill for new quarters in neighbouring Christchurch, becoming the Air Defence Research and Development Establishment (ADRDE). The Ministry of Home Security had acquired Malvern College for itself but chose not to use it, installing the Air Ministry's Signals Training Establishment, which occupied a series of huts on the school site instead. This soon evolved into the Radar Research and Development Establishment (RRDE) developing truck-mounted mobile radar sets. In early 1942, a raid across the English Channel was carried out to capture a German Würzburg radar set, installed at Bruneval on the French coast, and British commandos, along with a TRE technician, brought the equipment back for evaluation at Worth Matravers. The TRE's new home had always been in makeshift accommodation with an annexe in Durnford Preparatory School, whose pupils combined with another local prep school, and a training centre in Forres School in Swanage. Additionally, and more to the point, it now occurred to those responsible for security that with the French coast opposite, so recently occupied by the enemy, TRE had become just as vulnerable a location as had been Bawdsey Manor. Reports of a newly arrived German parachute unit just across the water from Dorset may have clinched the matter as TRE was moved, now with some justifiable urgency, into the by now under-occupied Malvern College.

In the next few years, TRE would develop crucial weapons that would significantly influence the war in the air and at sea. Airborne Interception (AI) radar aided night fighters to locate enemy aircraft on bombing raids; Air-to-Surface Vessel (ASV) radar greatly increased the success of RAF Coastal Command aircraft in locating U-boats; the Oboe blind bombing system enabled Pathfinders to pinpoint targets for the following bomber stream; HS2 radar allowed bombers to pick out targets on the ground, thereby improving on the hitherto dire inaccuracy of bombing; another airborne radar system installed in the form of an automatic gun-laying turret let air-gunners successfully target attacking fighters without ever seeing them. Other developments included many types of radar-jamming systems; the GEE navigation system adopted by the RAF and the USAAF; new types of electronic devices such as cathode ray tubes for radar displays; flight simulators and AI radar trainers; radio countermeasures for jamming or distorting the enemy's beams; and computer systems. By the end of the war, 3,500 people were working at TRE in Malvern.

Belhaven School in Dunbar was requisitioned by SOE in June 1943 as a Special Training School (STS 54b) for wireless operators. These were the members of the First Aid Nursing Yeomanry (FANY), an organisation that provided a cover, designed to confer the protection of combatant status on female civilian operatives. Following initial training at STS 54a in Oxfordshire, Belhaven offered its students advanced training, designed to hone their Morse skills by exchanging practice messages between Belhaven and STS 54a, 400 miles away. The women were trained to rigorously exacting standards as agents' lives might depend on the accuracy, consistency, and delicacy of touch of an operative's performance. It is possible that there was some operational communication between Belhaven and agents in Scandinavia, but the school's primary purpose was training. Graduates from Belhaven would move on to operational postings at places such as Grendon Underwood, SOE's HQ in Baker Street, or overseas to be nearer to their sources of information. The various sections of SOE required enormous amounts of supplies for their own agents and for supplying resistance organisations across Europe, and the Knoll School in Camberley was established as the SOE's main storage facility.

The 'Jedburghs' were three-man teams drawn from personnel across all the Allied nations, which would be dropped into Occupied France to co-ordinate the efforts of the French Resistance in impeding the movement of German reinforcements toward the invasion fronts following D-Day. Each team contained a wireless operator, 100 of whom were trained at Belhaven. Many of these men were already proficient as radio operators but their two weeks at Belhaven gave them the opportunity to familiarise themselves with their new radios. They, too, practised the exchange of traffic between Belhaven and STS 54a. Belhaven Wireless Station played a part in both naval operations in Norway such as the location of the German battleship *Tirpitz*, and in such clandestine operations as the destruction of the heavy water plant at Telemark. Once the Normandy front had been opened, the army's signals troops looked for direct radio contact with both the Jedburghs and SOE operatives.

The Royal Victoria Patriotic Asylum had started life as an orphanage for servicemen's children, and in the Great War, it had served as the 3rd London General Hospital run by the RAMC (TF). It then reverted to its pre-war existence as a girls' school, and in 1939, those ninety girls not at home with their families for the school holidays were evacuated to Pembrokeshire and the buildings were once again requisitioned for military use. Its first occupants were a RAF Barrage Balloon squadron operating on Wandsworth Common. After Dunkirk, the country was inundated with refugees, so it was decided that a central system of vetting these people was essential for the nation's security. The school was chosen as the location for this operation and known as the London Reception Centre. There was an annexe for females in Oak Lodge School, an LCC boarding school for the deaf at 101 Nightingale Lane, which had been evacuated to Northampton via Bognor. A Dutch intelligence officer, Colonel Oreste Pinto, made famous by the BBC *Spycatcher* programme in the 1960s, was put in charge, working with MI5 and MI9. Seeing an average of 700 people each week, it was his job to root out the potential spies and saboteurs who were seeking to infiltrate the country's defences and to constitute the fabled Fifth Column. One large room contained the personal effects of that day's intake of refugees, resembling, in Pinto's words, 'a cross between a customs examination and a vicarage jumble sale'. Apparently incriminating or unexplained items would lead to closer interrogation of their owners. Some 33,000 aliens passed through the centre during the course of the war with a comprehensive Central Information Index constructed to facilitate the cross checking of stories. Six spies were caught by Pinto, three of whom were executed at Wandsworth Jail. He admitted to only missing three enemy agents due, he maintained, to glitches in other sections of the Intelligence Service. It has become apparent, however, that Colonel Pinto made some false claims which inflated the substance of his successes. In all, nineteen enemy agents were caught, tried, convicted, and executed during the war, while others were turned as double agents, as part of Operation XX.

By the end of 1943, the vast numbers of coded signals handled every day at Bletchley Park and the pressing need to increase the number of *bombes* meant that GC&CS was running out of space. *Bombe* units were relocated to several other sites in north Buckinghamshire and the possibility of taking over Stowe School was mooted. However, this suggestion was vetoed at government level and the WRNS operatives moved to Stanmore and Eastcote instead.

Throughout the war, an arms race was conducted to develop new weapons. Cecil Clarke was a veteran of the Great War who ran a business in Bedford trialling innovative ideas, which attracted the attention of Military Intelligence's research department (MD1). He was encouraged to develop underwater explosives and invented the limpet mine, designed to be attached to the hulls of enemy shipping by naval frogmen, testing his prototypes in the new swimming baths, opened in 1935, of Bedford Modern School.

Use of School Buildings as Hospitals

Mill Hill School was evacuated to St Bees in Cumberland in 1939 making its 120-acre (48-ha) site available for new occupants. The Maudsley Hospital in Denmark Hill, Camberwell, had been taken over in the Great War as a military hospital and had pioneered the treatment of mental illness. Situated in an area of south London likely to be bombed, it was moved out to the vacated school buildings to become the 550-bed Mill Hill Emergency Medical Services (EMS) Hospital. Under the control of the Mental Hospitals Department of the LCC, it treated both military personnel and civilians for what was still then known as shell shock but might now more likely be termed post-traumatic stress disorder (PTSD). A range of treatments were employed including hypnosis; early semi-narcosis treatment using sodium amatyl injections to enable patients to work through their traumatic experiences; electro-convulsive therapy (ECT); and both individual and group psychotherapy. This latter treatment was developed at the hospital into the ideology of the therapeutic community, propounded by Maxwell Jones. Other eminent psychiatrists and psychologists also worked there during the war. These included John Raven who developed verbal intelligence tests such as the Mill Hill Vocabulary Test and Raven's Matrices; Hans Eysenck who became infamous for his views on inherited racial differences in intelligence, but pioneered work in behaviour therapy and explored the scientific study of personality; and Walter Maclay who laid the foundations for the Mental Health Act of 1959. Somewhat unsurprisingly, given the wartime circumstances of work overload and inadequate staffing; the complex nature of both illness and treatment; the awkward interface between the civilian and the military; and the strong personalities of the staff; the hospital was a hotbed of tension and professional disagreement. However, it can be argued that many of the innovative treatments and ideas which came out of Mill Hill in the war years proved of great benefit to the developing NHS. In 1946, the school returned, and the hospital went back to Denmark Hill as The Maudsley.

Campbell College in Belfast had been evacuated to Portrush with day boys attending the school's former junior department. The school was taken over as a military hospital and additional wards were accommodated in huts in the grounds. The 130 or so British general hospitals of the RAMC travelled the world with usually brief stays in Britain to refit and prepare for the next foreign assignment, but some were needed at home to treat the stream of casualties. The 20th General Hospital arrived back in Britain in May 1940 from France and after a brief spell in Leeds moved to Northern Ireland. From November 1940 until January 1943, it was based at Campbell College, eventually returning to France in June 1944. The 24th General Hospital spent nearly four years there between August 1940 and April 1944, overlapping for two of those years with the 31st General Hospital, before being deployed to India. The 25th General Hospital also spent time at Campbell College during the early months of 1944 prior to a move to France that autumn. In May 1941, the school was bombed with nineteen staff and patients being killed and some of the Nissen huts in the grounds being wrecked. Throughout the war some 34,000 patients were treated within the hospital. In the run-up to D-Day, the US military established over fifty hospitals for the reception of casualties evacuated from Normandy. In Bangor, County Down, the Central Primary School was taken over for use as a military hospital, as was the Friends' School in Lisburn, County Antrim and

St Swithun's School in Winchester was home to the 38th US Station Hospital.

Skegness accommodated two initial training establishments: the Royal Navy's HMS *Royal Arthur*, self-contained in the Butlins holiday camp; and the RAF's No. 11 Recruit Training Centre, scattered across a collection of hotels, cafes, shops, and a boys' home, whose station sick bay occupied the Seacroft Boys' School, now a care home. Taunton's School in Southampton, which had been evacuated to Bournemouth, served as a temporary hospital, and in Weston-super-Mare, Eastern House School became a Red Cross receiving station for casualties from the Bristol Blitz. The Blind School Hospital in Leatherhead took in casualties after the evacuation of British troops from Dunkirk.

Schools provided for other assorted wartime activities or functions. Devonport HS for Girls housed machine shops for the adjacent RN Dockyard and Southampton's Taunton's School was a staging post for German POWs, some of whom were downed aircrew. At West Coates in Edinburgh, Donaldsons School for the Deaf, an enormous Jacobean palace of 1841, in the style of the prodigy houses, which since 2007 has been converted to luxury apartments, served as POW Camp Nos 12 and 15. In 1944, the Jewish members of a Pioneer Corps unit at Oswestry in Shropshire were bussed to a Yom Kippur (Day of Atonement) service held in the assembly hall of Shrewsbury GS.

While schools were generally regarded as safer tenants than the military, large parts of Castle Howard were destroyed by fire while occupied by Queen Margaret's School from Scarborough. Lord Bath was a governor of the Royal School in Bath, which catered for the daughters of army officers. Prior to its outbreak, he had said that, in the event of war and the school's requisition by the military, he would take them all in at Longleat. Fortunately, Lord Bath appears not to have regretted his invitation as his 300 new lodgers settled in for the duration and, although he was confined to more modest quarters than he was accustomed, he did have plenty of riders for his horses. Not all billets fared so well. When the evacuated St Dunstan's College returned to Catford from Penarth in the autumn of 1945, it found the buildings full of rubble, classrooms dirty and littered with debris, and the playing fields, which had been used as a lorry park, resembling the Western Front. There had been five unexplained fires between 1940 and 1943, two of which had largely destroyed the Great Hall, and it would take five years to get everything put right.

Schools on the Front Line

Some schools found themselves in the forefront of what could have constituted the firing line, had the expected invasion taken place. The whole country was geared to resist invasion and, inevitably, existing buildings such as schools got caught up in these arrangements, and defence works could appear on school sites. The first line of defence was the Coastal Crust of anti-invasion measures, which included coast artillery batteries, and beach obstacles of wire, minefields, and scaffolding. The hinterland was then criss-crossed by linear defence lines consisting of anti-tank obstacles in the form of waterways, continuous ditches, or railway embankments, strengthened by barbed wire and minefields and backed by pillboxes, A/T gun-houses, slit trenches, and weapons pits. The most important of these barriers was the GHQ Line, which extended from the coast below Weston-super-Mare, through the Somerset Levels, along the Kennet & Avon Canal to Reading, the North Downs to the River Medway, and up across the Hoo Peninsula to the Thames. It then proceeded north through East Anglia and Lincolnshire to the Humber Estuary and onwards through Yorkshire and Northumbria into Scotland, finishing on the River Tay. Other defences included the Taunton Stop Line, which ran from the coast north of Bridgwater to the south Devon coast at Seaton; a series of Command Lines in East Anglia, South Wales, Kent, and Northumbria; and lines which followed rivers such as the Severn, Trent, Tame, Teme, Arun, Adur, and both Avons. Where important lines of communication met in towns or villages, all-round defensive schemes were prepared using roadblocks, wire, mines, A/T obstacles, and pillboxes. These latter positions were referred to initially as 'Anti-tank Islands' but subsequently became 'Nodal Points'. Everywhere there were vulnerable points, transport hubs, factories, and utilities, needing safeguarding. At Hampton GS, pits were dug all over the school fields to discourage the landing of gliders in an airborne invasion. Sixty cadets from Bishop Wordsworth Boys' GS in Salisbury's Cathedral Close were organised as a last line of defence behind the Home Guard in the event of an invasion. At Bolton School, an unusual pillbox, sometimes described as a firewatchers' post, is preserved, standing near the school's new Riley VI Form Centre.

Schools in the Coastal Crust Defences

In 1940, tanks containing a mixture of petrol and oil were sunk in the grounds of Caius School (now Shoreham College) at Kingston, Shoreham-by-Sea, to feed pipelines that would set the sea alight in the event of an invasion. In Sussex, the village of Lyminster, sitting behind the important port of Littlehampton with its shipyards, was fortified. Loopholes were inserted into walls commanding the main road to Arundel (A284) and after the children had been evacuated, the Pavilion School was turned into a strongpoint surrounded by barbed wire. The Duke of York's Military School above Dover had become an army transit camp and was fortified with a handful of pillboxes of differing designs. Three of them were semi-sunken D-shaped pillboxes with four loopholes facing front and a fifth one covering the entrance. The other two are square, with one of them incorporating a concrete table mount for a machine gun. Bognor was given all-round defences in 1940 and garrisoned by 9th Battalion, Hampshire Regiment. Battalion HQ was in Greenways School and 'C' Company was centred on Holyrood School. A detachment of the Royal Sussex Regiment's Infantry Training Centre from the barracks in Chichester was based in St Michael's School. Holmwood School in Hastings Road, Bexhill, was evacuated early in the war and occupied by an artillery unit. With invasion imminent in the summer of 1940, every available artillery piece was deployed to the South Coast, the likely target of Operation Sealion. The Great War-vintage 9.2-inch howitzers of 56 Heavy Regiment, RA, were emplaced in open sand-bagged emplacements, and their 6-inch guns on canopied platforms, in the Bexhill and Hastings area. The RHQ was established in the school, with a telephone exchange in an air-raid shelter on site. The regiment, re-equipped with modern 7.2-inch howitzers, fought in Italy in 1943, and the school building was turned into flats by the local authority, but is now, once again, restored to its original purpose as Worthingholme School. In Littlehampton, the Home Guard HQ was in East Street School.

Schools in the GHQ Line Defences

Sheephatch Camp near Farnham was one of thirty-six National Camps built in 1939 as educational holiday centres in peacetime or as evacuation centres in wartime. Each camp could accommodate 350 children in wooden huts. It was intended to house evacuees from Leyton, on the eastern edge of London. Just across the fields lies the GHQ Line with its gun-houses, pillboxes, and anti-tank obstacles, following the course of the River Wey. Further to the east along the GHQ Line lies Tonbridge, on the River Medway. The town lies to the south-east of London and was given all-round defences as an important nodal point, later upgraded to fortress status. The River Medway was lined with pillboxes, often two deep, and A/T emplacements along its length from Lingfield to Maidstone. Tonbridge was fortified with the castle as its centrepiece, where at the west end of the river wall was built an A/T emplacement, labelled 'Post No. 20' on a set of contemporary defence plans, which numbered the A/T emplacements along the river. This was built to house a 6-pounder gun previously mounted on Edwardian battleships against boarders in small boats and in Great War tanks. It covered the Big Bridge ('Great Bridge' on the 1940 plan), just 120 yards away. Above this, up on the castle wall, stood an infantry defence post, and an AA light machine gun was mounted at the east end of the walls. Roadblocks were placed across all entry points to the town, that on the Big Bridge consisting of large concrete blocks with slots into which could be inserted steel beams. Outside the Rose and Crown PH in the High Street, a few yards north of East Street, the pavement was blocked by A/T pimples and the carriageway had two rows of double slots for A/T rails or 'hair-pins'. These slots were covered with removable concrete covers to prevent them filling with water and mud, and the iron rails were stacked by the roadside for instant use. A barbed-wire barrier stretched the length of the High Street, with gaps in it to allow pedestrians to cross. Other roadblocks around the perimeter were less ambitious using movable obstacles and barbed wire mounted on knife-rests, which could be moved into place as necessary. Along the town's defensive perimeter, gaps between buildings were blocked with obstacles, and on the east and west, continuous A/T ditches were backed with barbed-wire aprons. On the west side, there were two infantry defence posts of sandbags and barbed wire, and a concrete infantry pillbox at TQ585469 or thereabouts, where three dykes meet on the present Weald Way. The outer defensive perimeter on its north-west side follows the edge of Tonbridge School's playing fields, and there were at least two defence positions on its length, one of which may have been a pillbox.

Not on the 1941 plan of the town defences, but revealed during building works at Tonbridge School, is a small, rectangular pillbox of unusual design, positioned opposite the Portman Park turning off the High Street, which was itself closed by a roadblock. The pillbox has an entrance in its thinner, west, rear face that lacks loopholes and backs onto school buildings. It would appear to have been designed specifically for that location in that its corner embrasures can be found in only a very tiny number of such constructions. The south face with two embrasures, one central and one at the south-east corner looks toward the Rose and Crown roadblock, and the east face with a central embrasure between the two corner ones, looks toward Portman Park. The north face which mirrors the south one overlooks the London Road junction where other defences were present. The 1941 plan appears to suggest a further pillbox at this spot and a third one about where Castle Street meets High Street, just south of the Rose and Crown roadblock. It is possible that neither of these other two pillboxes was built and that the school pillbox was substituted as a halfway compromise. By the beginning of 1941, there was a moratorium on building concrete defences as they were deemed to be expensive in labour and materials; allowed insufficient flexibility in defensive tactics; and encouraged a passive attitude in the defenders. It should be noted that it was General Ironside, an Old Tonbridgian and C-in-C Home Forces in 1940, who was responsible for the static defences of the GHQ Line when the army's lack of mobility gave him no alternative. The author of an article about the school in the war, written in 1981, mentions the extant pillbox but also 'another one built into the avenue gates'. The pillbox by the new science block has recently been rescued from obscurity and conserved as a memorial.

Schools in the Stop Line Defences

The Somerset town of Ilminster stood on the defensive line known as the Taunton Stop Line. This consisted of pillboxes and anti-tank obstacles that followed natural barriers such as railways and waterways. The Stop Line followed the line of the railway to the west of the town, which was turned into a nodal point, whose defences consisted of a continuous belt of barbed wire with a ditch connecting fourteen strongpoints. These defences skirted the grammar school field on which was planted one of the dozen pillboxes which surrounded the town. The local Home Guard shared the responsibility for manning these pillboxes with regular troops. One of the Ilminster platoons was commanded by a teacher from a school evacuated to the town from London, and one of its messengers in 1944 was a lad of twelve whose duties were confined to the town itself in case he got lost.

The River Avon Stop Line in Wiltshire ran from Christchurch on the coast up to Salisbury. Most of the villages marked river crossings and were defended. One such place was Downton where a pillbox was built in the corner of the school field to command the main road, which runs down the west bank, and the water meadows to the south of the bridge running down to the railway bridge, which might just about have been within range. On the opposite side of the road from the pillbox was a boomerang-shaped section post with a dozen loopholes.

Christ's Hospital School, south-west of Horsham, lay just below the northern section of the fortified River Adur Line which ran along the line of the river to the south of Horsham. At least one pillbox remains of those lining the riverbank close to the school's grounds. By the end of 1941, when the fear of invasion was diminished, manning these defences would have become the responsibility of the local Home Guard, which included the school contingent.

Schools in the London Defences

Merchant Taylors' School lies inside the Outer London Defence Line (Line 'A'), here marked by the River Colne. The river formed an effective A/T barrier and was supported by concrete pillboxes; roadblocks on the bridges which crossed the river; and A/T obstacles in the shape of concrete cubes and bent rail 'hair-pins'. To the west of the school where a minor road pierces the railway embankment, a large Type DFW3/27 octagonal pillbox stands within the school grounds. Over the north porch of the school's Great Hall is a further pillbox. This measures 16 feet (4.9 metres) by 15 feet (4.6 metres) and stands 13 feet (4 metres) above ground level. The Grade II listed Hall was built in 1931–3 and is the largest building in Europe to be constructed with 3-inch (5-cm) bricks. The pillbox was shuttered using similar bricks as a camouflage measure. It has four embrasures for rifles or light machine guns which are splayed both internally and externally and stepped to deflect incoming rounds. Two embrasures in the front of the pillbox face east to the river, 200 yards away across what, in 1940, was open ground. The single embrasure in the south side enfilades the front of the hall and beyond, but that in the northern face has always had a restricted field of fire owing to the projecting dining hall. The pillbox is accessed via a pre-existing door which originally opened onto a balcony on the porch roof. The Royal Commission on the Historical Monuments of England carried out an archaeological survey at the request of Hertfordshire County Council in 1995 prior to the intended demolition of the pillbox. The current (2020) image on Google Earth, however, shows the pillbox still *in situ*. In 1940, the older cadets of Merchant Taylors' School OTC formed a platoon of the local LDV unit based at Rickmansworth, so might well have manned those very defences which fronted their school.

Schools in Nodal Point and Vulnerable Point Defences

Lewes, in Sussex, was an important nodal point with road, river, and rail links. The centre of the town, including the castle, constituted the keep, whose eastern edge was formed by the River Ouse, crossed by the Cliffe Bridge. This bridge was covered by a pillbox designed to hold an anti-tank gun and slotted onto the pavement alongside the portico of Broughton's Ladies' School at 212 School Hill. It extended across the adjacent Number 213 and was camouflaged so cleverly with a paint job mimicking the house fronts as to appear invisible, the only recognisable feature being the large embrasure, which would have been masked. Although described as a Type 28a gun-house, it appears to have been a non-standard design, similar to one which stands in front of Newhaven Fort.

Arundel, also in Sussex, lay beside the River Arun Stop Line and was classified as a Category 'A' nodal point. To cover the roadblock at the end of Maltravers Street, the Free School, now the town's library, was defended with loopholes cut into its perimeter walls, two more at the east end, and five air-raid shelters in the school playground.

Ellesmere and Shrewsbury were two among eleven nodal points in Shropshire. The village of Ellesmere was ringed by a barbed-wire barrier with entry points mined and covered by weapons pits and sub-artillery positions. The village school, which lies in the shadow of the castle mound, stands in a re-entrant of the perimeter defences and may have been furnished with loopholes as a defended building. Shrewsbury School OTC is listed by Bernard Lowry as constituting 'K' Company, 1st Battalion, Shropshire HG. The battalion's other five companies, 'A' to 'E', were allocated to specified sectors of the town defences. An additional 'Z' Company was one of several companies expected to form a Great Western Railway (GWR) Midlands and Northern Home Guard battalion, spread across Shropshire, Cheshire, and North Wales. Shrewsbury's company, listed as No. 4 Company, would be tasked with defending the town's railway station. However, in his history of the cadet movement, Collins, drawing on Shrewsbury School archives, ascribes 'Z' Company to the school and quotes the relevant operational orders. These describe the school company's specific night-time role in the defence of the railway station, possibly, in an emergency, alongside the railwaymen responsible for daytime security, but usually on their own. Boys stood three-hour shifts in sections, one ran from 22:30 p.m. to 1:30 a.m., and the other from 1:30 a.m. to 4:30 a.m., and these duties were rostered with other Home Guard companies. There was a network of sentries based on the obvious VPs such as the signal box and the river bridges, with back-up from mobile patrols. Clear protocols were laid down for the conduct of sentries who worked in pairs and were armed with rifles and bayonets. They could issue challenges and ensure that only authorised routes were used through the station complex. This deployment would appear to bear out the apparent Home Guard policy (*cf.* Cranleigh and Dover College) of regarding school companies as 'bonus' units, providing flexibility to the defence plan. On the question of 'Z'

Company's GWR attribution, Lowry quotes a War Office document (WO199/342 in TNA) which details the GWR's plans for several Home Guard battalions. At stand down in 1944, however, there were just two GWR battalions, at Paddington and Swindon. It could have been that Shrewsbury School's 'K' Company morphed into the 'Z' Company that had failed to materialise, while its putative railway company-based membership would have been absorbed into others of the town's Home Guard companies. Across the country, after the initial improvisations of the invasion scares, regular army units were either despatched for overseas service or more closely immersed in training at home. This saw school contingents taking on more guard duties alongside Home Guard units as they assumed both a greater responsibility for home defence and for the preparation of youngsters for military service.

3

Youngsters in Defence of the Nation

'How old are you, son?'
'Sixteen, sir.'
'I didn't quite catch that.'
'Oh, eighteen, sir.'
'Very good, that's what I thought you said.'

There were many ways in which young people could actively help in the defence of their country whether they were still at school or had recently left, and this chapter seeks to explore many of those wide-ranging activities that could broadly be described as contributing to the military effort.

The Home Guard

When the Local Defence Volunteers (LDV) was first formed in the summer of 1940, seventeen was adopted as the minimum age for membership. In 1942, the Army Cadet Force (ACF) had been formed as the official successor to the Territorial Cadet Force and it was seen as constituting the first step in a progression for youngsters: ACF>Home Guard>Conscription>Basic Training. In 1942, the minimum age was lowered to sixteen on condition that parental consent was forthcoming. However, right through the war, many lads below either of these qualifying ages would manage to join the Home Guard in one capacity or another, while other initiatives might bypass such regulation completely. In May 1940, even prior to the establishment of the Local Defence Volunteers (LDV), Mr (later Sir Anthony) Eden, secretary of state for war, responding to a question regarding the 'watchfulness of the community in regard to parachutist attacks', reported: '... offers of assistance from certain pony clubs have been received and have been accepted in those districts in which their help can be of value'. The assistance being offered was for pony club members to carry out patrols looking out for parachute drops by enemy troops, and this was typical of many such initiatives which would run parallel to official measures.

Home Guard Units in Schools

At a time in the summer of 1940 when the LDV was first forming, the many schools with OTC contingents were in the strongest position to form fully equipped units, providing Home Guard units of either platoon or company size and integration into the Geneva Convention legitimated Home Guard would prove necessary for any OTC members who opted for combatant status. Among those who initiated LDV activities in the town was the adjutant of Oundle School's OTC contingent, which would become the nucleus of the six companies of the 3rd (Oundle) Battalion, Northamptonshire Home Guard (HG). The Battalion's 'F' (HQ) Company was commanded by an Oundle master and provided support, training, and expertise to the other companies. Masters commanded further companies or were responsible for signals, weapons training, or the supply and safe storage of ammunition. The battalion's 140-strong 'E' Company was based on Oundle School itself and was composed of officers and senior members of the OTC, along with other members of the school's wider staff. These two companies would take on the responsibility for securing nearby RAF Polebrook, operating Flying Fortresses even before the USA entered the war, but by 1942, an 8th USAAF bomber airfield. They would carry out patrols and mock attacks to test the airfield's supposedly lax defences. From the beginning, when boys were on guard duty on the school field, watching out for paratroop landings, they were each issued with a 0.303-inch rifle and two rounds of live ammunition and as one master later pointed out: 'such is Oundle discipline that none of the officers was shot either accidentally or deliberately'. Commercial lorries were commandeered from local firms' as necessary to provide mobility.

After Dunkirk, senior pupils at Millfield School in Somerset joined the LDV, carrying out nightly duties manning an observation post looking out for descending paratroopers and also manned roadside checkpoints monitoring traffic and checking drivers' papers. Evacuated from Norfolk to their new home in Newquay, Cornwall, Greshams School pupils joined the local Home Guard. During the school summer holidays, OTC members would often join the Home Guard in their home villages, carrying out patrols. At Christ's Hospital School, Horsham, seventeen-year-old OTC members automatically joined the school's Home Guard unit, which also contained masters and other school or estate employees. At the height of the invasion scare, a section would be taken by truck down to the coast at Angmering at night to carry out guard duties armed with loaded rifles. At Clifton, OTC cadets in the local Home Guard carried out nightly patrols on the Beggars Bush playing fields, later to become a US Army airstrip. A patrol schedule from midnight to 2 a.m. was followed by a brief sleep and then sentry duty until dawn. Eton College formed an LDV unit immediately, composed of staff and cadets over the age of sixteen. They wore their OTC uniforms with the necessary LDV armbands, which might suggest that a widely reproduced photograph of them drilling in top hats with shouldered rifles, was no more than a publicity stunt. Eton occupies an important position on lines of communication and near the strategically significant munitions factories of Slough, so there was plenty of work for the boys to do guarding VPs. Watches were mounted nightly in four-hour shifts looking out for parachutists and rifles and ammunition were issued to boys for all these sentry and patrol duties. School holidays might be given up to maintaining these activities through the summer. In Kirkcudbrightshire, Cally House was a residential centre for pupils in the fourteen to eighteen age group evacuated from Glasgow secondary schools. In 1942, there was a school platoon with at least fifteen members under the command of a mathematics teacher. Another local company was commanded by one of the school's physical education teachers. As well as the usual patrol and guard duties, the school unit was called out to fight heath fires and to locate crashed enemy aircraft.

Westminster School was evacuated to Bromyard, occupying several large houses including 'Buckenhill', 'Brockhampton', 'Clater Park', Whitbourne Rectory', Fernie', and 'Saltmarshe Castle'. The two larger houses, Buckenhill and Fernie, formed sections as part of the local Home Guard platoon, with several of the older boys, having attended training courses in their home bases during school holidays, taking on instructor roles. Although, initially, there was an official minimum age of seventeen, numbers of sixteen-year-olds were allowed to train so that on joining officially they would already have earned their proficiency badges. Welcomed and integrated into the local unit, they enjoyed the benefits to be had from a real involvement in local defence. Meanwhile, those boys who chose to stay in London, were also involved in Home Guard activities, also attending training courses at home in their school holidays. Boys and staff evacuated to Shropshire from Lancing bolstered the Ellesmere HG by carrying out observation watches on the castle mound, thereby releasing some WVS members for more productive duties. Boys from Maidstone GS marched in their OTC uniforms to enrol in the LDV at the earliest opportunity and Tonbridge School formed a platoon of the Home Guard and carried out guard duties on VPs. The school had a miniature range and boys also shot on the full-size open-air range. The results of shooting matches with other schools, of necessity being conducted by post, were reported in the school magazine. By 1942, Home Guard duties were claiming more time and reference is made in the school magazine to nights spent in the armoury. Exercises were carried out with local units and one night, an attack on the school guardroom by a couple of over-enthusiastic regulars was repulsed good-naturedly, but nevertheless, forcefully. Boys engaged in such nocturnal activities were permitted to spend the next morning in bed. This concession, however, was not extended to teaching staff. The school's secretary, a decorated lieutenant-colonel played a prominent part in the leadership of Tonbridge's Home Guard until his final retirement in 1945. The teacher in command of the school's OTC contingent also held a command position in the area Home Guard and rose to the rank of lieutenant-colonel. Senior OTC cadets at St Dunstan's College, during their stay in Reigate formed a school platoon of the local Home Guard company, carrying out guard and telephone duties and despatch riding. Merchant Taylors' School OTC, as we have seen, formed a platoon of its local Home Guard company.

Since those schools which were residential, sending their pupils home for the holidays, could not guarantee the consistent presence necessary to be included in regular patrol rosters, they tended, like university OTC, to be regarded as a bonus, and some were consequently organised as mobile reserves. Staff and over-sixteens in the OTC at Dover College evacuated to Poltimore House in Devon, formed the Mobile Reserve Platoon of the Bradninch Company of the 3rd (Cullompton) Battalion, Devon HG. As a military school the armoury was better stocked with weapons than 'the rest of the Devon Home Guard put together'. These weapons included Thompson sub-machine guns; Mills bombs; a Vickers heavy machine gun; and Lee-Enfield 0.303-inch rifles, sleeved to fire small-bore ammunition on the miniature range. It was this latter facility that the seventeen-year-old entrusted with caring for all this weaponry would find useful in early morning expeditions shooting game for the pot. As a 'mobile' platoon, those masters who were officers were entitled to petrol coupons. The platoon took part in many defence exercises attacking, in the guise of German paratroopers, all the local units, each time finishing up in the pub. A similar mobile platoon was also organised at Cranleigh School for the 5th Battalion, Surrey HG.

On the Isle of Man, over fifty of King William's College OTC members were absorbed into the Castletown Company of the Home Guard. The Man HG was unusual in having a clearly differentiated dual role. Not only would it maintain a tight network of coastal observation posts as part of the anti-invasion measures, but, owing to the presence on the island of internment camps, there would be an additional internal security dimension to their duties. While most of the foreign aliens might be expected to be quiescent, awaiting their release, interned members of the IRA or the British Union of Fascists might be more likely to attempt escape, as some did. As well as recruiting the senior cadets, the Home Guard on the island also attracted much younger lads as messengers or runners.

In many places, training became a reciprocal activity between schools and the LDV/Home Guard, especially where there was a close relationship as at Chigwell whose school armoury was the local Home Guard HQ. Very often, especially in the early days, NCOs in the OTC who had passed their Certificate 'A', often aged fifteen, found themselves in the position of instructing much older men, either in drill or in weapons training. A youngster from Haileybury, back home in Somerset for the school holidays became a temporary instructor in his village LDV platoon. Some military skills might have been acquired in a civilian setting and shooting was one of them. Boys, and girls, as young as thirteen with this particular skill could find themselves acting as instructors to home guardsmen three times their age. Some remembered being kindly treated but suspected some degree of covert resentment. But skill at shooting has clearly demonstrable and unarguable outcomes which would consolidate an instructor's legitimacy. A facility to strip down and reassemble weapons was also an advantage enjoyed by cadets with nimble fingers and fewer threats to their dignity over allegations of cackhandedness. Sometimes senior boys in the role of instructors, and their teachers in the role of Home Guard trainees, led to tensions. One teacher at Churchers College, a member of Petersfield Home Guard, complained to his headmaster after being likened to a 'lopsided marrow' while being drilled by one of his pupils. Some teachers were less conspicuous. A diminutive housemaster parading in the ranks of his school's HG unit was picked out by an elderly and short-sighted inspecting general. 'And what do you want to be when you leave school, eh?' Quick as a flash came the reply: 'Engine-driver, Sir'.

As new weapons appeared, notably the improvised guns known as sub-artillery, then familiarisation courses were run with Cranleigh School hosting such a course on the Blacker Bombard or Spigot Mortar. Beyond the conventional training in drill, weapons handling, shooting, and basic infantry tactics, some acknowledgement was made of the possible need to prepare to carry out guerrilla warfare. In 1941, the Boy Scout Association offered the War Office access to its expertise in fieldcraft, suggesting that cadets might benefit from such training. It was felt that the parade-ground had little to offer those fighting for their lives against an invading force, whereas the acquisition of survival skills might be more useful. Scouts were welcome to join cadet organisations but were urged to retain membership of their Scout Troops so as not to lose touch with scouting skills. This need was recognised by schools such as Winchester College, which attempted to balance the range of training needs. Another often-neglected field was the gathering of intelligence and its analysis and Whitgift School was one which developed its own intelligence course for senior pupils. Very often, such provision relied on the specific skills, experience, and enthusiasm of individuals who might introduce their cadets or home guardsmen to those activities not always present in the regular curriculum. By 1942, battle-craft had generally begun to dominate training to a greater extent and as the war progressed, training, which had initially been quite basic, became much more ambitious. At Sedbergh, the OTC's training manual for section leaders included sections on anti-tank warfare and house-to-house street fighting. Some of those who returned from service in the International Brigades, fighting in the Spanish Civil War, would become teachers and it is tempting to think that they might have passed to their pupils some of the skills of unconventional warfare which they had acquired fighting against Franco's regulars.

It was quite common for locally based teachers to take the lead in organising LDV units. In rural Scotland where schools might represent the only common social hub, schoolmasters often organised recruitment into the LDV. Lieutenant-Colonel Robinson, headmaster of Moseley GS, commanded 4th (Birmingham) Battalion,

Warwickshire HG, one of the first ten units in the city, with some of the school staff as officers. The Northamptonshire HG's 7th Battalion was commanded by a master at Wellingborough School who also commanded the school OTC and by 1944, he had almost 2,000 men and women under his command. In Somerset, No. 1 Platoon of the Yeovil Company of the 3rd Battalion, Somerset HG, was commanded by a master from Huish Boys' School, and the headmasters of St John's School, Clevedon, and Bradford Abbas School both served in their local Home Guard units, the former as a platoon commander. One of Tonbridge School's languages staff who commanded the school's OTC contingent had expected to be parachuted into France but was appointed to command of the local Home Guard instead. The second lieutenant commanding a platoon of the Street Company of the 9th Wells Battalion, Somerset HG, was a physics teacher who had been invalided out of the Regular Army with the rank of captain. The Home Guard platoon in Headley in Hampshire was commanded by the clergyman head of the local prep school, and the Petersfield unit by a language teacher from Churchers College who had been gassed in the Great War and suffered from deafness. A platoon based in a school now underneath Heathrow Airport was commanded by the head teacher with an assistant master as his deputy. A memoir from one of his rank and file would suggest that such *ex officio* appointments were not always terribly effective. Isolated and semi-independent units were able to develop more imaginative scenarios so, to be prepared for the interrogation of any German prisoners they might possibly encounter, the 1st Battalion, Banffshire HG, recruited one male and three female language teachers from Buckie HS as interpreters.

Teachers evacuated from cities or vulnerable coastal areas to a safer location also often joined the Home Guard. Three staff from Feltonfleet School including the headmaster joined the local Home Guard platoon when the school was evacuated from Cobham, Surrey, to North Perrott Manor House in Somerset. In Winscombe, some staff members who had been transferred from a London polytechnic to Sidcot School, enrolled in 'D' Company of the Axbridge Battalion of the Somerset HG. This must have raised some eyebrows since Sidcot was a Quaker school. The sergeant commanding the Simonsbath Platoon of the Exmoor Company was on the staff of a girls' school evacuated to what is now the Simonsbath Hotel, and the commander of an Ilminster platoon was a teacher from a school evacuated from London. In Shropshire, the local Home Guard was aided by a schoolmaster from Lancing, evacuated to Ellesmere College.

The participation of serving teachers in leadership roles or even in the lowlier ranks of the Home Guard, however, raised questions of priorities or even loyalties. Some of those teachers who were with parties of evacuated children decided on official advice that their primary duty in an emergency was to their young charges and therefore refused promotion or other military responsibility, remaining in the rank and file whilst others seemed not to be concerned by the potential conflict of interest. In Scotland, this concern became an issue when the Scottish Education Department (SED) asked teachers explicitly to consider the minimum nucleus of staff necessary for the welfare of children in an emergency such as an invasion, and to relate this to the number of staff who might properly be mustered with the Home Guard. The use of the word 'loyalty' to highlight the dilemma prompted some local authorities to discourage teachers from remaining with the Home Guard or joining at all. The SED sought to clarify matters by differentiating between the few 'full-time' members of the Home Guard and the many 'part-timers'. This failed to satisfy some authorities who proposed that, where loyalties were unclear, their teachers should immediately resign from the Home Guard. In the end, a two-tier system prevailed where there were teachers who were authorised to respond immediately to a call for muster, and others who would delay for up to forty-eight hours, in the interim giving all their attention to their charges. Even then, not all authorities could agree a common approach. Edinburgh opted for all its teachers to be in the immediate category while Glasgow assigned its teachers to the delayed.

Often, OTC armouries were the only source of weaponry in the early days of the LDV. The 5th Battalion, Wiltshire HG, at Swindon got its first rifles from Marlborough College OTC. A long-disbanded cadet unit had been reformed at Cheltenham GS in 1940 which supplied the local Home Guard battalion with a Lewis gun section, suggesting that these weapons had been hidden away for a generation. Whatever the circumstances, this was a very welcome addition when automatic weapons were in such short supply. As well as the usual weaponry which had remained in the school armoury; had been returned there; or had trickled down over time; some larger pieces might be obtained by schools. Christ's Hospital Home Guard possessed a piece of sub-artillery, a Northover projector, which launched SIP grenades through a 4-foot-long (1.25-metre-long) tube supported on a tripod. Apparently, only masters were allowed to fire it. As regular army units were issued with new weaponry, the Home Guard received hand-me-downs, and photographs exist of 2-pounder A/T guns on the school playing fields of two Somerset schools: Wellington and King's School, Bruton. Whether they were issued to school units or were simply being used for Home Guard drill on convenient open spaces is unclear.

Where school premises were taken over by large official organisations, their security and defence would become the responsibility of a dedicated Home Guard unit recruited from the workforce. The TRE Home Guard at Malvern was inspected by George VI in the College grounds when he and the Queen visited in 1944. Air Ministry employees at Wycliffe College, Stonehouse near Stroud, formed 'E' Company, 8th (Dursley) Battalion, Gloucestershire HG. Their task was to secure the 'Keep', the location chosen for the battalion's final stand before being overrun by the rampaging enemy. The Admiralty Signals Establishment (ASE) at King Edward's School, Witley, was part of a wider network of Admiralty research establishments in the Haslemere area. Between them they raised the 13th (ASE) Battalion, Surrey HG with HQ in Haslemere and one of its four or five companies based at Witley. The Ministry of Food in Colwyn Bay raised its own Home Guard unit which drilled on the Penrhos College playing fields.

Youngsters in the Home Guard

A contributor to a history of the Norfolk HG writes of how the presence of thirteen-year-olds was quite common, and this observation was echoed right across the country. From the earliest days of the LDV, there was a reluctance to turn away any keen volunteers, however young they might be. In Falmouth, a local vicar assembled a cycle patrol of lads who were officially too young to enrol. Elsewhere, some underage lads were actively recruited because they were physically mature for their age. A pair of strapping fourteen-year-olds in Glasgow had no trouble in joining the 3rd Battalion Renfrewshire HG. They were quickly issued with rifles and five rounds of ammunition and assigned to night-time guard duty and appear to have been present on the night Rudolf Hess parachuted into Scotland. Others were recruited because they possessed scarce skills. On the strength of his mathematical abilities, a fifteen-year-old schoolboy in Bristol was recruited into 17 AA Regiment (Gloucestershire) HG, the unit manning anti-aircraft rocket batteries, thereby releasing regular troops for duties elsewhere. After training at Horfield Barracks every evening for a fortnight, he was promoted lance-bombardier and joined Z1 battery at Easton in Gordano as a plotter. A Z Battery consisted of multiple twin rocket launchers, firing salvoes of 3-inch unrotated projectiles (UP), each of which weighed the same as the standard 3.7-inch HAA shell. In his account there were forty twin launchers, but the official record states sixty-four, the usual number organised into four troops of sixteen each. The plotting-room was in a protected command post and used a primitive form of gun-laying (GL) radar. Each twin launcher had a two-man crew, which meant that, along with those in the command post, often ATS personnel, a complement of approaching 150 operators was needed. Since almost everyone in the unit had full-time employment, they could only turn out every sixth night, meaning that around 900 personnel were needed at each of those three of Bristol's five Z Batteries, which were armed, hence the need to resort to skilled youngsters accepted as being old enough to be enrolled. Other teenagers manned ZAA batteries in London, Tyneside, Teesside, and elsewhere. As the war progressed and the threat of air attack was perceived to be decreasing, enthusiasm waned and absenteeism increased, with the result that fewer personnel were available to provide the necessary coverage. One sixteen-year-old in Bristol reported working three twelve-hour night shifts a week on the rockets alongside his full-time job in the shipyards. Given the sparse training, the tiredness of the crews on night duty, and the lethal nature of their projectiles, it is surprising that so few serious accidents occurred. One teenaged No. 1, later in life to become a judge, but in 1942 manning a ZAA site on Tyneside, relates how his command to 'Fire!' resulted in his two rockets streaking across the site at head height as his elderly No. 2, a shipyard worker, had neglected to elevate the projector from its horizontal position, possibly not having heard the relevant order as a result of the deafness, endemic in the ship-building industry.

Reported in *We Remember the Home* Guard, an even younger fourteen-year-old Les Garret in Sussex enrolled in the Home Guard in 1941. Although his teachers were aware of this, they preferred to capitalise on his maturity by giving him additional responsibility at school. Nights were spent up rickety church towers looking out for parachutists, or on patrol with fixed bayonets. Still only fourteen, Les got into hard-fought scraps as the uncompromising Canadian troops tested the Home Guard defences. Captured, and tied to a tree all night in a bruised and bleeding condition, he 'wasn't much good for school on the Monday'. In 1942, Les was transferred to one of the Home Guard units that had taken over the manning of coast artillery batteries from the Royal Artillery. The Aldwick battery, officially the Bognor Regis Battery and now forming the basement of a modernist beach-house, covered the coast from Selsey to Littlehampton in West Sussex. It was armed with a pair of 5.5-inch naval guns removed from a decommissioned ship in 1919 and kept in store at Priddy's Hard. The guns had an effective range of around 5 miles (8 km) and were accompanied by two searchlights. Les was made battery commander assistant and installed in the battery observation post. One perquisite of serving in a Home Guard emergency coast battery was that a five-hour stint on duty earned service rations. It was his job to plot the course of enemy ships using the crude methods available; observe the fall of shot; and relay orders to the gun crew using a Tannoy. The present writer, also at age fifteen, once found himself running the safety board, plotting targets on a live 25-pounder shoot with the TA on Salisbury Plain. As Les himself had commented, rather a lot of responsibility at that age. Such levels of responsibility came early for many of these youngsters. A schoolgirl who was taken on as a secretary by a Home Guard unit was required not only to type up reports, but to interview applicants and to judge their suitability. Girls had other, often unsuspected, skills as well. One group of young Girl Guides, taught to shoot by their parents, used to challenge the local Home Guard units to matches which they invariably won.

In Ibstock, another fourteen-year-old, employed at the local brick works, joined the works Home Guard. Too short to be comfortable with a rifle, he was issued with a Sten gun. He then transferred to the parent unit and became the CO's runner. As he was in a reserved occupation, he stayed in the Home Guard for the entire war, only doing his official military service afterwards. Although by the time he was demobbed in 1949, he had been in uniform for ten years, he was not allowed to apply for the Defence Medal as he had enrolled under the official age. Youngsters with specific skills had been quickly absorbed into the Home Guard. One eighteen-year-old office worker awaiting call-up volunteered and was instantly appointed as unit office manager with the rank of sergeant. Another way into Home Guard service was to have a father who was an officer. One fifteen-year-old and his group of mates were enrolled in his dad's company based on Hendon Technical College and shooting on the range at Mill Hill Barracks. By 1942, he had been promoted to corporal and sent to Hampstead Heath serving in a ZAA rocket battery and expected to direct older, by now conscripted, home guardsmen who really did not want to be there. A group of sixteen-year-olds volunteered to join a Home Guard

AA battery on Dulwich Common and were trained as plotters. One of them, on call-up, found himself posted to Little Horwood in Buckinghamshire, Special Communications Unit 7, and part of Section VIII of MI6/SIS providing secure messaging for forward units, in his case, the HQ 9th US Tactical Air Command, deployed to France soon after D-Day. His job involved the dissemination of ULTRA, the product of Bletchley Park's Enigma decrypts.

Both ARP and the Home Guard employed youngsters as runners or messengers, on foot or bicycle. One such messenger commenced his service as a fourteen-year-old Sea Cadet, recruited as a messenger by the Ministry of Information (MOI) located in London University buildings in Malet Street. He was on duty from 2 p.m. to 10 p.m.; stayed overnight in the Senate House; and then resumed his duties from 7 a.m. to 2 p.m. His role was to carry material between the MOI and the Admiralty for censoring. Operating at the height of the London Blitz he unavoidably got involved in ARP operations and was then recruited as a messenger in the Home Guard as one of its youngest members. At least four of the twelve battalions of the Worcestershire HG had an establishment of sixteen boy messengers per battalion. Four were attached to HQ Company with the rest distributed amongst the other five or six companies. The 5th (Halesowen) Battalion refers to these lads as 'cadets', possibly from an ACF company at the grammar school. One platoon in Sussex employed seven bicycle messengers, one for each day of the week, generally fourteen- to sixteen-year-olds whose duties were to carry messages between the Home Guard HQ and the police station. Other rural units used messengers to connect widely scattered observation posts, which lacked any alternative means of communication. The 3rd (Fulham) Battalion, County of London HG, made use of twenty cadets from the Princess Louise's Kensington Regiment Cadet Corps as bicycle messengers. Uniformed Boy Scouts and Girl Guides also acted as messengers for the Home Guard and were especially useful, at a time when few people possessed telephones, at turning out large numbers of men at short notice, simply by a thorough knowledge of their home localities and the power of the bicycle. Boy Scouts, as young as fourteen, had formal roles within the Home Guard as guides. If they were able to demonstrate the appropriate level of local knowledge, they would be employed on night exercises to ensure that troops, often unfamiliar with the area, found their way to their starting points. They were also valued as intelligence gatherers and general guides. Some of these Scouts wore armbands with the legends 'War Service Scouts' and 'National Service' and might be formally attached to Home Guard or ARP units. Girl Guides adopted the Army Pigeon Service as one of the beneficiaries of their fund-raising, with individual Guide companies also taking on the responsibility for looking after their local Home Guard unit's pigeons, maintaining their lofts, feeding, and flying them as well as managing their message-carrying roles. The skills of Sea Cadets were also exploited. Members of the Cotswold SCC crewed small craft carrying home guardsmen patrolling the Severn.

A typical temporary office building (TOB) erected for the use of decentralised government departments. Examples were built in Brislington, Cambridge, Cheltenham, Gloucester, Eastcote, Malvern, Worcester, and many other locations. This example was photographed in 2021 at Reading University's Whiteknights site.

Air-raid shelters built on the playing fields of Portsmouth GS when this whole area behind the Hilsea Lines was requisitioned by the Admiralty in 1939 as an outstation of HMS *Excellent*.

A standard Essex County Council school air-raid shelter at Silver End Primary School. (*Mike Bardell*)

An air-raid shelter braced with steel uprights and trusses prior to its demolition at Roger Ascham Special School, Cambridge, due to being deemed unsafe.

Above left: Boys digging trenches for cut-and-cover air-raid shelters at Oundle School. (*Oundle School archives*)

Above right: A blast-wall and protection for windows at Sherborne Boys' School. (*Old Shirburnian Society archive*)

One wing of the neo-Baroque school building added in 1927 to HMS *Ganges*, the Royal Naval boys' training establishment on the Shotley peninsula in Suffolk. The *Ganges* was evacuated to HMS *St George* on the Isle of Man in May 1940.

The chapel of Lancing College, initially requisitioned by the army and then by the Admiralty as HMS *King Alfred*, training mainly weekend sailors as 'hostilities only' officers in the RNVR, known as the 'Wavy Navy' for their distinctive cuff stripes.

The officers' mess of Portsmouth's Cambridge Barracks, renovated from a state of dereliction when the barracks became Portsmouth GS in 1926. The buildings were requisitioned by the Royal Navy in 1939 and the school was evacuated to Bournemouth.

Dame Bradbury's School at Saffron Walden served as HQ 65th Fighter Wing, 8th US Army Air Force, which had briefly occupied Newport GS. It controlled five fighter groups spread across the whole of East Anglia.

Badminton School in Westbury-on-Trym on the northern outskirts of Bristol became the base for a battalion of the Gloucestershire Regiment, converted into an AA searchlight unit, which had loaned its drill hall in Old Market Street, Bristol, to US troops.

St Dunstan's College in Catford housed clerical staff of the LCC, temporarily evacuated from County Hall; REME troops after 1942; and a first aid post for Lewisham ARP.

When Wycombe Abbey Girls' School was taken over by the USAAF becoming first Pinetree then Camp Lynn, administrative departments along with a medical facility were accommodated in the school's houses. Eventually, the site would grow to hold dozens of huts for the thousands of personnel.

Clifton College in Bristol served as the HQ of Omar Bradley's 1st US Army and much of his planning for the US element of the D-Day operation was carried out there. A communications flight operated from Beggar's Bush Field, the college's playing fields.

Rookesbury School outside Wickham in Hampshire became a marshalling area for troops prior to D-Day.

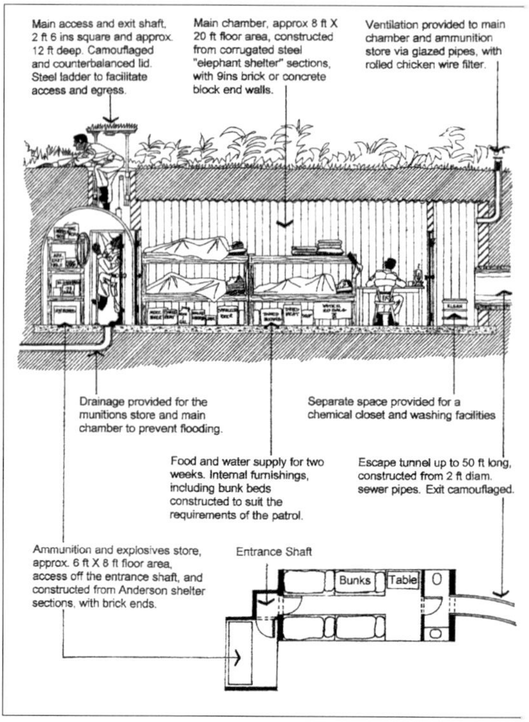

Above left: Boys from Gresham's School, evacuated from Norfolk to Newquay's Bay Hotel in Cornwall, sallying forth to carry out their Home Guard duties. (*Gresham's School archive*)

Above right: A reconstruction of an underground operational base (OB) as constructed for use by cells of the auxiliary units, the stay-behind element of the Home Guard. (*Mick Wilks*)

Cadets at Oundle School parade in 1940 wearing their OTC uniforms with LDV brassards without which they would have lacked legally confirmed combatant status. (*Oundle School archives*)

Right: Junior NCOs of Oundle School OTC preparing to carry out a map-reading exercise. (*Oundle School archives*)

Below: The School House Platoon of Sherborne School OTC. (*Old Shirburnian Society archive*)

Above left: Cadets of Oundle School OTC parading for inspection by their warrant officer instructor. (*Oundle School archives*)

Above right: Cadets of Sherborne School OTC parade for early morning bayonet practice in the summer of 1940, under the direction of RSM Brown. (*Old Shirburnian Society archive*)

Oundle School's Elmington Lodge rifle range used by the OTC and VTC in the First World War and by the OTC and the Home Guard in the Second World War.

Oundle schoolboys constructing a roadblock on the Benefield Road in the summer of 1940. Such efforts were less likely to provide a serious obstacle to the enemy's advance than to impede the movements of defending forces. (*Oundle School archives*)

A pillbox of unusual design at the Royal Military School, Dover, with the masts of Swingate Chain Home Radar Station in the background.

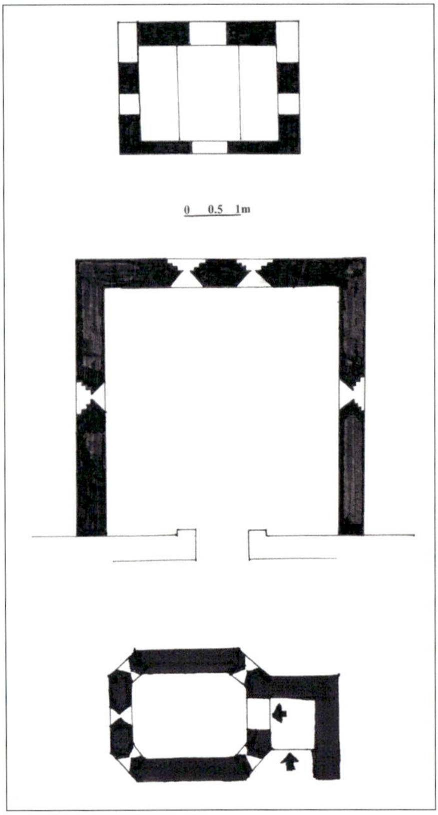

Above: The pillbox built onto the porch of Merchant Taylors' School Hall, constructed of the same 2-inch bricks.

Left: Plans of three pillboxes built on school premises. Top: Tonbridge School. Centre: Merchant Taylors' School. Bottom: Bolton School.

Dulwich Picture Gallery, now run as an independent charity, began as part of nearby Dulwich College. It was hit by a V-1 'doodlebug' in 1944 and Sir John Soane's original buildings, opened in 1811, have been restored and extended.

Sandhurst Road School, Catford, was bombed on 20 January 1943 resulting in the deaths of thirty-two children and six teachers.

Left: Damage to Braintree High School caused by an intruder aircraft. (*Mike Bardell*)

Below: The canteen run by the pupils of Sherborne Girls' School in use after the air raid of September 1940. (*Sherborne Girls' School archive*)

Ammunition boxes being made by schoolboys in Oundle School's workshops. (*Oundle School archives*)

Oundle schoolboys working in the school blacksmith's forge. The school was given contracts by the Ministry of Supply to make, among other things, firing pins for AA guns. (*Oundle School archives*)

Above: An Oundle schoolboy driving a tractor on a local farm. (*Oundle School archives*)

Left: Scouts collecting waste paper and other salvage. (*Oundle School archives*)

Over 1,200 home guardsmen died during the war, either by enemy action or in accidents connected to training, and these included some of those under eighteen, one of the two lads in the 23rd Battalion of the Warwickshire HG, killed during the July 1942 bombing of Birmingham, being a seventeen-year-old corporal. However, incidents concerning schoolboys could be entirely unforeseen and happier. In May 1941, a German pilot who had been shot down, surrendered to two boys from Sherborne School, out for an afternoon cycle ride. They flagged down a car whose driver, a home guardsman as it happened, conducted him to the police station. The incident was recorded in the school's Fire Watch Book, adding that the other three crewmen failed to escape the doomed aircraft and were burnt to death. Their teachers could also experience similarly unexpected events. There are several versions of the strange episode which took place in August 1940 in Sussex. One version has a German pilot landing his Gotha biplane on Lewes Racecourse to be met by an armed home guardsman accompanied by his evacuee companion, a modern languages teacher from Tooting Bec Secondary School whose charges were lodging with the Lewes County Boys' School. The pilot is reported as claiming to have got lost flying mail from Cherbourg to Jersey. He was sent to Canada as a POW and his aircraft, not deemed worthy of being issued to RAF No. 1426 (Enemy Aircraft) Flight, nicknamed the 'Rafwaffe', was repainted in RAF colours and put to good use, finally finishing up as an instructional airframe.

Youngsters in the Auxiliary Units

Nominally part of the Home Guard but operating in total secrecy and entirely independently were the Auxiliary Units, often referred to erroneously as the British Resistance Organisation. Local organisers in the coastal counties and several additional areas such as Worcestershire, the destination for evacuated government agencies, were tasked with recruiting small groups of men who would act as irritants to an occupying army. Each cell, or Auxiliary Unit patrol, was composed of eight or ten auxiliers who would set up one or more operational bases (OB) or hideouts. Recruits were men who knew the land and could live off it: gamekeepers, poachers, farmworkers, and so on, ranging in age, according to Lampe, from the early 'teens to the seventies'. They were trained to use a range of weapons and explosives, and it was their job to lie low while the invading enemy advanced over them, and then to harass them by disrupting their lines of communication; by blowing up railway lines; or by ambushing despatch riders. Training was continuous in the units' home areas, but members were also sent to Coleshill House on the Oxfordshire/Wiltshire border for specialist courses. In 1940–1, while a German invasion still seemed a certainty, the life expectancy of an auxilier, post-invasion, was reckoned at no more than a fortnight. The secrecy surrounding the organisation was carefully maintained by its membership until long after the war had ended, so when David Lampe published *The Last Ditch* in 1968, revealing their secrets, many of them were shocked. It is therefore unexpected to find that a Norfolk schoolteacher, having served as an auxilier from 1940–43, is recorded as relating the details of his secret life to his enthralled pupils, following an enigmatic radio report, referencing the Auxiliary Units, as early as the mid-1950s.

Many of those recruited as auxiliers had been Boy Scouts in the past, and the units would throw up a new generation of Baker Street Irregulars, following in the tradition of Sherlock Holmes or the Special Operations Executive. As with the Home Guard or the armed services, there was an official lower age limit for membership of the Auxiliary Units, and that most probably eighteen at the lowest. However, there appear to have been many instances of auxiliers who were very much younger than that as, like much recruitment in any situation, boys could be recommended by someone who was aware of their character and capabilities. Geoff Devereux had been a pupil at Worcester Royal GS, a member of the school's OTC, and had enjoyed a glittering career in the Boy Scouts achieving their top awards. Apparently on the recommendation of Major Asterley, the headmaster of Aymestrey School at Crown East and a company commander in the Malvern battalion of the Worcestershire HG, Geoff, still only seventeen and working in a Worcester engineering company as a student apprentice, was approached by an officer from Military Intelligence. He was sworn to secrecy and then invited to recruit and lead a patrol of the Auxiliary Units in the Broadheath area. He compiled a list of possible recruits, had it approved, and went ahead with the formation of his patrol, recruiting most of its members from amongst his contemporaries in the local scout troop. He was then released from work for a while and sent to Coleshill House for further training. The patrol's cover story was that they were a Boy Scout messenger service for the Home Guard. An OB was built by the REs and the patrol carried out practice operations in their area, based on the premise that, in the event of an invasion, they had every intention of surviving longer than the suggested fortnight. Geoff was called up in 1941 and would be commissioned into the Grenadier Guards. Other young auxiliers would utilise their newly acquired and specialist skills on joining the commandos but some might enjoy earlier, and more direct contact with these elite units. One cadet from Ayr Academy spoke of engaging in night operations in conjunction with the commandos.

It appears that there were talent scouts like Major Asterley, present in most Home Guard areas, looking out for likely lads to join the Auxiliary Units. One local organiser on Canvey Island was a schoolmaster who recruited suitable youngsters with Boy Scout experience, who knew their local area intimately but were still too young to join the forces. One seventeen-year-old newly enrolled home guardsman near Norwich was recruited by his employer who was a sergeant auxilier. The eight-strong patrol dug their own OB complete with its entrance hatch under a hollow tree stump, opened by pulling a wire secreted in a drainpipe. Some training was carried out with the army on the coast. Another lad was interviewed at the Norwich Drill Hall by a panel, clearly complicit in his recruitment as a sixteen-year-old. He joined a patrol with an OB in Rackheath Woods and was taught camouflage, weapons handling, the use of explosives, unarmed combat, and fieldcraft. In East Yorkshire, there were two fifteen-year-olds in the Cottingham North patrol and others in the Aldbrough, Westow, Wold Newton, Bridlington North, and Wharram patrols. Dependent on when they joined, their recorded birthdates suggest that some may have been even younger. Certainly, there were fifteen-year-olds acting as messengers within the patrols. One of the Worcestershire patrols was composed of mainly former pupils of King's School, Worcester, recruited as a ready-made unit. Mick Wilks is aware of a further group of fourteen-year-olds, from Worcester Royal GS, recruited into an organisation that was separate from the Auxiliary Units but which entertained similar ambitions. Some auxiliers did not need an intermediary to be invited to join the club. Geoffrey Bradford in Devon was appointed, aged sixteen, to the Auxiliary Units, bypassing the Home Guard for whose membership he was too young. His older brother was the county's intelligence officer or chief organiser, so his vetting by the chief constable and special branch was cursory, and he quickly took up his position in a patrol near Barnstaple. John Woodcock's recruitment was even quicker. As he had stumbled across the Bridlington North patrol's OB, to ensure his silence, it was felt advisable summarily to enrol the sixteen-year-old into the patrol.

Each OB was equipped with food and water; had two or more bunks; stored weapons and explosives; and was often only accessed by cleverly contrived hidden entrances and exited via equally invisible escape tunnels. Some were constructed by the auxiliers themselves, some by REs or Pioneer Corps personnel, and others by building contractors under RE supervision. Despite the emphasis on secrecy and concealment, some OBs were discovered by inquisitive youngsters. Two lads stumbled on the Beverley North patrol's OB in a quarry. They liberated a few flares and set them off. More serious was another case in the same area. Two curious schoolboys discovered the Beverley South patrol's OB, and this sensational discovery found its way into a school assignment to write a letter to someone living away from home, set by their teacher at Walkington Village School. Unfortunately, the intended recipient was an uncle incarcerated in a German POW camp and when the letter was read by the disbelieving local censor, who happened to be the leader of a neighbouring auxiliary patrol, the boys were in deep trouble. Dire threats of public disgrace ensured that their silence was procured and maintained; security was duly restored; and the site's location remained undisclosed, still generally unrecognised to this day. As well as the underground OBs, other buildings formed part of the auxiliers' infrastructure. In Herefordshire, Brockhampton School assumed an importance for the Jacob patrol. There was a dead letter drop in the school wall, and the head teacher acted as the patrol's courier. The school had also been identified as a likely potential German HQ or billet in the event of an occupation, so a familiarity with the layout might become important in the future. In 2016, pupils from Brockhampton PS were shown two of the Jacob patrol's OBs, excavated in nearby Warren Woods. Cockshut Hill School in Yardley, Birmingham, was opened in 1937 with a senior department added in 1941 and was the designated muster station for not only several Home Guard units, but also for members of X Branch who had received special training in sabotage techniques and clandestine warfare. These would have fulfilled a similar role to that of the auxiliers but, of necessity, organised in a different way in an urban setting. An Admiralty patrol in Bath recruited seventeen-year-olds who were awaiting call-up. They were a lot more visible in the town and when it was their turn to take the Thompson sub-machine gun home, the local kids soon sussed that they were not your normal home guardsmen. So much for secrecy. Those auxiliers who were in reserved occupations such as agriculture, were often able to serve throughout the war and were listed in an official return of 1944. Some were deployed to the Isle of Wight during the D-Day landings to guard against German retaliatory raids, and others were sent to Norway in 1945 to encourage the German garrison to surrender and disarm. After D-Day, auxiliers were generally assigned to observation duties, against the possibility of German airborne disruptive operations.

Although the commanders of the Auxiliary Units, first Colin Gubbins and then, when he was posted to run SOE, Bill Major, were both professional soldiers, many of the area organisers, or 'Intelligence Officers' were recruited from a range of professions including teaching. This also extended to trainers. Major Harston, training auxiliers in silent killing at Coleshill House, taught in a prep-school. The leader of one of the Essex patrols at Rayleigh was a teacher on Canvey Island who, incidentally, had enjoyed a parallel career as a smuggler, which had to be put on hold for the duration. The patrol sergeant of the Mechach patrol in Herefordshire was a Felsted schoolmaster, evacuated with his pupils to Canon Frome Court. Although Lancashire was not included in those areas which had an official Auxiliary Unit organisation, that failed to discourage local enterprise. Major Armstrong recruited a band of youngsters from the Home Guard and, in the privacy of Worden Hall near Leyland, trained them in fieldcraft, unarmed combat, marksmanship and camouflage. In the event of an invasion, these lads would have operated in the same way as would the auxiliers.

The Special Duties Section was a separate organisation that ran parallel to the Auxiliary Units but recruited and operated under similar conditions. Members were trained to use radios, which would be issued to them for concealment in a secure place, known as a Control Zero Station. Operators in an area would communicate with a central clearing house which would then relay information to a central control. In Matlock, Peter Attwater, a fourteen-year-old ARP messenger and ATC member, was recruited by Military Intelligence as a stay-behind radio operator. In the event of an invasion, it would be his job to pass orders to the Auxiliary Units and to forward their reports on enemy strengths, vulnerabilities, movements and orders of battle. One fourteen-year-old girl, daughter of a country GP in Norfolk, found herself required to sign the Official Secrets Act. Her father, like many country doctors, was a member of the Special Duties Section running a civilian outstation, part of a network supplementing that of the Control Zero Stations and keeping a radio transmitter in his surgery's coalhole. She learned to receive and transmit, using codes and used her cover as a breaker of horses to ride around the countryside delivering messages to auxiliers. Finding she was being harassed by soldiers she took a large, ferocious looking dog around with her. As well as this network of Control Zero Stations and civilian outstations, there were further stay-behind arrangements. In Worcester, the headmaster of Worcester Royal GS and the county's director of education were primed to man a transmitter, located in a brick building next to the canal in the St John's area of Worcester. Their task would have been to broadcast official messages to the populace for as long as they remained undiscovered as the occupying German forces converged on their hideout.

While youngsters were being recruited to work in covert organisations at home, others were being prepared for similar work abroad. From its inception in 1940, SOE was constantly looking for people, usually with linguistic abilities, to carry out undercover assignments in occupied Europe and some of those selected were very young. Yvonne Baseden joined the WAAF aged eighteen and as a French speaker was considered suitable for work in France. As 'Odette', she was parachuted into France, captured, survived Ravensbrück concentration camp, and returned home, her bravery recognised by numerous awards. Sonja Butt was barely fifteen when war broke out but managed to join the WAAF at seventeen and a half. She was the youngest SOE agent sent to France, as a courier for the Headmaster Circuit, and she, too, unlike many of her colleagues, managed to survive the perils. At least a further dozen or more men and women joined SOE as teenagers, some of them still only twenty years old at war's end if they had managed to survive.

Young People in the Air Raid Precautions (ARP) Service

Some local authorities were extremely quick off the mark enrolling ARP workers. By November 1938, Winchester had recruited almost 1,000 personnel, two-thirds of whom were already trained. Others, however, would take a much longer time to get anywhere near the projected complement considered necessary for the task. In September 1939, the London Borough of Hampstead had established a permanently staffed control room in the town hall but had recruited only 220 of the 1,100 wardens needed to man posts, and only three of the required forty-five messengers to liaise between the sections of the service and to ensure that warnings were broadcast. First aid training had commenced before the war using Fleet Road School. Basingstoke's Civil Defence organisation had 813 people on strength, of whom fifty-four were messengers. Nationally, by June 1941, Civil Defence employed 216,000 full-time and 1,235,800 part-time personnel. The fire services employed 85,821 full-time and 139,300 part-time personnel augmented by the 67,024 full-timers and 125,973 part-time auxiliary fire service (AFS) staff.

The cost of maintaining these services with uniforms, vehicles and equipment, provisions, welfare, undertakers' costs, training, first aid kits, and air-raid shelters constituted a major drain on the Exchequer and undermined the development of an efficient war economy. Not least, it proved difficult to find volunteers to carry out ARP work from a dwindling workforce being drawn on for military, agricultural, administrative, educational, industrial, medical, and maritime functions. It is therefore totally logical that the nation's youth should be seen as contributing to a potential solution and the official establishment of an AFS unit had, in fact, always included one 'youth'. The government had consistently stipulated that nobody under sixteen would be allowed to work in ARP, but there were children around, who, as young as ten, had helped their parents make people aware of the dangers of aerial bombing before the war. These would continue to work unofficially and there were some who had passed their ARP examinations aged fourteen but would have to wait a further three years before being formally accepted into the organisation. Many youngsters found the passive behaviour of being bombed extremely stressful and much preferred to get out there and be doing something more positive, even if, initially, it was acting the casualty in an ARP exercise. One boy in Selkirk, six years old in 1939, whose father was an ARP instructor, spent many hours strapped to a stretcher, being lowered from a variety of windows including a particularly inaccessible dormer in his granny's house. He was also allowed to engage in fire training, crawling into burning sheds to extinguish blazes. To ensure realism, his local butcher provided bones to be dressed up with paint and putty and attached, it is to be hoped temporarily, to healthy limbs to simulate protruding breakages.

Many Scouts and Guides had participated in pre-war Civil Defence exercises and were determined to use the skills they had gained. In January 1939, thirty of Rochdale's Boy Scouts had already signed up to ARP duties. In the early days of the war, Girl Guides were involved with helping young children to put their gasmasks on correctly; Scouts and Guides were involved in digging public air-raid shelters; and were helping people to erect initially, Anderson Shelters and, later, Morrison Shelters as in Rochdale, where Boy Scouts erected them for the town's old folk. Ranger Guides might be organised into decontamination squads, prepared for the casualties of the expected deluge of chemical weapons, turning their canvas toilet tents into portable outdoor screens. Some of these activities became challenging experiences, misadventures they would happily have missed or, worse still, ones they even failed to survive. An eleven-year-old Boy Scout in Newcastle upon Tyne in June 1941 happened to be passing the spot where a seven-year-old girl had fallen into a bomb crater near her home. Tying a rope around his waist, he attempted to reach her, but both, along with two AFS men who also entered the crater, were overcome by gas fumes and died as a result. During the Blitz, another duty performed by Boy Scouts was being despatched to locate unexploded bombs and to report on their state and location. They also helped to clear up after raids where they were quite liable to come across body parts and headless corpses. A group of Scouts from four bombed cities travelled to the United States in 1942 to brief their counterparts who had been recruited into the US Civil Defence services and wished to 'be prepared'. They, no doubt, relished the opportunity to share their most gruesome experiences with their transatlantic cousins.

Young teenage messengers were recruited by the AFS, the police, ARP and the voluntary first aid organisations. These were initially members of the Civil Defence Cadet Corps, although this name seldom appears in official records or personal memoirs as the term 'Messenger Service' is much more frequently used. Boys still at school reported this service as giving them a status amongst their peers and a degree of respect from their teachers. In West Ham, the messengers, aged between fourteen and sixteen, were organised by Councillor Gillman and were known as 'Gillman's Dare-Devils'. Giving her age as sixteen, the fourteen-year-old Charity Bick in West Bromwich became a despatch rider for ARP. In the middle of one of the worst raids of the war, she made repeated trips between her ARP Post and Central Control, through bomb-blasts, fires, and debris, becoming the youngest person ever to have been awarded the George Medal for outstanding service in the worst conditions imaginable. In Bristol, the Boy Scouts Association was given the job of organising the ARP Messenger Service. Each ARP division was allocated a chief messenger officer who appointed senior messengers in charge of groups of twenty to twenty-five lads, most of them Boy Scouts, with six of them based at each ARP wardens' post. The number of these messengers, most of them in the sixteen to seventeen age group, reached a total in Bristol alone of around 1,000 over the war years. Several boys aged fourteen to sixteen died while on duty as messengers during air raids with at least four killed while on duty in Clydebank, one fourteen-year-old messenger in Bristol and another in Liverpool. Similar roles were performed by sixteen-year-old Boy Scout volunteer ARP messengers in London, Hull, and other cities. Frank Davis, a seventeen-year-old Boy Scout working as an ARP messenger, was on patrol in Bermondsey during an air-raid in December 1940. He had already carried out one rescue following which he was caught in a bomb-blast at Holy Trinity, Dockhead church and killed while attempting the rescue of a fellow Boy Scout messenger. In Eccles, a Boy Scout messenger was drowned when his ARP post, occupying a cellar, was flooded by burst water pipes during a raid that killed eleven people in that one building. During the raids on Norwich of 1942, a fifteen-year-old ARP cycle messenger, who had lied about his age to join, was repeatedly blown off his bike by bombs as he continued to deliver messages, extinguishing incendiaries as he encountered them, and receiving a gallantry award for his bravery. In Birmingham, the Boys Brigade, equipped with bicycles and tin helmets, provided a messenger service for the ARP. Boy Scouts in Belfast joining the messenger service were issued with an official card that listed the principal ARP centres and gave instructions for calling in by telephone if unable to attend when called out. In 1943, sponsored by the *Yorkshire Evening News*, the Grand Theatre in Leeds staged a show called 'Youth Marches On'. Against a backcloth of a bombed and blazing building the city's messenger boys with their bicycles performed a musical routine to packed and appreciative houses every night. It was not necessary to belong to any specific organisation to display initiative and courage in the bombing. In Birmingham, a seventeen-year-old hotel porter was awarded the city's civilian gallantry award for single-handedly tackling fires across several city centre properties.

Teenagers also served as messengers for the General Post Office (GPO), delivering telegrams. Throughout the war, Dover was under constant bombardment by heavy artillery on Cap Gris Nez firing the 20 miles (32 km) across the Channel. Here, the role of the GPO messenger was particularly vital and was carried out under fire. Boys aged fourteen-and-a-half could start, but 'part-timers' began as young as twelve. These younger boys had to fit their weekly twenty hours' duty around school and other commitments and many of them found themselves having to provide comfort to those to whom they had just delivered the worst of all possible news.

Fire Services

Boy Scouts as young as thirteen were recruited into the fire service, which was attracted by their firefighter, first aid, and pioneer badges. They generally served as messengers, making themselves aware of which local houses had telephones, and guiding fire crews to emergency water supplies. The girls at Edgbaston HS formed their own AFS detachment in 1940 and were trained by their school caretaker to fight incendiaries with stirrup pumps and buckets of sand. In August 1941, all local fire brigades and the volunteer AFS detachments combined as the National Fire Service (NFS). This would ultimately lead to the central direction of resources and a standardisation of equipment. Girls who had been accepted by the WAAF or ATS but told to stay at home until they were eighteen, often joined the NFS, which accepted them at seventeen and a half. After a month's training, they were driver/firewomen, clerks, telephonists, or cooks. Early in the war, as their leaders were called up, fifteen-year-old Guide patrol leaders had stepped into the breach and run troops, thereby gaining important leadership skills that equipped them for the teamwork that firefighting demanded. For boys becoming messengers with the NFS in 1942, there was a further attraction when they were kitted out with uniform. This consisted of navy-blue battledress with red badges and lanyard topped by a stiff-peaked cap with red piping and the same NFS badge as the firemen themselves. A cape and leggings for cycling in bad weather were also issued as well as a service gasmask and a tin hat with an NFS transfer. The availability of this kit and the payment of a bicycle allowance for messengers drew lads away from ARP which made no such provision.

One boy in the Forest of Dean was determined to become a fireman but his age prevented him. Eventually he managed to get taken on at sixteen by the Gloster Aeroplane Company who were setting up a works brigade. Initially his service alternated between drilling and training, but once the factory was bombed, suffering multiple casualties, his work began in earnest. At the height of the various blitzes, the pressure on firemen and women was so great that young teenagers were taken into the service. There are many cases of sixteen-year-old volunteer AFS messengers being promoted to firemen in the London Blitz. Several local Scout Troops in Croydon were recruited specifically to provide support for two local hospitals. Rostered in dozen-strong groups, each of which was on duty every third night, they were trained in firefighting techniques. They manned mobile units and were qualified to use the pressure hoses, using standpipes as fire hydrants. They were also proficient in coupling up their hoses to the water points in the hospitals' second- and third-storey wards.

Additionally, groups of boys aged between thirteen and seventeen were known to form their own independent shadow volunteer fire services, taking the appropriate action if they saw bombs or incendiaries landing. One such group in Wapping, the self-styled 'Dead End Kids', consisted of children aged from ten to seventeen, some of whom had returned from evacuation during the Phoney War. Led by the son of a Poplar refuse collector, they pitched in during the East End blitz dumping unexploded bombs into the river; breaking into bombed and burning buildings to rescue trapped victims and carrying them to safety; getting people out of shattered shelters; rescuing animals and stifling incendiaries. Their leader's sister was thirteen and their specialist climber was just ten. Such dangerous exploits were bound to result in tragedy and, one night, two of their members were killed when a wall collapsed on them as they tackled burning incendiaries. Volunteer firefighters in towns unaffected by the bombing could not escape the horrors, as they were often called out to help in neighbouring areas that were undergoing heavy attacks. As well as receiving medals from their own organisations, several young teenagers were awarded the George Medal in recognition of their heroic actions during the Blitz, but almost 200 teenage messengers died performing their various roles during the war, all of them heroes, but many unobserved and therefore not fully recognised as such.

When fire-watching became compulsory, many teenagers found themselves on top of high buildings smothering incendiaries and dismantling those that had failed to ignite. Boys from Oundle School served as firewatchers around the town. In Winchester, older boys at the Peter Symonds School performed fire-watching duties in fours with a master and were then allowed the following day off, being expected to make up the schoolwork they had missed. At Burnage HS, boys over fourteen could volunteer for fire-watching and two teachers and four boys were on duty each night, sleeping on camp beds in, respectively, the staffroom and the library, with supper left out by the school kitchen. In every town and city, groups of Scouts and Guides were organised to patrol rooftops as firewatchers, looking out for incendiaries and quenching them with buckets of sand and stirrup pumps.

The Police Service

In built-up areas, thirteen-year-old volunteer police messengers rode their bikes around the streets equipped with a whistle and a tin hat alerting people caught out in the street to air raids. In some areas, their bicycles were painted yellow hence their 'canaries' tag. Although recruited into the police, ostensibly as fifteen-year-old messengers, those youngsters in many cases were expected to fulfil the duties of police cadets whose role had been suspended for the duration. Lads on night duty might find themselves in sole charge of a police station, dealing with everything from reports of air raids, to crashed aircraft or even criminal activities. Whenever possible, the duty officer was to be left to sleep as he had been on duty all day, and would be again on the following day, and the constables on night duty were out patrolling the streets.

The Royal Observer Corps (ROC)

As flight gained in popularity during the interwar period, many youngsters developed a strong interest in aircraft. So as the new airfields appeared in the landscape, boys would cycle round the countryside hoping to spot unfamiliar aircraft. Some of them such as Michael Bowyer in Cambridge would go on to write about aviation history. In 1937, the ROC formed No. 10 Group in York. Observers came from several local employers but were brought up to their required strength by recruiting Rover Scouts. As in many other places, schoolboys at Oundle School formed a Spotters Club in 1942, soon amassing over 100 members, learning to distinguish the various aircraft in the skies above them. The *Aeroplane* magazine produced the weekly *Aeroplane Spotter*, price 3*d.* (62p), which featured silhouettes and specifications of aircraft for young spotters. School-based spotters' clubs competed against each other to identify aircraft on lantern slides, Reigate GS taking on and beating Purley County School in two fixtures in 1941. This interest and activity often brought boys into the ROC, to be included in duty rosters. As early as 1929, an aircraft spotting post had been set up on the roof of Steyning (Sussex) GS and in 1936 the observation tower of Bridlington GS provided the site for a post, as did the roof of Springfield House at Wycliffe College near Stroud, in 1938. The New Cross/Dulwich post in south London was re-sited in 1940 to the roof of Haberdashers' Aske's Hatcham GS. The Crawley post was re-sited to Copthorne School tower in 1942 and equipped with the Granite system, which used flares to warn returning aircraft of their dangerous proximity to high ground. Observers occupied church towers, the roofs of tall industrial buildings, and bleak, exposed hilltops. Eventually huts, affectionately (or not) known as rabbit hutches, were provided, affording some shelter in the most exposed locations. Some observer posts built their own raised platforms with a covered area and even bunks. Parallel to such official ROC activity was the informal use of spotters on factory premises. This was one way of postponing the downing of tools in the factory until the last possible moment as both warnings delivered too early and the many false alarms were costing valuable work time. One fourteen-year-old working in an aircraft factory in Norwich spent two hours every day on the roof looking out for incoming hostile aircraft. Supervised by an officer in the works Home Guard, he was soon recruited into more active participation.

ROC units also recruited from the ATC. Cadets who had acquitted themselves well in the aircraft recognition competitions found themselves being headhunted. The ROC in Driffield, East Yorkshire, was uniquely equipped with a GL radar set for night operations and required a couple of able and keen cadets to provide extra manpower during daylight hours. They were trained in the operation of the post-instrument—the Micklethwaite height finder that, despite its name, was not peculiar to Yorkshire. Less formally, Boy Scouts and Girl Guides acted as spotters of enemy aircraft from the rooftops. Younger children ran their own unofficial play versions of these organisations' activities and, later in the war, some schools had rotas of quite small children spotting Doodlebugs for real.

So concerned were Admiral Ramsay and the planners of Operation Neptune that trigger-happy AA gunners on the D-Day invasion fleet would be unable to distinguish between hostile aircraft and those of the Allies, that they recruited ROC personnel to sail aboard the freighters and landing ships on the big day. These ROC personnel wore a 'Seaborne' shoulder flash and were given the temporary rank of petty officer. One of those recruited was the seventeen-year-old Ian Ramsbotham from Stoke-on-Trent. Ian had passed his aircraft recognition tests with flying colours and reported for duty at the Royal Bath Hotel, Bournemouth. Here he was given further training with help from the Rafwaffe, passing ever more stringent tests. He then served on merchant ships supplying the invasion force for a few weeks as temporary PO Ramsbotham, was given an honourable discharge, and returned to Woolaston School with some stories to tell. Probably among the youngest wholly legitimate participants in the D-Day operation, his underage status had enjoyed official sanction.

At the end of the war, the ROC was stood down and spotting posts were usually made secure. The geography teacher at Aske's GS, however, decided that the post on his school roof would make a splendid weather station. When, in 1948, members of the reconstituted ROC arrived to reclaim Post 19/Y.4, they found the locks had been changed; the post instruments and chart table had been exchanged for a Stevenson screen and a rainfall gauge; and there was a large 'KEEP OUT' sign on the door.

Underage Military Service

Following a question posed in the Canadian Parliament in 1965 relating to underage enlistment in the Canadian armed services in the Second World War, the ensuing debate revealed the specific cases of six named individuals. These were a wing commander, a colonel, a major, and three senior NCOs, all of whom had enlisted at ages ranging, amazingly, from nine to thirteen between 1936 and 1939. It was seriously suggested, in the context of their retirement that, rather than being rewarded for their years of service, they be charged with perjury for lying about their ages. Just as in the Great War, underage enlistment proved widespread but there were also legitimate ways of serving whilst still a minor, and often still of school age.

Underage Military Service in the British Army

Although the former practice of enlisting youngsters as drummer boys had ceased by the end of the nineteenth century, and the recruitment of boys as musicians was terminated in the 1930s, boys as young as fourteen were still able to join up without difficulty, especially in areas of high unemployment or meagre or uninspiring employment opportunities. Even in 1940, underage youngsters were being taken into the army. The military authorities, in fact, although they could not openly admit it, found these lads very welcome and certainly preferable to reluctant conscripts. Many of these young lads were eager, fit, and enthusiastic; they were untainted by the pacifism, which pervaded some younger elements of the population in the 1930s; and they might be more easily receptive to receiving orders than those drawing on a greater experience of life. However, the government could not be seen to be condoning the recruitment of child soldiers, so the official process of army enlistment was laid down as voluntary membership of the Army Cadet Force from age fourteen to seventeen; then another year as a volunteer in the Home Guard; then enlistment at age eighteen and basic training at an Infantry Training Centre or a trade school. Some of those boys who had enlisted on false pretences were unmasked and discharged, but others remained undiscovered or had a blind eye turned to them as it was quite possible that their officers or NCOs had done the same thing in the previous war. In this way, the odd sixteen-year-old found his way into a POW camp in 1940 and spent the next five years there.

After Dunkirk, the large influx of eighteen-year-olds was accommodated in Young Soldier Battalions, usually numbered 70th in the order of the county line regiments. Though intended as purely training formations, the crisis of the next twelve months when invasion was expected meant that many of these semi-trained youngsters found themselves in the frontline, prepared to defend the coast against invasion and airfields against air raids and the possibility of an airborne assault. The 70th (Young Soldier) Battalion of the Suffolk Regiment defended airfields in East Anglia and that of the Queen's Royal West Surrey Regiment, having relieved a TA battalion in Southern Command, was assigned to Civil Defence duties until 1943. While guard duties were often tedious, they were far from safe. The Essex Regiment's YS battalion suffered nine fatalities and sixteen serious injuries while defending North Weald airfield against an air raid. Some youngsters were recruited into the commandos where they underwent intensive physical and tactical training and those who met the demanding standards were soon in action. This meant that there were sixteen-year-olds on the disastrous Dieppe raid of 1942. More underage boys volunteered throughout the war and some of those ended up, still only sixteen, landing in France on D-Day.

However enthusiastic might be the youngsters, the shortage of instructors meant that unsuitable officers and NCOs were posted to these YS units, one reason why many had been disbanded by 1943 when men with more recent experience could be assigned as instructors at the army's reorganised primary training centres (PTC). If the instructors were of poor quality, complaints were also recorded regarding the quality of the conscripts: they were poorly nourished, ill-educated, and badly socialised, many of them having grown up in urban or rural poverty, often in orphanages, had left school at eleven and had been in reform schools or Borstals. The attraction of a uniform and free food meant that for some, enlistment offered the only opportunity to escape poverty or criminal habits, but that was not what the army wanted or needed. However, some instructors did have recent experience to share. Having enlisted at fifteen and having weathered various attempts by the army to determine his true age, one soldier was finally returned home from the Middle East as, even at eighteen, he was still ineligible for foreign service. However, his home posting was as an instructor at a PTC, working with new recruits who were, in fact, his contemporaries. By the end of the war, those youngsters who had gone in underage, so long as they survived, had become veterans by the age of nineteen or twenty.

Underage Military Service in the Royal Navy

Naval officers had traditionally started out as midshipmen often aged as young as twelve and sent to sea at once. This had gradually changed as officer-training courses at venues such as the *Osborne* on the Isle of Wight and the *Britannia* at Dartmouth were introduced. During the 1930s, boys could enter Dartmouth RN College at thirteen to complete their education and be prepared for service as permanent naval officers. This system would continue at Dartmouth throughout the war and then at Eaton Hall, the Grosvenor family's pile in Cheshire, to which the *Britannia* had been evacuated in 1942 following bomb damage. In 1936, the Special Entry scheme brought in eighteen-year-olds and attracted a wider range of entrants. After 1939, as the navy recognised the need for thousands more naval officers, further new systems were introduced for hostilities only (HO) officers. Potential officers could be sent to undertake a six-month course at a university prior to going to a basic training centre such as the *Ganges* and then specialist officer training at HMS *King Alfred* at Hove and Lancing College, becoming RNVR midshipmen aged eighteen or nineteen. Seamen, however, were still being recruited as young as thirteen for immediate service on HM ships. When the old battleship HMS *Royal Oak* was torpedoed at Scapa Flow in the Orkneys in 1939, 125 boy sailors, out of the 165 on board, were among the 833 lives lost. The cruiser HMS *Fiji* was sunk off Crete in

1941, covering an evacuation of British and Commonwealth troops, and eight boy sailors on board were lost. One of them, a Royal Marine bugler, was, at fourteen, thought to be the youngest serviceman to be killed on active service. There were boys lost whenever a capital ship was sunk: these included the battleships and battle cruisers HMSs *Hood*, *Prince of Wales*, *Repulse*, and *Barham*, and the aircraft carriers *Courageous*, *Ark Royal*, *Glorious*, *Hermes*, and *Eagle*. Additionally, the three escort carriers and twenty-seven cruisers that were lost all carried boy sailors. When the cruiser HMS *Ajax* returned home after her victorious action against the German pocket battleship *Graf Spee,* it brought home the seventeen-year-old Tubb twins who already had several years' service behind them, to be feted by the Simon Langton School in Canterbury. Fishing communities traditionally saw their school-leavers following their fathers and brothers onto the trawlers. Many of the newer craft had been built at the behest of the Admiralty during the 1930s with a view to their wartime requisitioning with many of the skippers standing by as RNR officers. On the outbreak of war, crews, many of which contained boys of fourteen upwards, were automatically committed to naval duties including escorting coastal convoys, minesweeping, servicing harbour defences or patrolling the sea lanes for submarines. Many of these trawlers and drifters were sunk by enemy aircraft, by mines, in collisions and in storms. The Commonwealth War Graves Commission lists the names of thirteen boys under the age of fifteen across the naval service who died in action at sea, but those records are, in all probability, far from complete. Fishing fleets around British coasts were regularly strafed by enemy aircraft.

Underage Service in the Wartime Merchant Navy

We have seen how large numbers of boys as young as twelve could be serving on merchant ships during the war. The Registrar General of Shipping and Seamen has calculated that, overall, over 32,000 merchant seamen, representing 27 per cent of the total workforce, died as a result of enemy action. Boys aged fourteen and fifteen served as deck boys, galley boys, stewards' boys, or cabin boys on every type of ship from the Cunard Line '*Queens*' to tiny coasters. A fifteen-year-old was lost when SS *Athenia* was torpedoed in 1939, and two brothers of fourteen and fifteen were lost on SS *Fiscus*, torpedoed in 1940. They had joined the ship only a short while previously on the strength of a forged letter from their father giving his permission. The youngest boy to die as a merchant seaman was under fourteen and a half having lied about his age to sign on and was killed when SS *North Devon* was attacked by German aircraft off the Norfolk Coast in July 1941. Four close friends from Liverpool, aged from fifteen to seventeen, were killed when SS *Almeda Star* was lost. The motor fishing boat *Courage*, sailing out of Scarborough, crewed by a skipper and three teenagers, was bombed in March 1940. Of the 700 British boys serving on Norwegian merchant ships by 1943, at least sixty-six lost their lives. This represents 20 per cent of the 323 British seamen killed on Norwegian ships during the war. It should be noted that the Norwegian shipping authorities accused the British mercantile marine of getting their boys trained at their expense as they appeared not to serve very long on Norwegian ships. Survivors of sinking ships were sometimes rescued by the enemy and uploaded onto prison ships until they could be landed and taken to POW camps. Many boys from fourteen upwards spent up to five years in such camps, often being made to work in dangerous conditions, maltreated, and starved. In one camp in 1943, the senior British officer counted 150 boys among the 3,000 prisoners, 5 per cent of the camp's population.

Underage Military Service in the RAF

It was harder for boys under the official age to join the RAF, mainly because of the higher standard of education generally demanded of recruits in the form of examination certificates. Selection for pilot training was effectively limited to those whose parents could afford the costs of a secondary education. Enlistment in the RAF became such a popular aspiration for many boys that it became necessary to demonstrate not only the requisite level of academic achievement, but also an established commitment to the service. Boys joined the Air Scouts and progressed to the ADCC and the ATC so that, aged seventeen, they had some leverage. Many lads knew they would not make aircrew but were content to join for general duties just to wear the uniform. Despite the hurdles, there were, nevertheless, boys who made it into the skies while being anything up to three years underage, blagging their way through the recruitment process and maintaining a plausible cover story. One such appears to have been Nathan Max who was still on the Liverpool Institute's roll in 1938 and was just sixteen when he joined the RAFVR and was trained as an air gunner.

The Intelligence Services

By the time of the Japanese offensive in Malaya and the Dutch East Indies in early 1942, the government was waking up to its total unpreparedness for fighting a war in south-east Asia and a scholarship scheme was launched to rectify at least one deficiency. Dulwich College was one of the few secondary schools in London that had stayed put throughout the war, and thirty of its seventeen-year-old boys were recruited to attend Japanese language classes at the School of Oriental and African Studies (SOAS) with a view to being employed by the military as interpreters, translators, and Y-Service listeners. For the duration of the course lasting five terms, the boys lived in the college, travelled to SOAS every morning for their lessons, then returned to Dulwich for afternoon school. Alongside fellow students who were serving military personnel and women who would go to Bletchley Park as codebreakers, they were taught largely by the Japanese wives of British diplomats. On completion of their course, the boys were posted to military units, generally in India, and given the task of intercepting and interpreting Japanese radio traffic.

Some lucky boys stumbled across their own opportunities to play spy-catcher. One pupil at Hymer's College in Hull was on holiday in Cromer in the summer of 1939. As he was studying German, he was delighted to discover that the couple at the next table were German, so engaged them in conversation. Put off by their reluctance to respond, he became suspicious and determined to follow them on their clifftop walk next day. He watched as they carefully observed and photographed a Queen Bee pilotless aircraft, a target drone from the AA camp at Weybourne. Back at the hotel, he announced his discovery to ridicule. Fortunately, he had been overheard by a retired RAF NCO who was clearly still linked into official channels. The lad was later informed via the RAF that the couple had been detained at Dover as they tried to leave the country with their observations. Children leaving school during the war and seeking employment could seldom anticipate what they would end up doing. One sixteen-year-old, assigned to clerical work, found herself in Baker Street working in an office as secretary to Wild Bill Donovan, who was learning the ropes as director of the Office of Strategic Services (OSS), SOE's United States equivalent.

Children of Occupied Territories

On the islands of Jersey and Guernsey, British children came into daily contact with the occupying forces of the enemy. As on the mainland, their schooling was disrupted as their schools were requisitioned and supplies of stationery and other materials gradually dried up. One source of resentment was the imposition of compulsory German language classes on the school curriculum. Children could fight back in a number of ways with participation in a campaign of chalking or painting 'Vs' on any available surface, particularly German military vehicles being one. Fortunately, while for those adults being caught it was a serious matter involving possible deportation, the occupation authorities took a more lenient view with children, who merely got a home visit from a plain-clothes field policeman (*Feldpolizei*). Hitler regarded all uniformed youth organisations as paramilitaries, dedicated to the advancement of Britain's imperial establishment, so had banned them all. Therefore, another way of resisting the German occupation authorities was to belong to an underground Guide or Scout troop as this would be construed as a subversive activity. Several troops continued to operate and one on Jersey met in the hayloft of a remote farm. However daring and rebellious it might have seemed to the participants, it soon became clear that it was not a game when one of their teenage troop-leaders and his father were both deported for a minor offence and died in concentration camps. Girl Guides on Jersey also continued to hold undercover meetings in defiance of the German regulations, even managing to go camping on members' farms. As the availability of food, material, and other commodities grew evermore scant, Guides did their bit to make do and mend. The Boys' Brigade also contrived regular secret meetings and emerged on Jersey's Liberation Day in full uniform with their band playing.

For entirely different reasons, however, there was another, wider group of youngsters, who often found it difficult to make their contribution to life on the Home Front or were denied the chance altogether. These were some of the 70,000 German, Italian, and Austrian nationals who were liable for internment as enemy aliens under the British Government's Regulation 18B, suspending *habeas corpus*. Even though around 80 per cent of the German and Austrian aliens were Jews who had fled Nazi persecution and arrived in Britain as *bona fide* refugees in the spring of 1940, thousands were nevertheless still interned. If many of the Germans and Austrians were recently arrived refugees, then many of the Italians had lived in Britain for decades and regarded themselves as British citizens. All those over sixteen who intended to remain in Britain after the outbreak of war were required to report to the police with their documents. Children under fourteen were exempt and merely required always to carry an Alien Certificate of Registration. Any softening of attitudes toward enemy aliens was soon eradicated by fears of invasion in the summer of 1940, exacerbated by memories of the vaunted 'Fifth Column' of the Spanish Civil War. This prompted wholesale internment of enemy aliens, however friendly, and led to a total abandonment of previous categorisations. Thus, those interned included in their ranks many sixteen-year-olds, some of whom were in their school sixth forms. This was particularly noticeable at schools like Boothams, in York, one of twelve Quaker schools, including Great Ayton in Yorkshire, Reading's Leighton Park School, and Wigton in Cumbria, which had been taking in refugees. Exemption from internment had to be sought through tribunals to which could be submitted testimonials from head teachers and, in the case of those evacuated away from home, host families. Membership of uniformed organisations, indicating a willingness to serve their adopted country, might also help official assimilation. However, for a sixteen-year-old, the twenty-year residency qualification, applied to Italians, was of little help. Some children of school age were interned with their mothers on the Isle of Man and were able to attend self-help schools established within the camps but many of these children were released and reunited with their families only after at least a year's incarceration. Even some of those 10,000 children who escaped from Germany on the *Kindertransport* and were taken in by Britain could be in trouble. By attempting to write letters of reassurance to their parents back in Germany, some were charged with the serious offence of corresponding with the enemy and interned, and it could then take a year to secure their release. Some children were even transported to Canada or Australia, and some of those may have perished when their ship, SS *Arandora Star*, was torpedoed *en route* for Canada. The records of who were on-board show no internee under the age of eighteen but are recognised as being incomplete or inaccurate. However, at least seventeen of the Merchant Navy crew were teenagers, including one of fifteen and another of sixteen.

One particular problem for child refugees was the tensions attached to identity—something possibly to be discarded, but if to be retained, something to be concealed.

British wives of German and Austrian nationals automatically lost their British nationality as did their children, and were required to register with the police. Unaccompanied refugee children who were likely to have been orphaned might choose to be formally adopted by a British host family, taking on a new identity. When a child refugee became old enough for military service, his name would very often be changed to conceal his Jewish origins were he to be captured by the enemy. The establishment of a Foreign Legion had been suggested and rejected on the grounds that expatriate Poles, Czechs, Belgians, and Norwegians could all enlist in their own national armies in exile. Initially, the only real option for other aliens to engage in military service, was to join the Auxiliary Military Pioneer Corps, which became, simply, the Pioneer Corps in 1940. This military labour corps recruited over 2,000 aliens from the internment camps, rising to more than 5,000 a year later. Despite its usefulness in carrying out physically demanding and often dangerous tasks, this regiment was popularly regarded as the British Army's sink unit. Consequently, service in its ranks was the cause of much resentment among educated and skilled aliens who saw themselves as being denied more productive work than the physically demanding but mentally unchallenging labouring tasks of the Pioneer Corps. While most of its recruits were thus limited to menial tasks and manual labour, a fortunate few were enabled to use language skills to interrogate prisoners of war and to gain intelligence from captured or intercepted documents. Geoffrey Perry was born in Berlin, emigrated to Britain in 1936 aged fourteen, joined the Pioneer Corps, and was commissioned into the Intelligence Corps in 1944. After the fall of Berlin, it was he who arrested Lord Haw-Haw as he attempted escape. After 1942, it had become possible for more of 'His Majesty's Loyal Aliens' to transfer into other arms of the services and some became commandos, fighter pilots or officers in other combatant units. Others joined organisations such as SOE or served in branches of the intelligence services. One even joined Churchill's bodyguard. Such assignments inevitably involved new names, new numbers, assumed religions, and changed histories. There were opportunities for girls from refugee backgrounds as well, often in support services requiring higher-level skills. Alice Gross volunteered for the WAAF and trained as a photographic interpreter, involved in identifying the V-1 launch sites by recognising their distinctive hockey-stick shape from aerial photographs. However, such opportunities were generally open only to those with specific skills whose acquisition was often beyond the reach of most youngsters. Even when relevant skills had been gained, useful military employment was not assured. One refugee lad had spent two years in the ATC but his application to join the RAF was rejected out of hand once his German nationality was admitted. Moreover, the Royal Navy was always over-subscribed and took the line that those British applicants should be given preference even when aliens might be better qualified.

On a different war front altogether, a world away from 'blighty', were the children of British expatriates working in the Far East: Malaya, Singapore, Hong Kong, the Philippines, and China who were interned in brutal and incompetently run camps by the Japanese occupying army. Their full story has been told elsewhere but it is important that their ordeal which, at the time, barely impacted on the public consciousness at home, is remembered. Living in squalor, on starvation rations, in permanent fear of brutal treatment by the guards, subject to the whole range of tropical diseases with little medical attention and few drugs, and very often orphaned or separated from parents and siblings, these children spent up to five years striving for some sort of normality at best but basically, survival. Despite boys over twelve years of age being classed as adults and put to work, some of the camps even managed to run schools, putting children through public examinations that qualified them for university entrance at the end of the war. Some 20,000 British civilians were interned of whom around 4,000 were children or juveniles and the ratio of children to adults in most camps was around 1–1.5:8. Although surviving records are inadequate, the mortality rate for these civilian internees was around 10 per cent, as opposed to the rate of 30 per cent in the POW camps, so it must be assumed that somewhere between 400 and 500 children died from disease and malnutrition, a result that was entirely avoidable. Many of those who survived suffered from recurrent health problems and conditions such as osteoporosis caused by dietary deficiencies and the long-term effects of disease.

Preparing the Fourteen to Eighteen Age-Group for Military Service

Prior to the Great War, there had been a surge in membership of uniformed youth organisations as a counterbalance to the government's refusal to countenance conscription or any form of compulsory military training. The primary role of the patently military officers' training corps (OTC) and the Territorial Cadet Force (TCF) had been to provide potential officers and NCOs to the Regular Army. Additionally, the Boys' Brigade (BB), the Church Lads' Brigade (CLB), and, to a lesser extent, the Boy Scouts all had a demonstrable, paramilitary dimension and were able to apply both their civic and military skills during the Great War. However, the post-war reaction against overt militarism meant that the following decades saw organisations relinquishing the more patently militaristic dimensions of their several identities and adopting the following aims:

> ... fostering the virtues of citizenship among the future men and women of the race. Love of country without insularity, mutual help yet independence, the ability to act quickly in cases of emergency are principles which the movement [Ranger Guides] seeks to instil. They are concepts on which the empire was founded and upon which it will be maintained.
>
> Quoted by Edwards

The economies forced on the government by the effects of the Depression of the 1930s saw military budgets slashed and cadet organisations consequently all but disappeared. By the time war broke out again in 1939, many local groups had lapsed, so units of the various cadet corps depended for their formation on local initiatives that very often came down to personalities willing to organise such companies. To take one county, Bedfordshire, as an example, in 1942, Miss Olive Brown of Dunstable formed No. 186 Company of the Girls' Training Corps and two years later, she formed No. 15 Girls' Nautical Training Corps, with TS *Preston* as its HQ in the Old Mill in West Street. Although the Sea Cadet Corps had been in existence for many years, the Dunstable unit (No. 15) received recognition from the Admiralty only in 1942. There were OTC contingents at Bedford GS, Bedford Modern School, and the Ashton GS, Dunstable. An ATC unit, No. 134 Squadron, was started in Bedford, drawing in part from Great Barford's ACF company some of whose members had been wooed and wowed by the USAAF, which had invited them to explore the insides of B17 bombers at Thurleigh. To improve the fitness for service of youngsters, Major S. J. Parker had proposed a National Youth Service Corps in early 1941. Apparently, there were soon nearly forty branches established, but information regarding this organisation is meagre and only in Nigeria has the organisation had a lasting impact. Across the country, the membership of the various pre-service training organisations, numbering half a million boys at any one time between 1940 and 1944, would contribute 80,000 conscripts per year to the nation's armed forces, all of whom had undergone some degree of relevant training. Some schools insisted on membership of the Home Guard, ARP, or the firewatchers as did Strode's GS, Egham. Figures reported by Sian Edwards as having been compiled by the Scouts and Guides national organisations themselves, record membership of the Boy Scouts in 1941 as 305,760 and of the Girl Guides as 400,236, both totals increasing significantly in 1945 by 54 per cent and 16 percent, respectively. If the Scouts and Guides represented conformism and service to the community, then the Woodcraft Folk, with a membership in 1945 approaching just 3,000, offered a more political slant with its members, drawn largely from working class youth, being encouraged to adopt critical thinking and revolutionary attitudes and to acquire a dual understanding of civic duties and rights rooted in socialism.

The Officer Training Corps (OTC)

The Territorial Force, which formed in 1908, saw the public school as its prime source of officers for both itself and the Regular Army. Universities and other higher education institutions would have Senior Training Corps contingents, and schools would constitute Junior Training Corps. However, all these corps were usually referred to informally as the generic OTC or just 'the corps', and here, only the term 'OTC' will be used. Since the war, schools have had Combined Cadet Force (CCF) contingents, and universities remained as OTC. During the Great War, the high wastage rate among young officers compelled the War Office to look to recruit from a wider pool: grammar school boys, young professionals, supervisors, or foremen, as well as candidates from the ranks of the NCOs and the success of this democratisation of the officer cadre led to a shift in official attitudes. In the Second World War, this change in the War Office's attitude to the officer who lacked a public-school education was manifested in the imposition of size limitations on the OTC, not altogether prompted by financial constraints, which would not be allowed to exceed 30,000 cadets across 183 schools, and the possession of Certificate 'A' would, no longer, provide an automatic route to a commission. However, many of those schools which maintained OTC contingents made membership compulsory. Blundells School in Tiverton, Winchester, Tonbridge, and Chigwell all expected their pupils to join the corps. Dover College had been evacuated to Tiverton after being bombed, and then moved on to Poltimore House near Exeter, where membership of the OTC and Home Guard was mandatory. At Chard School, membership was voluntary, but for those who committed themselves to membership, the regular parades were compulsory. However, if a boy wanted to be a legitimate member of the armed forces, he would have to join the Home Guard as membership of the OTC did not, by itself, confer combatant status. Outside those schools with established OTC, any schools wanting to raise cadet contingents from 1940 onwards were directed along the ACF route, affiliated to their local line regiment. So, Slough GS Cadet Corps would join the 1st Cadet Battalion, Oxfordshire & Buckinghamshire Light Infantry. While general attitudes might have changed, there were still some which remained entrenched. As had been the case in the Great War, certain schools' OTC were regarded as particularly fertile recruiting grounds, producing the right sort of chaps, and Eton, Rugby, Charterhouse, and Winchester were among those regularly visited by officers from prestigious regiments such as the Rifle Brigade and the KRRC to encourage boys to seek commissions with them when the time came.

The Army Cadet Force (ACF)

In 1923, the government, faced with the costs of the Great War and signs of the coming economic depression, had attempted to save money by summarily shutting down all cadet forces. Led by Viscount Allenby and others determined not to abandon the cadet movement, the British National Cadet Association (BNCA) was formed as the managing body for cadet organisations. By around 1930, the government was having second thoughts regarding its abdication of responsibility and the decision was reversed in principle. Not until the later 1930s, however, were LEAs being actively encouraged to promote activities for boys in the fourteen to twenty age group including pre-service cadet organisations, and only in 1942 did the War Office officially take back control of what had become the ACF. From its inception, boys were encouraged to join the ACF, but much of the impetus came from the boys themselves requesting that units be established. Many of these cadet units originated in schools which often made their facilities available on drill nights. During the time it spent in Reigate, sharing facilities with Reigate GS,

St Dunstan's College maintained its OTC contingent, parading in the local drill hall, with older members serving in the local Home Guard. Additionally, there was a cadet company of younger boys in the Middle School with a lower age limit of fourteen and a half. Reigate GS had formerly run an OTC contingent, but in 1935 had switched to becoming 'D' Company, 1st Cadet Battalion, Queen's Royal West Surrey Regiment, but membership of the two organisations would probably have overlapped. Following the establishment of the ACF, the Home Guard often provided instructors and many cadet units were formally affiliated to Home Guard units. St Saviour's PS in Shirland Road, Maida Vale, provided the base for both local Home Guard and ACF units. Typically, the Doncaster ACF unit was affiliated to the 46th (Doncaster) Battalion, West Riding HG, itself badged as the King's Own Yorkshire Light Infantry and such links quickly became the norm. Schools in Yeovil started an ACF unit in early 1941 that affiliated to the 7th (TA) Battalion, Somerset Light Infantry. Very often, teachers over the age of enlistment became ACF officers and one, at Ilminster GS, had a heart attack and died on a route march with his lads, who were surprised to discover that he had been seventy-six years old. The County Territorial Associations (CTA) initiated further units. In late 1941, cadet companies for boys from fourteen years of age upwards, with HQ in Peterborough, were raised by the Soke of Peterborough and Huntingdon CTA and half the projected strength of 600 had been recruited by early 1942. In some areas, there were also Junior ACF contingents for those under-fourteens who were keen to join.

Once the National Service Act came into force and the responsibility for the ACF fell on the War Office, recruiting levels that had been repressed by the government would rise and provision of uniforms and equipment would improve. While schools may have been one of the driving forces behind the initial take-up, the majority of ACF recruits would have already left school and entered full-time employment. Four-fifths of the membership of an 'open' ACF in Cardiff were employed full-time in manual, agricultural, or clerical jobs. Factories in Scotland, such as the Nobel's explosives plant at Ardeer, raised their own cadet units. An engagingly enthusiastic account of involvement in all aspects of military training, as well as sport, the band, and camping, was written by a lad who was an apprentice marine fitter in a Grimsby shipyard. A former Boy Scout, he managed to fit in all this ACF activity with fire-watching and messenger duty with the Home Guard and ARP. In fact, so enthusiastic was he that, despite having to fight to get out of his reserved occupation, his ACF service led to a twenty-five-year-long career in the Royal Engineers. This was just the sort of lad the military were desperate to attract.

By 1941, the changing nature of the Home Guard saw it moving away from its former role of predominantly static defence with minimal armament, to the adoption of a more offensive posture. This involved greater mobility; general access to a wider range of weaponry; an increase in involvement in manning AA guns and rockets as well as field artillery and heavy coast guns; and the expansion of MT units. The continued success of these ventures rested on the consistent involvement of young men. However, just as many youngsters were gaining proficiency at these new tasks, they were whipped away to join the regulars. At the same time, when in 1942 the upper limit for conscription was increased to fifty-one, many middle-aged members were also lost. Responding to this double-ended attrition, the military authorities therefore made every possible effort to engage youngsters in the ACF as a preparation for joining the Home Guard prior to being called up. Links between Home Guard units and the cadets were therefore to be encouraged. In Scotland, where the local regiments maintained a more visible presence, a feature which extended to their Home Guard affiliates, parading with their pipe bands, Home Guard battalions were actively involved in recruiting youngsters into the ACF, and these cadet units were then formally affiliated to their local Home Guard. The movement also spread to Northern Ireland which, for political reasons, had never formerly been permitted volunteer forces. Strong contingents were raised by the former headmaster of Campbell College and by the Royal Inniskilling Fusiliers who provided NCOs as permanent instructors. The Royal Belfast Academical Institute (Inst) raised a cadet company of the Royal Ulster Rifles in 1943. Across Britain and Northern Ireland, the ACF and the OTC totalled, respectively, 190,000 and 30,000 in late 1943, for the ACF, an 80 per cent increase since 1942. Officers were recruited from teachers, retired regular officers and NCOs, and territorials. Commissions could be granted to suitable candidates over the age of sixteen and might be held concurrently with a commission in the Home Guard, but if the holder became eligible for call up then the commission had to be relinquished. This latter stipulation would suggest that a significant number of commissioned officers in the ACF were under eighteen.

For cadets being trained in either OTC or ACF units, Certificate 'A' was the gold standard. Along with the normal first aid and physical training components, the syllabus consisted of foot drill and arms drill; fieldcraft; map-reading; and signalling. Once rifles became available shooting could take place, and weapons training would include the use of automatic weapons. Training in infantry tactics was also upgraded. Given that the new forms of warfare relied more heavily on individual initiative and the contribution of junior leaders, so effective communications assumed a greater significance, and a stronger emphasis was placed on message writing and the clarity of orders. ACF cadets were perceived as being the source of the army's next generation of junior NCOs so the functions of the section leader formed a prominent part of training: organisation and equipment; battle drills in defence and attack; the selection of fire positions; and the issuing of fire control orders. Imaginative and challenging exercises were held, and camps were organised to facilitate extended intensive training. As the army became ever more technical—the REME had been formed in 1942—so courses were introduced for boys to gain technical qualifications embodied in Certificate 'T', awarded in conjunction with Technical Colleges, giving boys the opportunity to gain trade qualifications.

Incentives were introduced to motivate units to gain as many passes as possible since this had a direct bearing on the duration and content of conscripts' recruit training. Hence large numbers of boys graduated from the ACF with the Certificate 'A' qualification and had very often gained specialist skills such as Morse code or weapons handling. Ironically, however, they were often advised by old sweats to conceal this knowledge when they joined up, awaiting their chance for subsequently impressing their instructors with their quick learning. Despite this old soldier's advice to boys—'never volunteer for anything'—many might still expect to be fast-tracked as junior NCOs or even potential officers.

Where possible, particularly in towns and cities, joint training with OTC, ACF, and the Home Guard took place. Cadets would be trained in shooting, drill, fieldcraft, map-reading, and so on up to three nights a week. Facilities could be shared as at Lewes whose ACF platoon used the Home Guard's miniature range in the Old Naval Prison. In Somerset, two cadet NCOs from Ilminster GS were drafted in as instructors at the newly formed Chard ACF unit. On the back of its Home Guard experience (see Chapter 2), Shrewsbury School supplied a demonstration platoon for a night patrol training session for the county ACF at its summer camp. By the last years of the war, more camps were again taking place, and VJ Day found the Reigate ACF camping in the grounds of Charterhouse School. Co-operation, of necessity, stretched to common membership, as OTC and ACF cadets participated in Home Guard operations, often under the leadership of officers holding responsibilities in both organisations. The War Office recognised this by building on the experience of an officers' course held at Malvern in 1941, and instituting an OCTU for the ACF, many of whose candidates would have also been serving in the Home Guard. JF Wolfenden, headmaster of Uppingham School, who perceived the importance of providing social as well as military training to produce citizens as well as servicemen would, no doubt, have approved of the social mixing that resulted from these overlaps and collaborations. The present writer's memories of attendance at a joint ACF/CCF course over the 1961–2 New Year with the Royal Artillery at Woolwich and Larkhill are naturally vague, but there are recollections of only friendly teamwork whilst manhandling 25-pounder gun/howitzers in the snow. What did signify at the time was that we CCF cadets could not quite understand why we all had our Certificate 'A' badges up, but no stripes, while just Part 1 qualified our ACF colleagues as lance-bombardiers.

It should be remembered that between Dunkirk and D-Day, the vast majority of the British Army was encamped in Great Britain and Northern Ireland, alternating garrison duties with training activities. This meant that it was often possible to draw on these troops for cadet training activities. King's School, Bruton in Somerset, appears to have established useful links, involving regulars in their field days with scout cars and anti-tank guns. Similarly, Latymer Upper OTC were trained in weapons handling, including automatics and the 2-inch mortar, by the Welsh Guards. These relationships were made easier when ACF units were affiliated to line regiments. At their summer camps in Wales, the cadet battalions of the King's Own Shropshire Light Infantry benefited from demonstrations mounted by regulars ranging from the REME's vehicle-recovery units to the RAC's armoured vehicles, and to spectacular escapades by the Royal Marine Commandos. In 1945, three years after the War Office resumed responsibility for the ACF, the BNCA became the ACF Association, a registered charity, continuing to this day, to support the work of the ACF.

The Air Defence Cadet Corps (ADCC) and the Air Training Corps (ATC)

The ADCC was set up in 1938, by Air Commodore Chamier, a former Royal Flying Corps pilot, to train young men in aviation-related skills. The first two squadrons were established in Leicester and Watford, quickly rising to forty-two by the end of the year, many of them based on schools, with teachers serving as officers. From early in the war, cadets worked on RAF stations doing all sorts of useful jobs such as filling sandbags and loading belts of ammunition into aircraft. Following pressure from the ADCC's Yorkshire Committee, the Air Ministry recognised its usefulness and, in February 1941 reinvented it by Royal Warrant as the ATC with HM King George VI as air commodore-in-chief, describing it as 'the royal road to the Royal Air Force'. It would henceforth be subject to regulations formulated by the Air Council which specified sixteen as the minimum age for enrolment. Recruitment to the ACF was suspended for six months in 1941 to allow boys to join the newly established ATC and in Stoke Newington, the ACF and ATC detachments occupied adjoining four-storey houses in a terrace on Albion Road. Boys over sixteen who were physically fit and wished to join the RAF could enrol. They had to pass a compulsory PT test involving minimum standards for runs and jumps, balancing speed, and endurance. Within a short time, there were 400 ATC squadrons in existence. Fosters GS and Sherborne School combined to establish No. 617 Squadron in 1941 under a teacher commissioned into the RAFVR. The boys drilled at school with days out at RNAS *Yeovilton* and HMS *Dipper,* the Fleet Air Arm station at Henstridge. Colyton GS formed No. 1067 Squadron with three teachers as officers, and seventy members of the Nottingham Battalion of the Boys' Brigade formed No. 1059 Squadron. The headmaster of Lewes County Boys' School raised No. 464 Squadron in April 1941 with three flights consisting of sixty cadets from the County School; forty from the evacuees of Tooting Bec School; and ninety from other schools needing extra mathematics instruction before they could be considered for entry to the RAF. The cadets also acted as ARP messengers as part of their service. Scarborough HS formed No. 739 Squadron in May 1941, quickly recruiting over 100 members. The headmaster of St Dunstan's College raised an ATC unit in Reigate, and Westminster School, evacuated to Bromyard, maintained an ATC squadron training on aircraft recognition and practising Morse code. Sufficient competence was achieved to enable boys to proceed to the navigation and mathematics elements of the training syllabus, which would gain them their proficiency certificates. The ATC in Fairford was based at Farmor's School where thirty boys received instruction and a Rolls-Royce Kestrel engine was installed in the school's woodwork room. Manchester GS had an ATC unit from 1942 but many of the staff were elderly, limiting the number who could be involved as officers. They had talks, visited RAF stations, went gliding and flew in a de Havilland Rapide. The cadets from nearby Burnage HS visited RAF Ringway and went aloft in Airspeed Oxfords, Rapides, and Douglas Dakotas. One boy got a trip in a Fairey Swordfish, an open cockpit biplane known as the 'string-bag'. Some cadets got to tag along on practice bomb-runs on the ranges in The Wash, and one 'lucky' cadet was taken from RAF Syerston in a heavy bomber dumping faulty bombs into the sea. As the ATC developed, air cadets might provide training in aircraft recognition to AA or ROC personnel. Reminders that there was a war on were sometimes salutary. The huts in Trent Road, housing the HQ of the Nottingham ATC were destroyed in an air-raid and a fourteen-year-old and two seventeen-year-old cadets from Buxton were killed when the Lancaster in which they were flying crashed.

Pre-entry training for the RAF was organised by Wolfenden at Uppingham and courses to introduce potential aircrew to service life were held at institutes of higher education, such as Loughborough College, which also ran summer schools for ATC cadets and their instructors. Stowe School's ATC contingent was honoured by a visit from Air Commodore Chamier in 1943. By this time, the Air Ministry had allocated ten aircraft—Airspeed Oxfords and de Havilland Dominies to the ATC whose cadets were desperate to get airborne. For many, it was a question of being in the right place at the right time, or else having contacts. Many individuals write of having flights in all types of aircraft, sometimes even being taken on operational flights with Coastal Command. What was needed, however, was a systematic approach to get numbers acquainted with life in the clouds. An ATC Gliding school had been set up at Kirkbymoorside in Yorkshire, in 1942, the first in a planned provision of 100; by April 1944, some 1,300 ATC cadets had achieved various stages of proficiency. The provision of flying experience for most though would remain very much, a matter of luck. Some ATC squadrons constructed their own mechanical flight simulators which forced them to habituate pre-flight procedures. Some cadets, such as those at Chard, were fortunate to go up in dual-control aircraft which put them a bit closer to the flying experience. Cadets who were bound for university and hoped to fly with the RAF were permitted to join University Air Squadrons for six months and be taught to fly. Some ATC units were based in schools, particularly technical schools, where if, as was the case in many places, the headmaster also commanded the ATC squadron, the practical and the theoretical could run together and such happy conjunctions attracted high levels of enrolment. Across the country, membership leapt tenfold from the original total of a little under 20,000 in 1940 to 200,000 by the end of 1942. These were distributed in 366 'closed' school units, and 1,043 'open' units, which any boy satisfying the entry requirements could join. Especially fortunate units such as No. 414 (Epping) Squadron was based at RAF North Weald with constant access to modern fighter aircraft. By 1944, however, improving fortunes in the progress of the war meant that ATC numbers were cut back with fewer boys being recruited. This also affected those cadets who had committed themselves to the RAF and dismay was expressed in parliament regarding the diversion of keen air cadets into the mines or the army, representing a loss of trained and enthusiastic entrants to the RAF which had declared itself as over-manned. This situation was so dispiriting for the ATC's membership and leadership alike that, by the spring of 1945, numbers were rapidly falling away. Concern was expressed by Members that in the new 'air age' youth must be afforded the opportunity to prepare themselves for service in military or civil aviation (noted in *Hansard* 1945-03-06 Column 1933). During the war, fifty-five ATC cadets died as a result of enemy action, and some 100,000 boys passed into the RAF with 25,000 more entering the Fleet Air Arm.

Air Scouts

Although Baden-Powell, the founder of the Scout Movement, demonstrated a keen interest in the contribution of aviation to warfare, right up until the late 1930s he felt that for most Scout Troops, access to aircraft would be so unattainable that forming an Air Scout category was impracticable. Other aviators were keen supporters of scouting and an airman's badge was available from 1911. Claude Graham-White, well-known for his flying demonstrations and ownership of his Hendon aircraft factory, would make flights to his old school in Bedford to stimulate interest. However, this badge could be gained simply by attendance at lectures on aeronautics and aircraft recognition, which were backed up by a specially commissioned set of seventy-two lantern slides but had few active elements. It was suggested that Scouts could train as observers of aerial activity on the ground and gain expertise in reporting aircraft movements. Thus, it was not until 1941 that the Air Scouts were formed for those boys, keen to prepare for service in the RAF but too young for the ATC with its entry age, at the time, of sixteen. The organisation built on earlier arrangements which had involved Scout Troops in aviation-themed activities such as gliding. By January 1943, the movement could amass 1,000 Air Scouts at an exhibition in London, which promoted interest in the RAF. The Air Ministry loaned a Link Trainer and a power-operated gun-turret, but there appears to be little evidence that Air Scouts ever got off the ground more than figuratively. In some places such as Rochdale where, by 1943, the Air Scouts had begun to work in conjunction with the neighbouring Royton ATC, boys might have made more progress. Not until 1951, however, would the Air Scouts as a sub-set of the scouting movement, obtain recognition from the Air Ministry and be permitted to sport the RAF roundel.

The Sea Cadet Corps

The Sea Cadet Corps (SCC) had its origins in a political pressure group when, in the years leading up to the Great War, the Navy League believed Britain's security depended on the existence of a strong and well-manned Royal Navy, promoting the Blue Water doctrine. By 1910, it had raised the Boys' Naval Brigade and set up training ships, alongside other unaffiliated initiatives. While many of these units performed useful service in producing semi-trained lads for the Royal Navy throughout the Great War, the Admiralty remained ambivalent, showing little interest in supporting or even recognising them. Numbers of sea cadets gradually rose through the 1930s until the international situation prompted a surge in 1937–8, largely funded by private donations. This produced a cadre of cadets willing, were war to break out, to join the Royal Navy for the duration. In the summer of 1939, there were 9,000 cadets in 100 SCC units. Astonishingly, the Admiralty requested an increase in these figures to 25,000 cadets in 250 units, but still declined to offer finance or official recognition, but as the war progressed, numbers picked up. Cotswold Sea Cadets parading in Cheltenham in April 1940 mustered 320 cadets from the surrounding towns. Cirencester's Sea Cadets had to parade above a shop in the town's Castle Street, but by 1944, they were fielding a drum and fife band and had contributed twenty-five recruits to the Royal Navy. Not until February 1942 did the Admiralty show real interest, and then it was a sudden intention to take control. Training would henceforth be under the direction of naval officers, but the Navy League hung on to overall control of the movement and would continue to provide finance. Throughout 1942 and 1943, the SCC doubled in strength to 50,000 cadets, to a great extent remaining self-financing. All over the country, new units appeared, many of them raising the money to build their 'Training Ships' in which their training could take place. These ranged from simple huts to redundant chapels and converted barns, to stone frigates with lifeboats slung on davits, upper-level decks, and masts, replicating a ship's layout, as at Dudley's TS *Centaur,* or the even more realistic TS *Undaunted* in Bromley. In 1942, following this long-awaited recognition by the Admiralty, a Sea Cadet Corps, one of many new units, was formed in July in Peterborough, recruiting seventy to eighty cadets in the fourteen to seventeen age group, and meeting at Brook Street School, now Peterborough City College. A Sea Cadet unit was started in Wisbech in 1944 with two loans of £400 for equipment and premises. Although one of these loans was interest-free, a minimum of £100 had to be repaid annually. The Northampton unit bought a barge that could accommodate groups of cadets for weekend training sessions on the Nene, while at Heybridge in Essex a veritable flotilla of small boats was available to units within travelling distance. Elsewhere steam yachts, cutters and ketches were acquired for cadets' use. The Navy League was loaning out thousands of pounds to subsidise all these developments on land and water, while local fundraising was an ongoing feature of units' programmes.

Cadets learned general seamanship skills of boat handling, naval discipline, physical fitness and signals, along with navigation, shooting, and meteorology. From 1943, new subjects were introduced including gunnery, wireless-telegraphy, naval aviation, and electrical engineering. Once the Admiralty had taken charge of training, then a tighter regime could be introduced to govern qualifications and the quality and duration of instruction. Free uniforms were also distributed, and *per capita* grants were introduced based on the age and proficiency of cadets. All this effort was directed at reducing the amount of time young recruits to the Royal Navy would spend in basic training. The resultant dividend can be seen in the specific training of signallers. A converted houseboat initially, and then Grenville Hall in Slough served as training centres for Sea Cadets receiving intensive training in semaphore and wireless telegraphy. Every four weeks, from 1941, twenty-four-strong cohorts of cadets graduated and were accepted into the navy at seventeen. During the first six months of 1943, almost 550 trained cadets went into the Royal Navy's Communications Branch, and across the country, SCC units competed to prepare boys for acceptance onto this path. Membership of the Navy League Sea Cadet Corps in Nottingham was promoted specifically on the premise that cadets were eligible to gain special entry into the Royal Navy based on their successful training as signallers and telegraphists. Following the success of the signals training, a similar scheme was set up in 1944 for the Mechanical Branch of the navy, seeking to prepare sea cadets as potential petty officers covering all aspects of engineering in a course spread over eighteen months. Those who successfully completed this course were graded as provisional mechanics and were assured of a place in the navy. Cadets could also undertake a month's course qualifying them, aged seventeen, as junior ordinary seamen or, if they passed at a lower level, deck boys, in the Merchant Navy. As well as these concentrated courses that aimed at specified outcomes, cadets could attend summer camps which were simply intended to familiarise them with service life. In 1943, such camps, many of which were held near naval bases enabling cadets to visit ships and dockyards, were attended by some 15,000 sea cadets.

Although the headmaster of Bath College had expressed support for the sea cadets, in principle, back before the Great War, it was only in 1942 that first Harrow and then Sherborne set up SCC units, to be followed by other such schools, expected to produce candidates for the RNVR officer training courses at HMS *King Alfred*. Traditionally, the Royal Navy had selected their potential officers at the age of thirteen, so this was an entirely new approach. Even more radical was the introduction of the 'Y' Scheme in 1941, generally understood to be aimed at attracting potential officers into the Royal Navy, Fleet Air Arm, Royal Marines, and the Royal Air Force by grabbing them early. Candidates had to be seventeen years old, in good health, and in possession of the school certificate or else a letter signed by their headmaster stating that they had attained the requisite standard but explaining the reasons for their not having the actual certificate itself. It was further expected that candidates should have been exemplary members of the SCC or the ATC for at least a year before they reached the age of seventeen. The Royal Navy's experience of the scheme was disappointing, as although the scheme strengthened links with some schools, it was felt to have fallen short of its objectives with fewer than 40 per cent of those accepted onto the scheme being put forward for possible commissions, while a similar number remained as ordinary seamen and only around 10 per cent attained advanced technical levels. Mismatched expectations on both sides were apparently held to be responsible for producing this shortfall.

The Royal Marines were still recruiting fourteen-year-old boys as trainee bandsmen throughout the war. Recruitment of both officers and other ranks generally followed the pattern of the other services drawing on volunteers and conscripts. Not needing so many highly trained technicians, their participation in the RN's 'Y' Scheme was intended to identify exclusively potential officers. In the event, it was felt that standards were not sufficiently high for this purpose, with only 25 per cent of candidates ultimately commissioned into the Marines in 1944.

The Sea Scouts

The Sea Scouts began life in 1908 and achieved Admiralty recognition by serving as auxiliary coastguards during the Great War. After 1939, the Admiralty made continued recognition dependent on meeting specified proficiency criteria and accepted the organisation's seamanship training as qualifying Scouts to join the Royal Navy. Such troops enjoying this Admiralty recognition were limited, and remain so, to just 105 among the 400-odd in existence. The research ship *Discovery* was moored in the Thames in 1936 and became a temporary Sea Scout base. During the war, it was the HQ and depot ship of the River Thames Emergency Service, a collection of small craft acting as floating ambulances in the London Blitz with Sea Scouts acting as telephone operators, signallers, and stretcher-bearers for the service. The Sea Scouts, by now 27,000 strong, repeated their duties of the previous war as coast-watchers and signallers for the Royal Navy ashore.

Sea Scouts were involved with the little ships that supported the Dunkirk evacuation. The motor picket boat *Minotaur*, an ex-naval steam pinnace, was one such boat, converted as a training vessel, manned by Sea Scouts, which crossed from Ramsgate and ferried troops from the beaches to the transports, constantly under fire. She eventually returned fully loaded and guided other boats home on the nine-hour-long voyage. Sea Scouts from Cornwall to Essex manned more of these little ships. A former officer who survived the *Titanic* sinking took his 58-foot power yacht *Sundowner* to Dunkirk with a Sea Scout as deck hand. Dodging enemy fighter aircraft, they brought 130 men back, crammed into every possible space.

Voluntary Uniformed Organisations for Girls

The National Association of Training Corps for Girls (NATCG) was formed in 1942 by the Board of Education, under Florence Horsburgh, as an umbrella organisation for the Girls' Training Corps, the Girls Venture Corps Air Cadets, the Women's Junior Air Corps (WJAC), and the Girls' Nautical Training Corps. All these organisations, open to fourteen- to twenty-year-olds, were dedicated to preparing girls for service to the community and, particularly, as pre-service training for conscription as eighteen-year-olds. Although they were unaffiliated to the armed forces, service personnel were often involved in their training and military drill and practical skills were on the curriculum, along with first aid training. All these activities, however, took place—entirely dependent on links made at a local level, and there could be no expectation—on the part of the organisers of girls' groups of official support. Although some organisations (the Boys') were official and others (the Girls') were not, there were some examples of co-operation. At RAF Uxbridge, Girls' Training Corps, ATC, and ACF units co-existed, training together and enjoying joint access to shared facilities. In Chingford the girls of the WJAC squadron trained alongside the boys of No. 63 Squadron ATC.

The WJAC had been formed in 1939, largely independent of the Air Ministry, but with the purpose of preparing girls for service in the Women's Auxiliary Air Force (WAAF) and the Air Transport Auxiliary (ATA), which would deliver aircraft from factory to RAF station. Its uniform was based on the WAAF and its core programme with the addition of motor maintenance, was similar to those of other organisations. Additional topics, however, such as AA operational duties, radio location, signals, and engineering, were soon introduced as being relevant to what might be asked of the girls on call up. Role models among its officers included the high-profile ATA pilots, Diana Barnato Walker and Freydis Sharland, but it was still down to local initiatives to form units. The Gravesend unit had recruited 130 members by the end of 1942, eagerly awaiting delivery of their uniforms. No. 260 Squadron was based at Lewes County Girls' School from May 1942. Girls aged sixteen to eighteen could join alongside the Junior No. 3200 Squadron for girls aged thirteen to sixteen. In parliament, in July 1941, the secretary of state for air was asked a question regarding the Air Ministry's attitude to offering support to the WJAC. His reply revealed that the organisation had received no official support from the Air Ministry and that, given that the WAAF was presently recruiting girls aged seventeen and a half, nor would it be justifiable to offer any support in the future. His department had gone no further than advising unofficially on questions of uniform 'in order to avoid unintentional breaches of the law' (noted in *Hansard*: Vol. 372, Column 1326). However, despite the Air Ministry's strictures, WJAC units continued to appear in uniforms indistinguishable from those of the WAAF/WRAF. The band (incidentally, the first of its kind) of Streatham's No. 6 Squadron WJAC, could be seen leading a 'Salute the Soldier' fundraiser procession in April 1944. This was just one more instance of voluntary organisations choosing to disregard rules they regarded as unnecessary, pointless or downright daft. Eventually, a limited number of aircraft was made available for WJAC girls to experience flight.

The Girls' Training Corps (GTC) formed in 1941 taking girls aged fourteen to twenty and adopted the motto: 'To Serve and Train for Service'. Its object was to prepare girls for service in the ATS so trained its members in first aid and other ARP duties; aircraft recognition and Morse code; marksmanship and map-reading; courier and messenger work; all alongside physical training and the fostering of independence. Soon, over 120,000 girls had joined, providing their own basic uniforms and attending training sessions at units based in localities using public buildings. In 1942, the twenty-strong No. 646 Company was based at Somercotes Infants' School in Lincolnshire, and in Brighton the local company trained at the Royal Pavilion. The Girls' Nautical Training Corps (GNTC) was formed in 1942 to prepare fourteen- to twenty-year-old girls ultimately for service in the Women's Royal Naval Service (WRNS), the Wrens. Its curriculum consisted of naval drill and seamanship along similar lines to the Sea Cadets. The organisation had its equivalent in Canada known as the Wrenettes, not to be confused with a later Tamla-Motown band. The Girls' Friendly Society (GFS) was an organisation founded in 1875 to support girls from the age of twelve working in hitherto unfamiliar, mainly urban, situations. It provided social and domestic facilities for girls and women in factories, offices, and the hospitality industry, but membership came predominantly from the domestic service sector. In 1942 the GFS launched its War Training Scheme for girls in the fourteen to eighteen age group. This covered everything from ARP procedures to housecraft and worked in collaboration with the Board of Education and the LCC.

Girl Guides

Like the Boy Scouts, the many thousands of Girl Guides in Britain in 1939, performed many of the tasks that arose from the circumstances of war from meeting troops off the Dunkirk evacuation flotilla, feeding them and distributing dry clothing, to the more mundane, but vital, tasks of rolling vast numbers of bandages in hospitals up and down the land. Many of their activities have already been detailed above but many more must be added (see also Chapter 5). Guides were particularly active in the general welfare and medical arena, particularly connected to evacuation and ARP. Concerned for people displaced from their homes by bombing, and the permanent problems produced by homelessness, rationing and food shortages, Guides had an important contribution to make with their homecraft, nursing, social, communication, and cookery skills. The 2nd Cirencester Abbey Company placed a notice in the *Wiltshire & Gloucestershire Standard* in July 1940 advertising their availability for:

> (1) Hay making, fruit picking or weeding or any odd farm jobs evenings or holidays as most are still at school; (2) Wooding on behalf of old people; (3) They are willing to look after evacuee children on Saturdays and Sundays.

No doubt there were plenty of takers.

Boy Scouts

Under the slogan 'The Boy Scouts Are Carrying On', by the end of 1940, the movement had trained 53,000 of its members to fulfil roles related to the nation's survival. We have already seen (see also Chapter 5) how some of these activities involved intense danger during air raids, working in ARP as messengers, first aiders, stretcher-bearers, firefighters, firewatchers, and ARP wardens, some of them earning bravery awards and experiencing the immense satisfaction to be gained from helping people and saving lives. Other duties involved intense boredom and physical discomfort during patrols and guard duties at remote reservoirs or in desolate coastal areas. However, the bulk of Scouts' activities related to collecting money for munitions or comfort funds for service personnel; gathering salvage for recycling, especially paper, cardboard, glass, and metal; and growing fruit and vegetables to supplement dwindling food-stocks. Alongside all these activities came labour at forestry and harvest camps; acting as orderlies in hospitals; helping out at evacuation centres; and conducting evacuees to their billets.

Other Uniformed Youth Organisations

The Boys' Brigade (BB) and the Church Lads' Brigade (CLB) had begun in the nineteenth century as paramilitary organisations in a framework of, respectively, non-denominational and Anglican Christian teaching. After the formation of the Territorial Force in 1908, many companies affiliated to the Territorial Cadet Force (TCF), although the official line was against placing these organisations in thrall to the War Office. Parallel girls' organisations such as the Girls' Life Brigade (GLB) were also formed. During the Great War, the boys' dummy drill rifles had been exchanged for real ones as they took on duties guarding public utilities and transport hubs while many companies carried out first aid and further such services to the community. Thousands of the older boys enlisted in the services, winning medals, and becoming casualties and many of the girls joined voluntary aid detachments working in Red Cross hospitals or on ambulance trains. In 1926, the BB shed its military past and combined with the Boys' Life Brigade with a joint membership of 100,000 boys in 2,000 companies, celebrating its golden jubilee in 1933. In Scotland, the BB acquired a former orphanage, Balrossie School in Kilmalcolm, for use as an outdoor training centre. The advent of war in 1939 saw most of the older boys enlisting, leaving the younger ones to apply their first aid training in the numerous blitzes or to join the AFS. In Glasgow, the BB was often more popular than the ACF and recruited accordingly and in Nottingham, the BB maintained a boy messenger service for the ARP. From the evidence of wartime diaries and newspaper reports, it would appear that organisations such as the CLB, BB, and the GLB also supplied the vital service of helping to keep the social fabric together with concerts, plays, church parades and gatherings. Along with the YMCA and the YWCA, they provided an outlet for the young people themselves and a service to the Forces and the wider community. The Government Circular 1486 of 1939 had brought a significance to youth work as a relatively novel concept. Change was in the air and, as Roberts points out, the new BB and GLB companies raised in Norton-on-Tees in 1941 and 1942, began life fighting for space in the backroom of a church competing with the Home Guard, the AFS and the emergency hospital in the requisitioned church hall. By 1945, however, they numbered over sixty twelve- to eighteen-year-olds, and enjoyed the use of their local secondary school.

4

Schools under Attack

Although the nation had been braced to defend against a seaborne invasion, when the enemy attacked it was from the air. This chapter, therefore, examines the effect of the bombing campaigns waged by the *Luftwaffe* on schools and their communities between August 1940 and April 1945. One of the lessons learnt in the Great War concerned the vulnerability of public buildings holding large numbers of people. There had been in existence a number of conventions to which nations had ostensibly subscribed which included prohibitions on attacking civilian shipping or hospital ships; the use of poison gas; and the targeting of civilian targets by aerial bombardment. While the first two had been wilfully ignored by the *Kaiser*'s forces, the primitive nature of bomb-aiming techniques made it difficult to adhere to the last stipulation. In the first daylight raid of the Great War, on 13 June 1917, a squadron of fourteen German Gotha bombers descended on the East End of London. One aircraft dropped a 50-kg (110-lb) high explosive bomb on the Upper North Street LCC School in Poplar. It fell through the school's three floors before exploding in an infant classroom. Eighteen children were killed and nearly forty more seriously injured. These deaths accounted for over 10 per cent of the civilian deaths from bombing that day. The presence of memorial plaques reminded people of such dangers from the air and raised fears of their repetition since by the time of the outbreak of the Second World War, bombing accuracy had undergone but little improvement. Anti-aircraft gunfire and barrage balloons represented little more than an attempt to force the bombers to stay at heights at which accuracy might be difficult to attain and while this might have achieved some protection for specific targets, it effectively promoted promiscuous and indiscriminate bombing.

Bombing and Strafing Attacks on Schools

In urban areas, even when major bombing offensives were ostensibly aimed at centres of industrial activity and their associated housing areas, schools would inevitably be hit simply due to the density of the buildings around them. However, even rural sites, including schools, would still become targets for opportunistic attacks. Oundle School was strafed in July 1942 when the boys were, fortunately, not in residence. A German aircraft pulled out of an attack on Christ's Hospital after, it was suggested, mistaking the figures in their long-skirted Tudor coats for girls or monks, and flew off to strafe a school in nearby Horsham instead. Cadets drilling in the playground of a Southampton school, and on the field at Churchers College, Petersfield, were strafed by Messerschmitt fighters. Eton College suffered bomb damage to Upper School and to its chapel some of whose windows had to be replaced, while Dover College, as HMS *Lynx*, was shelled by the cross-Channel guns located on Cap Gris Nez. Few schools ever had the opportunity to observe the fight-back at close quarters. At Hilly Fields in west Lewisham, a HAA battery was located next door to Brockley County School, and the Latymer School field in Hammersmith was occupied by a barrage balloon. Following a broadcast warning from Lord Haw-Haw, Eastbourne College as HMS *Marlborough* was bombed by German aircraft, which were engaged by a LAA Bofors gun mounted on the school's memorial tower. No aircraft was hit but the bombs missed their target.

Some of this activity appears to have been opportunistic and random. A boy in Sidcup remembers walking to primary school with his friends along Sherwood Park Avenue and being machine-gunned by a Messerschmitt 109. Some instances of aerial bombing were completely unpredictable, particularly the hit-and-run 'nuisance' raids of the middle years of the war. In June 1943, a bombing raid on Margate saw an infants' school hit. Fortunately, the children were off-site having their dinners and escaped injury. Elsewhere in the town, ten people were killed, and a rest centre was set up in the Royal School for Deaf Children, which had remained open throughout the war. Braintree's worst raid came in February 1941 when the high school was damaged by a bomb which fell close by.

Areas on the flight paths of bombers making for target areas suffered from enemy pilots jettisoning unused bombs on their way home. This was especially prevalent at places on the bombers' homeward routes out of London. Aircraft suffering from battle damage or mechanical failure crashed in unpredictable and unexpected places. The log of ROC No. 18 Group at Colchester recorded an enemy aircraft crashing at 'Downhall School, Sheering', on 14 September 1940, with two survivors of the crew of three, apprehended. Walthamstow Hall School in Sevenoaks was severely damaged in September 1940 just as the London Blitz was beginning. Even as a German bomber crashed on the adjacent tennis courts during the Battle of Britain, the staff and thirty-seven boarders sat tight with lessons taking place in air-raid shelters equipped with bunks. The younger day girls and boarders were then evacuated to Shropshire, sharing Attingham Park with girls from Edgbaston Girls' School, Birmingham, only returning to Kent in 1944, just in time for the V-1 and V-2 onslaught. Gravesend was bombed in August 1940, when Colyer Road School was burned out and the TS *Cornwall* was sunk. The next month, Gravesend County

School for Boys was damaged when hit by two bombs. Four bombs were dropped on Charterhouse early in 1941, and at St Andrew's Convent School in Leatherhead, five nuns were killed and many of its buildings destroyed. At St Peter's Primary School in Croydon, a bomb fell on the air-raid shelter in March 1944, killing three people. Reigate GS was damaged by cannon fire in September 1940, delaying the start of term and three boys evacuated to Reigate from St Dunstan's College were killed in the space of a few months. At Tongham, near Aldershot, the school roof was blown off by a near-miss and not repaired for a year, with no school at all for the first three months, followed by nine months in the village hall. The Royal Naval School in Twickenham, the country's oldest girls' boarding school, was destroyed by bombs in 1940 and was evacuated, initially to Fernhurst, and then, in 1942, to Stoatley Hall, Haslemere, where it remained until 1995 when it amalgamated with another school as the Royal School. In February 1941, a bomb landed very close to Purley Oaks School but failed to explode immediately. Only when RE bomb disposal operatives arrived did the bomb explode, killing six sappers and severely damaging the school. West Green (C of E) School in Crawley was destroyed in a raid carried out, mercifully, at a time when it was unoccupied, and Tonbridge School had a narrow escape when a 250-kg (550-lb) bomb landed just 15 yards from the chapel, smashing windows but causing little other damage. In Petersfield, Churchers College hosted Emanuel School from Battersea, evacuated there in 1939 after its buildings had suffered bomb damage and working half-days in the classroom and half-days on the school field. Early in 1941, the school was bombed and strafed while the Emanuel OTC were drilling on the field. Although minor damage was caused there were no casualties in the school. Nevertheless, the school recommenced some teaching back in London with around 100 boys in 1943.

More frequent than those individual random events was the collateral damage to schools caused by planned air raids involving large numbers of aircraft attacking larger targets. Beginning in July 1940, many towns and cities across Britain were bombed, and Aberdeen's Victoria Road Primary School became the first Scottish school to receive bomb damage. Other towns and cities went on to be heavily bombed, and some of them like Plymouth, effectively obliterated. The general criterion for a major air raid was the dropping of 100 tons or more of bombs—HE, parachute mines, incendiaries, and oil bombs. London suffered fourteen such attacks and Birmingham, Merseyside, and Plymouth, eight each. The other worst-hit cities seeing severe damage accompanied by high numbers of casualties were Bristol, Portsmouth, Southampton, Coventry, Manchester, Glasgow/Clydeside, Cardiff, and Hull, with Belfast, Leeds, Newcastle, and Sheffield close behind. Some smaller centres suffered by their vulnerable location on the south or east coasts, and others through their proximity to intended targets. By mid-1941, over 30,000 people had been killed and 20 per cent of schools in England and Wales damaged by bombing. Subsequent bombing campaigns and the V-1 and V-2 attacks saw the total of deaths reach over 60,000. Of as much import to daily life, particularly that of children, was the fact that for every fatality in bombing raids, thirty-five people were rendered homeless. While the press sustained a picture of high morale among the inhabitants of bombed cities, and children were often sheltered from their parents' anxieties, the constant fear of death and destruction remained inescapable, particularly for children whose world picture was necessarily limited.

While extensive damage could result from a one-off event—a single heavy raid on Aberdeen in April 1943 damaged twenty-four schools—it was generally the more sustained onslaughts which impacted most on targeted urban areas. The following examples show the severity of the assault on some of those targets with a particular emphasis on damage to schools, and on casualties amongst their occupants. Although terminologically inaccurate since bombing campaigns might last for months and *Blitzkrieg* was, by definition, a short, sharp shock, the word 'Blitz' is used here as it is the word most used in local histories to indicate a measure of severity and the perceptions of both helplessness and defiance which intensive bombing generated.

Belfast

Belfast was a centre of the armaments industry with Harland & Wolff building warships, including capital ships, for the Royal Navy and Short Brothers constructing aircraft for the RAF including the Stirling heavy bomber and the Sunderland flying boat. Between 7 April and 6 May 1941, Belfast suffered four heavy air raids with that on the night of 15–16 April causing 900 deaths, after London, the heaviest loss of life in a single raid. Very few children had been evacuated from the city, and army families continued to live in Victoria Barracks, which was severely damaged when it became a target for the bombers. Although the Belfast Royal Academical Institute escaped damage, it deemed it sensible to teach its younger pupils at alternative sites away from the danger area. Over 50,000 houses were damaged or destroyed, rendering 100,000 people homeless, many of whom fled the city. The Strand Public Elementary was one of two schools destroyed. Initially, there were only four public air-raid shelters in the whole city, and those but poorly designed, leading to terrible injuries with people becoming buried in collapsing buildings, especially those living in the shadow of high mill buildings which crumpled on top of the surrounding houses. Improvised shelters such as the crypt of the Clonard Monastery took in as many as they could. When small local shelters were built, they were unfortunately of the design where blast would blow out the brick side walls and drop the concrete slab roof onto the occupants below, and many residents died in this way. The Stormont government had been reluctant to prepare for war and had cancelled orders for firefighting equipment. This resulted in an inadequately resourced ARP service being quickly overwhelmed and grateful for the help which arrived from the Republic, responding quickly to their urgent calls for help. An initial digitised list of the first 650 casualties, in alphabetical order, of the 900 or so from the biggest raid, has been released by the Commonwealth War Graves Commission.

It shows that from this total, thirty-nine (6 per cent) children of five years old or younger; forty (6 per cent) children aged six to twelve; and fifty-one (8 per cent) between thirteen and eighteen were killed in these raids. These figures include the Douglas family of Ballynure Street where the mother and her five young children all under nine died. A second heavy raid in early May showered incendiaries down to create a firestorm and caused a further 150 deaths. One of the sites damaged in this raid was Campbell College, in use as a military hospital with large numbers of Nissen huts and occupied by Nos 24 and 31 British General Hospitals, RAMC. Nineteen patients and staff, including several Pioneer Corps orderlies, were killed. A first-aid party based in the Grove Elementary School was forced to move to a neighbouring school after an unexploded bomb caused the evacuation of 200 people.

Birmingham and the West Midlands

Prior to the outbreak of war, arrangements had already been made to evacuate large numbers of children and when the time came, schools were closed while air raid shelters were built in their playgrounds. The first raid came in August 1940, hitting industrial targets but also the cultural centre of Birmingham. A total of seventy-seven raids (eight of them classified as 'major') occurred, particularly in November 1940, with three coming on consecutive nights, when schools in Sparkhill and Yardley were destroyed. On one of these nights alone, 400 tons of HE bombs, incendiaries, and eighteen parachute mines were dropped. Further raids in April 1941, when Nuneaton was one of the towns hit, and in July of the following year, took the death toll to over 2,000 with 3,000 serious injuries, putting Birmingham among the most heavily bombed British cities in the war. Within the conurbation, Wolverhampton, West Bromwich, Dudley, and Tipton all suffered raids which caused multiple fatalities and destroyed extensive areas of housing.

Bristol

Over 1,300 people were killed in a series of air raids mounted with the general aim of destroying Avonmouth Docks and the Bristol Aeroplane works at Filton but causing indiscriminate devastation across the city. The most destructive raid came on Good Friday 1941, when parts of Colston Girls' School were burnt out. One of its pupils was standing on the roof of an adjacent building with her father, who was an ARP warden looking out for incendiaries. She witnessed the fall of the bomb that demolished her school's art room, library, and some junior form rooms. Private houses were taken over to allow the routine of the school to continue. The ARP control centre for the Bristol region was at Badminton Junior School in Westbury-on-Trym. As in other cities, schools were used as ARP posts and some of the city's twenty-six AFS sub-stations were located in schools including Ilminster Avenue School in Knowle and Windmill Hill School in Bedminster. This latter was bombed and suffered five deaths. In September 1940, the Cathedral School was bombed, injuring the headmaster. St Nicholas School was almost destroyed, with just enough left standing to accommodate a wardens' post. In the intensive raids of November, a fourteen-year-old messenger, having rescued a baby from a burning building, was killed by bomb fragments while delivering a message to the central police station. At Hillcrest School in Totterdown a shelter, its walls covered in children's graffiti was recently rediscovered under the school playground but deemed unsafe; it has been backfilled.

COVENTRY

As recorded in a 1,200-word article in *The Times*, published in February 1940 and widely read throughout Europe, Coventry manufactured the tools for a large part of the British munitions industry and was also the location for factories, both established and shadow, producing aeroplanes and armoured vehicles, and hence of crucial importance to the war effort. This fell little short of a clear invitation, so it was no real surprise when it came to be regarded as a legitimate target for aerial bombing by the *Luftwaffe*. Consequently, on the night of Thursday 14 November 1940, the city was hit by Operation *Mondscheinsonate* (Moonlight Sonata) when a force of over 500 bombers, led by pathfinder aircraft, descended on Coventry. Some even had time to return to their airfields in France to rearm and refuel before re-joining the assault. Although the scientists had found ways of jamming or bending the familiar *Knickebein* beam by which German bombers could locate themselves over selected targets, the *X-Gerät* system which used a combination of six such beams would take longer to counter. The allegation that the raid had been anticipated via Enigma decrypts but that the defensive response had been suppressed in order to protect ULTRA has been dismissed. As in other Victorian city centres, industrial premises lay cheek by jowl with houses, schools, and hospitals. Coventry's first recorded daylight attack by a dive bomber had been on the Standard Company's paint shop, next to the Henry Parkes School in Canley. The November raid on the city in which 500 tons of HE bombs, parachute, and petroleum mines and incendiaries were dropped, caused total devastation, killing over 800 people, but children still tried to get into school the next morning. One fourteen-year-old pupil attempted the journey to Leamington College for Boys but having walked 4 miles through ruined streets to the train station was turned away. The next day, a Saturday, he borrowed a bicycle for the 10-mile journey and on arrival was sent to the headmaster for failing to produce his homework. Although Bablake School buildings largely survived the raid, its staff and pupils were soon moved away to Lincoln. Two later raids in April 1941 brought a further 300 tons of bombs raining down on the city. The King Henry VIII GS, damaged in the first raid, had also moved to Alcester by the time of the later raids of April 1941 by which time, its buildings were described as derelict. Over 1,200 people had been killed in these three raids.

Glasgow and Clydeside

Understandably sceptical over the need to construct anti-invasion defences in the west of Scotland, an area perceived as being remote from the war, the myriad local authorities involved in the Glasgow region were late in assembling an ARP organisation and when the first German aircraft appeared in June 1940 they were met with shock. The first serious raid on Glasgow occurred the next month when several targets were hit and an oil bomb severely damaged St David's School, Townhead. For the next six months, mainly lone raiders attacked airfields and munitions factories causing civilian casualties and damage to homes. By early March 1941, radio intercepts pointed to an imminent heavier raid on the region. On the nights of 13 and 14 March 1941, over 250 German aircraft deposited 400 HE bombs on the compact Clydeside town of Clydebank, completely devastating the town and its services, killing around 500 people, a significant proportion of the town's population, leaving many of the town's schools burnt out, the rest severely damaged, and three-quarters of the town's 47,000 populace homeless. Although the town was a prime target with the Admiralty oil storage tanks, John Brown's shipyard, the Beardmore engine works, and the Singer factory manufacturing Sten guns, insufficient precautions had been put in place. Initial enthusiasm for fire-watching had waned and there were not enough stirrup pumps, hoses or ladders available. Firefighting efforts would be hampered by lack of petrol for the fire engines and incompatibility of equipment between different fire crews. There were 462 ARP wardens, of whom fifty were full-time, but some of their ARP posts lacked telephones, which placed a heavy reliance on the ninety teenage messengers, many of them from the Boys' Brigade and the Boy Scouts. When volunteer fire-watchers did come forward, leadership was lacking, and so their efforts remained largely uncoordinated.

When the onslaught came there was immediate devastation. Boquhanran School had been set up as one of the town's two first aid posts but was soon hit by HE bombs forcing an evacuation. Clydebank High School on its new campus on Janetta Street took over, but it, too, was hit by a parachute mine that caused major damage. The school would end up housing a mortuary. Bankhead School in Knightswood was a key AFS depot, first aid post, and local control centre, but when it received a direct hit from a parachute mine, twenty-one AFS firemen, five ARP personnel, eleven first aiders, and two messengers were among the forty-six people killed outright. At least three teenagers on ARP duties were killed along with seventy other children. Six children under fifteen were killed at the wardens' post in Janetta Street. Eight schools were completely wrecked, and three others were severely damaged, with three of the town's designated rest centres, and all three AFS sub-stations destroyed. The North Elgin Street School first aid post, destroyed by a parachute mine, saw its occupants moved outside into the playground shelters. Another parachute mine badly damaged the Cloberhill Public School in the Great Western Road. Hyndland School had been the venue for the Boys' Brigade's PT class before the first raid and then became sanctuary for those 500 inhabitants whose homes were destroyed in the ensuing raid, which left twenty-one of its neighbours dead including several from the Boys' Brigade company. The first aid post in nearby Notre Dame HS was put out of action by blast damage and Dalmuir Infants' School, also housing a first aid post, was flattened.

The attacks were witnessed by a seven-year-old girl whose fire-watcher father had taken her onto their Glasgow tenement rooftop, and by schoolchildren 4 miles (6.2 km) away on the western edge of Glasgow, who climbed up to the roof playground of St Joseph's school to get a better view of the conflagration. Glasgow itself was heavily bombed on those same nights and suffered 647 deaths and getting on for 2,000 serious injuries. A parachute mine landed close to St Mary's School in Kilmun Street, Maryhill, killing eighty-three people in the surrounding buildings. The stone frontage of the school survived but the rest of the building, which had housed an AFS station, was wrecked. The patients from Redlands Hospital were evacuated by Boy Scout stretcher bearers. In Paisley, a 500-kg (1,100-lb) unexploded bomb was discovered on the ground floor of Possilpark School having fallen through the roof.

It has always been thought that the number of deaths in Clydebank far exceeded the number declared by the authorities. Although Glasgow suffered a higher official tally of casualties in these raids, it was the proportion of deaths in the local population of Clydebank which had so impacted on the town. The shattered population attempted to get back to normal. One of the Clydebank refugees gave birth in the headmaster's study at the Hermitage Academy in Helensburgh, and Whitecrook School became a hostel for the 'blitz bachelors'—those members of John Brown's workforce who had previously lived in the digs which had now been destroyed but were desperately needed back in the shipyards.

Across Scotland, thirty-two schools had already suffered bomb damage by February 1941, prior to those hit during the Clydebank raids. Raids on Greenock in May 1941 caused damage to all but two of the burgh's public schools amid a general feeling that the devastation had been compounded by a lack of organisation. One Greenock headmaster found hundreds of people in his school, designated as a rest centre, but with no provision for caring for its customers or for feeding them. He was forced to commandeer mobile canteens and trust to the industry and good sense of the WVS. By the end of May, the total of bomb-damaged Scottish schools had risen to 117 with around a fifth of those rendered unusable, resulting in a second wave of evacuations. School rolls from Dumfriesshire and Ayrshire to Perthshire ballooned, and schools, already full to bursting, were overwhelmed by a combination of disorganised (private) flight and supposedly planned (official) schemes. The number of Scottish schools suffering severe damage by July 1941 was 145, representing 4.5 per cent of stock.

Kingston-upon-Hull

Hull suffered under a campaign of aerial bombing second only to London's which lasted right through from summer 1940 into 1945 with V-1 'Doodlebugs' being air-launched from Heinkel III bombers during Christmas 1944. Nearly 90 per cent of the city's buildings were damaged or destroyed and over 1,200 people killed in eighty-two raids. The conditions were brought vividly to life by the accounts of the children from fourteen of the city's schools, written for official use (see Chapter 1). Children saw their homes and schools destroyed and, even if their school survived, some could not attend at once as all their clothes had been burned. Bombed-out schools included Drypool C of E School; the 1,400-place secondary girls' Estcourt Street School; Thomas Barton Holmes School where only the infants' department would be able to continue; Lime Street primary school; St Joseph's RC girls' and infants' school; the Convent School; the junior department of Sidmouth HS; and Daltry Street School which was able to reopen in 1942 as a mixed primary school. A total of 11,000 school places were lost through bomb damage. The Central Secondary School for Girls, later to become Newland High School for Girls was bombed out and its pupils moved into a teacher training college until they were able to return to their rebuilt school. Hull Girls' HS, Riley Technical High, St Mary's GS, and Malton Street special school were among those schools evacuated *en masse*. The ninety-eight girls and twenty staff of the Boulevard HS went to Scarborough where they occupied the Esplanade's Astoria Hotel as both residence and schoolrooms. After the war, ten primary schools had suffered so much damage that they had to be entirely replaced and the city had opened twenty-five brand-new schools by 1960. Bridlington, up the Holderness coast, whence Newland High School had been evacuated, suffered over forty incidents with the worst raids during May 1941.

Leeds

Nine serious raids and many smaller ones were carried out on Leeds aiming for its heavy industry and aircraft factories and causing nearly eighty fatalities. The most damaging was on 14–15 March when 25 tons of bombs were dropped on the city wrecking the infants' department of St Peter's School. While this attack caused widespread damage, in tonnage, it amounted to only a quarter of the total set as the criterion for a 'major raid', hence locals labelled it ironically as the 'Quarter Blitz'. In recognition of the city's vulnerability as an industrial target, in early September 1940, children from 200 schools had been evacuated to small towns in the Yorkshire Dales. In some cases, entire schools were evacuated with St Hilda's School going to Ackworth, the Quaker school near Pontefract, and Roundhay Girls' HS to Otley but others being sent much further away: West Leeds HS and Allerton Girls' HS to Retford, and Roundhay Boys' GS to Lincoln. Amongst the dozens of buildings damaged or destroyed in the heaviest raid were Richmond Hill School, its pupils being evacuated to rural Lincolnshire, St Peter's School and St Vincent's RC Girls' School.

LIVERPOOL

Liverpool was first bombed in August 1940 and its last major raid was in January 1942. Gwladys Street School in Walton was one of those destroyed in September 1940 along with Garston's Banks Road School. October saw Holy Trinity School in Richmond Park hit by a bomb, but the worst case was in November 1940 when nearly 300 people were killed, and housing and two Aigburth schools, the Vale High School and St Ann's, were destroyed. Then, on 29 November, 300 people had taken to the underground shelter under the Ernest Brown Junior Instructional Centre in Durning Road, Edge Hill. This was thought to be safe as the reinforced concrete roof of the boiler room would provide added protection. However, the school took a direct hit from a parachute mine that collapsed the building, bursting the boilers, and flooding the basement with scalding water. At least 166 people were killed, including more than forty babies and children. Rescue workers struggled to extract survivors, of whom a bare thirty were unscathed and, after two days, a twelve-year-old girl became the last to be rescued before the site was sealed as a mass grave. This was followed by three consecutive nights of bombing in early-December. Further raids came in early May 1941, when eight consecutive nights of bombing caused nearly 2,000 deaths. By early 1941, Merseyside had 132 AFS sub-stations, many of them in school buildings and was rapidly recruiting firefighters. As in many other cities, schools met many ARP functions. Holly Lodge School provided the premises for initially an AFS Station; then a Divisional Fire Service HQ with a communications centre and a field telephone office; an area stores office; and workshop facilities. The school for the deaf in Melville Place was used for ARP training and many were used as air-raid shelters and those with deep basements, despite the danger of a direct hit, were often preferred to the damp and exposed Anderson shelters. Everton's Heyworth Street School was one such facility where children enjoyed a singalong accompanied by accordions and increased the volume to drown out the sound of the explosions. One night, though, a landmine demolished many of the surrounding houses and the school took in the survivors. However, the bombing became so bad that the many offers to transport them to outlying schoolrooms and church halls were gratefully accepted. In January 1941, St Vincent's School for the Blind in Yew Tree Lane was hit. On 4 May, Liverpool suffered its worst attacks with widespread devastation and high loss of life. Two more schools, in Anfield Road and Leyfield Road, were hit with further damage to others over the next few nights, and a shelter at Addison Road School was hit. The next day, St Sylvester's Infants' and Junior Schools were bombed, as were Bootle Boys' Secondary and Lambeth Road Schools two days later. By late 1941, the new NFS organisation had established many more fire stations and had set up another training facility in School Lane, Culcheth. The Melville Place School and Fazakerley Open Air School were two of the five rendezvous points for reinforcement firefighters coming into the city from other areas. At the end of the bombing, there had been nearly 4,000 deaths in ninety raids, including nearly seventy firefighters and a boy messenger.

LONDON

London's first major Blitz continued over fifty-seven consecutive nights through September and October 1940 during which 13,000 tons of bombs and many thousands of incendiaries were dropped, causing 20,000 deaths and massive damage to the docks, housing, and infrastructure. Probably the worst raids, however, were on the night of 29 December 1940 when 20,000 bombs including 130-odd tons of HE and vast numbers of incendiaries caused devastation. The conflagration surrounding St Paul's Cathedral and spreading over the East End and the docks was reported as being visible up to 25 miles away. The West End also suffered from the raids if less severely. Although most of Westminster School had been evacuated to Herefordshire, the school continued to operate next to the abbey and both buildings were bombed. The school cloisters were damaged, and the Upper School Hall was completely burnt out. In another raid the Abbey's Choir School was wrecked. An air-raid shelter was built in the College Garden and a firefighting team was based in Little Dean's Yard to aid the defence of the abbey, which suffered extensive damage. Mayfield School in Putney was temporarily evacuated to Woking while bomb damage was being repaired.

A great many LCC schools were in use by the ARP services, and many of them were bombed with consequent loss of life. Like many of London's board schools, Abbey Road School had been built in the nineteenth century, but at the beginning of the war, it was evacuated, and the buildings taken over by West Ham Fire Brigade as the Bridge Road ARP depot and ambulance station. On 'Black Saturday', 7 September, it received a direct hit from a bomb that killed thirteen firemen. The three-storey Marner Street Board School in Bow was hit and severely damaged, losing its roof, all its glass with two-thirds of it becoming unusable. In Rotherhithe, Redriff School suffered damage to all four floors. These first raids of September 1940 on London's East End caused the destruction of hundreds of homes. Several particularly devastating raids had hit the area around Canning Town, leaving hundreds of residents homeless. One bomb had landed in Martindale Road but had not detonated so people were told that they would be evacuated to safer parts. In the meantime, they were directed to gather outside South Hallsville School on neighbouring Agate Street to be ready for when the buses arrived. For some reason, the buses never did arrive, either because they could not penetrate the rubble-blocked streets, or because they had been misdirected. Some accounts report that people had spent three days waiting there. Whatever the reason for the non-arrival of the promised transport, by nightfall on 10 September, with another raid imminently expected, over 600 people had taken shelter in the school. Images of the bombed buildings suggest two concrete-framed buildings, one with two floors and the other with two floors and an attic storey like the nearby Hermit Road School. The two-storey building had a concrete roof, covered in asphalt to form a roof playground. With nowhere else to go, people went into the basement so that when the school received a direct hit from a parachute mine, the concrete structure collapsed on top of them, killing some outright and burying many more alive. There is a longstanding dispute over the number of deaths as there is no record of how many were in the school's basement to start with. The official report at the time recorded seventy-seven, roughly the number of bodies recovered to be buried in a mass grave. At the time, however, many survivors and local observers thought this to be a gross reduction of the true figure in order, either to cover up the administrative shortcomings of the evacuation authorities, or to avoid damaging the morale of those being so regularly bombed. When the queen visited the area on the fiftieth anniversary of the tragedy, the figure was stated to be as high as 740. General consensus appears to put the number of deaths at around 400. The matter is complicated by a number of factors: the site was tarmacked over, effectively converting it into a war grave for an unknown number of people; children had been evacuated leaving parents and siblings behind who became victims, themselves leaving unidentified children unclaimed at the war's end; and survivors spoke of families who were happy to disappear and to be counted as victims of the tragedy.

A week later, another school being used as an AFS sub-station (35U), Saunders Ness School on the Isle of Dogs, was hit by a parachute mine at 11 p.m., killing twenty-six people outright. These included a mobile first aid unit, which had only just arrived at the school. The four-storey, flat-roofed building collapsed trapping many underneath the rubble and it was three months before the final body was extricated. A few weeks later, yet another AFS sub-station (24Z), the Ricardo Street School in Poplar was hit on 1 November, burying a dozen firefighters, five of whom subsequently died from their injuries. Before the week was out on 6 November, the Cavendish Road School in Balham, AFS sub-station (86W), was hit and twelve male auxiliary firefighters and one female driver were killed. The school would not reopen until 1950, becoming the Henry Cavendish School in 1989. Two weeks on, and Invicta Road School in Siebert Road, lying between Greenwich Park and Charlton, was hit by a parachute mine. The school was AFS sub-station 54X, and it being a relatively quiet night, there were many personnel on site. Over twenty people were extricated alive from underneath the rubble, but fifteen people perished including twelve AFS firefighters and the school caretaker. Among the dead was a fireman who had courageously saved the school from destruction in an earlier attack and was in line for the George Medal. At least four bodies were apparently never recovered. Two neighbouring schools—Halstow Road and Charlton Central—were also bombed that night.

The Old Palace School in St Leonard's Street, Bow, was taken over for use as an AFS sub-station. On the night of 13 April 1941, the fire crews were assembling in the school playground at 1:30 a.m. to be given their deployments and duties. Just at that moment, a parachute mine came through the roof and tumbled down a stairwell. Two teenaged firewomen, one of them a telephonist, in the watch room were killed in the explosion and thirty-two firemen were killed by the blast or by being buried under the falling masonry. The two women and eleven of the firemen were from the London Fire Brigade and the other twenty-one had come in from Beckenham, on the outskirts of London, to help their beleaguered colleagues. Two of the Beckenham contingent were teenagers, one a motorcycle despatch rider, and the other, a messenger. On the same night, Mulgrave Place School in Woolwich was hit, killing a firewoman, a fire brigade section officer and a messenger. Grove Lane School in Denmark Hill, now Lyndhurst School and once an annexe of the military hospital which became the Maudsley, was used as AFS sub-station 48Z and was also bombed, as was Sayer Street School, formerly next to the Elephant & Castle railway station. In the City of London, the Cass Foundation School was severely damaged.

Sandhurst Road School had suffered damage on 7 September 1940 when a bomb hit an adjacent shed made of iron and timber, owned by the War Department and used as a store for the RAF. However, the school would suffer the worst attack of the war over two years later. On 20 January 1943, a German Focke-Wulf fighter-bomber, one of a flight of twenty-eight, dropped a single 500-kg (1,100-lb) bomb on the school. It was lunchtime and many of the children were gathered in the very spot where the bomb hit. Thirty-two children, between the ages of five and fifteen, and six teachers were killed at the scene, and a further six children died in Lewisham Hospital from their injuries. Witnesses reported observing the aircraft circling the school before selecting it as its target. A second aircraft strafed the playground and surrounding streets. The school was four storeys high and might have been mistaken for a factory, although the German pilot seemed to think he had hit a block of flats. According to an eyewitness, prior to bombing Sandhurst Road, the aircraft had attempted to bomb the neighbouring Downderry School but had hit an adjacent house instead. For some unresolved reason, there had been no warning from the sirens, so no steps had been taken to get the children into the shelters, and it was thought that there might have been a technical problem with the alarm mechanism. Civil Defence workers including a heavy rescue squad were quickly on the scene, but little could be done to save the worst hit victims. Beyond the forty-four dead, around sixty more were seriously injured but survived their injuries, although several lost limbs and spent up to eighteen months in hospital. Some went to East Grinstead for facial reconstruction and at least one has never completed a regime of ongoing surgery. Although it was thought that the German pilot who, it was reported, had waved at the children, was shot down after the raid, in reality he was only killed later that year. In the same raid, the playground of Evelyn Street School, Deptford, was shot up with a child killed and others injured.

Manchester and Salford

Just prior to Christmas 1940, the Greater Manchester area suffered two major devastating raids on successive nights in which nearly 300 tons of HE bombs and nearly 40,000 incendiaries were dropped on the first night, with a further 200 tons of HE and 7,000 incendiaries on the second. These killed nearly 700 people and severely injured over 2,300. Public shelters included the use of an abandoned canal tunnel opened in 1839 to link the River Irwell and the Rochdale Canal, designed to accommodate 1,350 people in sixteen bays separated by blast-walls. A further 1,600 people could shelter under the cathedral steps, and Piccadilly Gardens was surrounded by shelters for those caught on local transport during a raid. Manchester GS had long moved out of the city centre to its present site in Rusholme. One of its original buildings was destroyed in the bombing, as was the school's outdoor activity base, the Owls' Nest near Lyme Park, which had occupied a former army hut since 1920. In 1939, Manchester schools were evacuated northward to Horwich and out as far as Blackpool, Preston, and Fleetwood; into suburbs such as Altrincham or Cheadle; or to the more rural Glossop on the edge of the Pennines, but many children appear to have returned during the Phoney War. Burnage HS was evacuated to three towns in Staffordshire in September 1939, but most of the boys had drifted back home by Christmas. One night, soon after, the school was bombed and its hall with its newly installed organ was destroyed. By this time, shelters had been constructed at the school and, elsewhere in the city, two schools had been taken over as rest centres, and others damaged, though the censor prevented the press from identifying them.

Newcastle upon Tyne and the North-East

Owing to the presence of the extensive shipbuilding yards and Vickers-Armstrong's vital munitions plants, the city was a prime target for bombing raids and underwent sustained aerial assault from the summer of 1940 through to the end of 1941. On 1 September 1939, over 30,000 schoolchildren and 13,000 mothers with young children were evacuated from the city's schools into the small villages and towns of rural Northumberland and Cumbria. A further 4,300 children were evacuated in July 1940 following the first air raid on the city, which had taken place on 2 July. The Royal GS was evacuated to Penrith, only returning in October 1944. On 28–29 July 1940 some of the twenty-five HE bombs dropped in a straight line across the city hit the Heaton Secondary Girls' School, killing the caretaker's wife who was attempting to warn people of the danger and destroying the dining room and classrooms. The school was open for pupils who had returned home from evacuation in Whitehaven. Only after several months of repairs and the construction of shelters was the school able to reopen fully. A dozen more HE bombs fell on open land and in the grounds of the Heaton schools in September 1940. The next month saw errant barrage balloons in Elswick causing superficial damage to Rutherford College Girls' School. More serious were the raids in April 1941 which severely damaged Cambridge Street School and the senior department of Bell Terrace School, a rest and emergency feeding centre, as well as St Oswin's School in Tynemouth. One of a stick of six HE bombs landed in the playground of Rectory Park Infants' School in Sunderland but fortunately no children were hit. Chirton Council School on Billy Mill Lane, North Shields, was wrecked by a parachute mine on 16 April 1941. Schools which became rest centres for those whose homes had been destroyed included the Jubilee Schools in Union Road and North View Schools in Byker, St Dominic's School, and Sandyford Road School. A heavy raid on North Shields at the end of September 1941 wrecked the Holy Trinity School and destroyed five classrooms at the Queen Victoria Council School. Although the children were immediately transferred to the Western Board School, owing to the particularly protracted and bureaucratic procedures involved in getting a crown property repaired, it was a whole two years before they could return and, even then, it would be a further three years before the entire claim had been settled and work completed. However, on a happier note, despite all these setbacks, the city managed to open the brand-new Whickham View School, complete with its very own swimming pool, in May 1942. Its Art Deco buildings, completed in 1938, are Grade II listed and currently used by Newcastle College.

Many children were among the 400 people or so people killed in further raids over the eighteen months of raids, and in one incident, 107 people, including forty-two children, died when a bomb hit their shelter in a factory basement in North Shields. By the end of the war, almost 300 air raids had been carried out against targets in the Northern Civil Defence Region centred on Newcastle which included Gateshead, Durham, Sunderland, and Teesside.

Nottingham

Despite the presence of the extensive Chilwell munitions depot, the ROF in Kings Meadows, Rover's shadow factory, and numerous other plants engaged in war production, Nottingham sustained only one serious raid, in May 1941, but there were ten others that caused fewer casualties and less damage. The city was well prepared with an efficient ARP organisation and adequate shelter provision, which included caverns under the castle. Several schools were requisitioned including Ronald Street and Wells Street Schools as first aid posts. Station Road Schools in Beeston, along with other schools, was prepared as an emergency communal feeding centre and the list of Nottingham's seventy-one designated rest centres, detailed in the city's comprehensive handbook of 1942, contains the addresses of twenty-seven schools. Mercifully, much of this provision proved unnecessary, although those raids that did occur caused nearly 200 deaths and widespread damage to property and infrastructure.

Plymouth

With its naval base and dockyard, Plymouth and Devonport offered prime targets for the bombers and was one of the top four most heavily bombed towns, undergoing fifty-nine serious raids and suffering nearly 1,200 civilian deaths. All schools closed for three weeks on 1 September 1939 to cope with the arrival of hundreds of London children *en route* to their allocated reception centres in Cornwall. The first bombs fell on 6 July 1940 but some 6,600 HE and 200,000 incendiary bombs were dropped over a period of two months in the spring of 1941. Almost all the town's public buildings, including twenty-six schools, were totally destroyed with raids continuing into May 1944. In one raid in March 1941, the maternity ward at the City Hospital was hit, killing three teenaged nurses and nineteen babies and young children along with teenaged new mothers. One eleven-year-old girl, one of only three survivors, was pulled alive from the rubble but had lost four members of her family among the seventy-six people who were killed when a shelter received a direct hit in April 1941. Boys from Hyde Park County Secondary School were moved to Montpelier School, attending on a split-shift arrangement and Johnston Terrace School was completely destroyed. Devonport High School for Girls received a direct hit from a parachute mine, the site of whose crater still being marked by variations of ground level in the tennis and netball courts added in 1952. The pupils were evacuated to Tiverton and the remaining school buildings then housed firefighters and a dockyard machine shop. With a steady increase in the volume and frequency of air raids, the town's population halved as so many residents left and most of the children were evacuated, beginning on 3 May 1941, with 2,000 leaving for billets in rural Devon and small towns in Cornwall. On some nights, up to 50,000 of those people remaining in the town would trek out to the safety of Dartmoor to avoid the constant raids. In March 1942, Leslie Stephens, by then in army uniform, became, albeit belatedly, the youngest recipient of the BEM for outstanding service as an ARP messenger, receiving his medal from King George VI at an investiture at Buckingham Palace.

Portsmouth and Gosport

Portsmouth suffered three major raids among the sixty-seven that hit the town between July 1940 and May 1944, with 930 civilian deaths. In one of the earliest raids in August 1940, a theatre was hit during a matinee performance and eight children were killed. On one night in January 1941, 350 tons of HE bombs and 25,000 incendiaries were dropped and hundreds of houses and eight schools were destroyed. Trinity Church Boys' School in Gosport's South Street was one of those wrecked in 1941, and most schools were evacuated wholesale, Portsmouth GS going first to Winchester and then on to Bournemouth where boarders occupied three houses and three further houses were used for teaching, and Hilsea School went to Leigh Park at Havant. However, some schools remained open and former pupils have recollections of crouching under their desks during air raids. A direct hit on a shelter at Arundel Street School killed forty-seven people and injured a further 430. Raids specifically targeting the naval installations were responsible for the shifting of whole departments out of town, some of them to schools such as Roedean, Lancing, Eastbourne College and King Edward's School, Witley (see Chapter 2).

Sheffield

The city suffered its heaviest raids on 12, 13, and 15 December 1940 when nearly 700 people were killed and 1,500 seriously injured. Out of the city's 154 schools, 106 of them, including Attercliffe Council School, Phillimore Road, and Duchess Road Schools, were damaged, and eight of them were destroyed. Cumulatively, according to the Department for Education's own estimate, this effectively took 15,000 school places out of use. At least one school, Pye Bank, was used by a Civil Defence ambulance unit, another on London Road served as an AFS station, and many were designated as rest centres. Schools also provided the necessary premises for the war emergency voluntary hospitals co-ordinated by the city's pre-NHS unified health service—Westfield Health.

Southampton

During November 1940, Southampton was heavily bombed, with the Supermarine factory at Wolston (manufacturing Spitfires), the General Motors plant, and the docks (which handled much of the nation's military traffic) being the main targets. However, as well as the aircraft factory being destroyed, it was the newly opened civic centre that bore the brunt. A 250-kg (550-lb) bomb penetrated down to the art gallery on the lower floors where a party of schoolchildren were having a lesson in the basement, killing fifteen of them along with twenty-one other staff and visitors. In some fifty-seven raids, over 600 people were killed and a further 900 seriously injured.

As well as these major cities, smaller towns were hit with large loss of life and accompanying damage to property. Five such targets are singled out below, along with accounts of the raids on the cathedral cities, and other related incidents.

Dover

The town of Dover was under constant bombardment throughout the war both from aircraft only a few minutes' flying time across the Channel and, following its occupation in mid-1940, from the batteries of heavy guns that operated from the Pas de Calais. Batterie Todt and the Batterie Grosser Kurfurst on Cap Griz Nez, Batterie Lindemann, now under the Channel Tunnel access, and Batterie Friedrich August at Wimille, between them fielded thirteen guns from 280-mm (11-inch) to 406-mm (16-inch), plus a further nine 280-mm (11-inch) railway guns. Over 250 people were killed in Dover over the four-year assault, with nearly 500 houses destroyed and many more damaged. A total of 2,226 shells, 464 bombs, and three parachute mines hit the town, and there were over 3,000 alerts. Dover College, the Duke of York's School, and Dover County School for Boys were all hit by bombs or shells. The Duke of York's Royal Military School was subjected to a low-flying cannon attack that caused a great deal of damage but caused no casualties among the troops billeted there. Dover College, housing HMS *Lynx*, was regularly both shelled and bombed.

PETWORTH

At mid-morning on 29 September 1942, a lone German aircraft is presumed to have been attempting to bomb troops camped in the grounds of Petworth House in West Sussex. There were eighty boys present in Petworth Boys' School that day, and it was there, during playtime, that three bombs landed without warning. Twenty-eight boys, the headmaster, and a female assistant teacher were killed along with a female worker in the adjacent laundry. The ARP action officer's minute book records a succession of requests for rescue parties, doctors, a mobile first aid post, and ambulances to attend. Up to forty seriously injured boys and residents from neighbouring houses were treated at the Red Cross centre and the first aid centre at the Cottage Hospital prior to being taken to hospital in nearby Chichester. By mid-afternoon, there remained sixteen unaccounted for as the rescue workers and Canadian soldiers tried to shift the rubble that had trapped so many. A WVS canteen was requested for the rescue workers who continued searching overnight.

The aircraft that bombed the school was one of three Ju 88s that were carrying out nuisance raids over southern England that morning. One eyewitness was under the impression that the aircraft was being fired on from the ground. Another stated that it was being pursued by a Beaufighter. Both felt that the pilot had jettisoned his bombs to make his getaway. The inference to be drawn from that would be that the deaths were accidental.

Canadian soldiers of the Toronto Scottish Regiment and the 7th Anti-Tank Regiment were present in the grounds of Petworth House, where three tented camps had been set up to accommodate almost 4,000 troops, so would have represented a legitimate target. However, another theory suggests that Petworth House was specifically targeted in order to disrupt an important conference or planning meeting.

RUSHDEN

At the beginning of October 1940, the Alfred Street School in Rushden in Northamptonshire received a direct hit from one of eighteen HE bombs, which were dropped in a line across the town by a lone, low-flying German aircraft. Four adults and six children aged seven and eight were killed, but fourteen survivors were dragged from the ruins, several of whom had received life-changing injuries, still being reported by the local press five years on. Three of the children killed were evacuees from Canterbury Road School in Colchester. A second bomb had landed in the playground damaging shelters and walls. As so much of the school was unusable, the school shut for ten days and some classes were relocated to St Peter's Sunday School and Mission, the Scout Room, and the Adult School. Later the next month, fourteen of the Colchester children, along with two of their teachers, had to be transferred from the Newton Road School when it, too, was forced to close temporarily while air-raid damage was repaired.

Ashford

Within two months of the attack on Sandhurst Road School in Catford, the same unit struck again, this time at Ashford in Kent. On 24 March 1943, flying in at rooftop height in a carbon copy of the Catford attack, the aircraft hit several sites in the town, killing fifty people and seriously injuring nearly eighty more. One bomb landed on the junior department of the Victoria Road PS, destroyed two classrooms completely and severely damaged other areas of the school. Fortunately, unlike at Catford, warnings had been sounded and the children had all reached the nearby shelters safely, eighty of the girls having barely vacated in time the two classrooms, which were soon to be wrecked. In the same raid, Beaver Road Boys' Junior School was destroyed but, amazingly, there were no casualties among pupils or staff at either school.

Sherborne

The town of Sherborne, lying on the borders of Somerset and Dorset, lies where the A30 trunk road from London to the West Country crosses an important north–south link down to Weymouth, as well as the railway line linking Salisbury and Exeter. The town was therefore a nodal point in the anti-invasion defences with a garrison based in the town and using the Boys' School's facilities, and its own Home Guard unit, the 4th Battalion, Dorset HG. A force of 150 German bombers attacked the town on 30 September 1940, destroying houses and an infants' school, causing eighteen deaths and numerous serious injuries. Bombs fell on the Boys' School's playing fields and among the buildings. Windows, including one of stained-glass, were shattered; 20,000 tiles were dislodged and roofs lifted; and serious damage was caused to the museum, science laboratories, art school, and other teaching spaces. Bombs fell in the school's courtyards and in the surrounding roads, leaving large craters. The Girls' School's sanatorium received a direct hit, and it would be a few weeks before the final unexploded bombs were tracked and dealt with. Fortunately, the shelters, so diligently organised, proved effective. At least one bomb detonated near the armoury and the roof of the OTC rifle range was damaged. The cost of interim repairs came to a total of £1,277 (£63,850).

The Baedeker and other Bombing Campaigns

The bombing raids of 1942 on Exeter, Canterbury, Norwich, Bath, and York were consciously designed to cause maximum destruction to England's cultural treasures as described in the Baedeker tourist guidebooks. In Bath, St Peters School in Dorset Street took a direct hit; severe damage was caused to Twerton School; and a bomb fell in the grounds of Kingswood School, at the time in use by the Admiralty. In Exeter, in a raid on 4 May 1942, much of St Sidwell's primary school was destroyed and lessons were switched to neighbouring schools. Part of the school was saved when teachers living nearby managed to pick up and neutralise some of the 10,000 incendiaries that fell on the city. Blast from the 75 tons of bombs which fell that night blew the roof off Ladysmith School. Hele's GS was requisitioned as an emergency feeding centre for the hundreds of homeless, and as an information centre posting news of casualties and damage. Over 150 people were killed that night and nearly four times as many seriously injured. Canterbury suffered over thirty air raids throughout the war but the heaviest was in June 1942 when thirty German aircraft dropped bombs and incendiaries causing widespread damage and loss of life. The number of deaths has been reported as between thirty-three and fifty-five. In the June raid, the Simon Langton School, which was acting as a clearing house for evacuees, was damaged by bombs, as was King's School in the cathedral precincts, but four other schools in the city were totally destroyed. In York, Poppleton Road JS received a direct hit in the biggest raid in April 1942 which claimed twenty-three lives in the area that night. Other deaths occurred in the houses next to Shipton Street School, and St Peter's School was damaged. The Manor Higher Grade School was deemed to be beyond repair and the Queen Anne Secondary School lost all of its widows and ceilings when a stick of five HE bombs fell on the school field destroying the fortunately unoccupied, air-raid shelters. In all, 115 people died in York including thirteen children under twelve, and four teenagers. In a further raid in September 1942, the tenth sustained by the city, incendiaries dropped on the Blue Coat School were dealt with by the Master and senior pupils. Norwich endured four raids in the spring of 1942. The brick and flint-built grammar school in the Cathedral Close was hit by thirty-six incendiaries. Unusually, it proved fortunate that the school was not on holiday as it meant that the headmaster and senior boys were on hand to use stirrup pumps and sand to extinguish the many fires that started in the ancient wooden roof.

Apart from enemy action, there were further dangers associated with flying accidents. One such accident resulted in one of the worst incidents in the war, involving children's deaths. In August 1944, a refurbished B-24H Liberator bomber, one of a pair being delivered to the USAAF's 2nd Combat Division from Warton Air Base Depot in Lancashire, was attempting to land, having been recalled due to the approach of a particularly savage storm. Arriving back at the very height of the storm, the pilot attempted unsuccessfully to abort the landing. The aircraft ploughed into the village of Freckleton and one wing hit the infants' department of Holy Trinity School. Being full of fuel, it immediately exploded, killing thirty-eight children and two teachers. The crew of three died in the crash as did eighteen other servicemen and civilians on the ground in adjacent parts of the village. In other, fortunately less disastrous incidents, a Blenheim came down on Tonbridge School with resultant damage to buildings caused not only by the impact but also from the explosion of its bombload, and in January 1944, a Wellington bomber of the RAFVR on a training flight from RAF Worksop crashed at night in the grounds of Worksop College, killing the crew of five.

The V-1 attacks

The first V-1 'Doodlebug' of the 2,500 to fall on London fell in Bethnal Green in June 1944. As the campaign intensified, a junior school in Croydon, soon to become London's worst hit borough, was struck, but the children were ensconced safely in the school's shelters. On 19 July 1944, a V-1 hit Woods Road School in Peckham, killing twenty-four people in an adjoining row of houses in Harders Road Mews. Fortuitously, the pupils were sheltering at the far end of the building and the only injury was to a teacher cut by flying glass. The main aiming point for the V-weapon launches was thought to be North Dulwich railway station, so its surrounding area and the neighbouring Borough of Croydon received a disproportionate number of strikes, with 144 V-1s landing in Croydon alone, and a further eighty-five in the neighbouring Boroughs of Lambeth and Southwark. On 10 July, a V-1 hit Dulwich College causing severe damage to its south wing which contained science laboratories and the OTC's rifle range. It happened in the late evening and caused just three casualties but not until 1960 was this part of the school rebuilt. Under a fortnight later, the College's Picture Gallery was hit by another V-1 at 2 a.m. The majority of the paintings had been removed to safety but any left behind were destroyed. Dulwich College Preparatory School had been evacuated in the first weeks of the war to Cranbrook, but by June 1940, it was decided to go further away and a hotel in Betws-y-Coed was chosen, where the younger pupils stayed until the end of the war. The college itself had been evacuated to Tonbridge School early in September 1939, but the project was not judged a success and it had returned to Dulwich by the end of the year and remained open there throughout the war.

In north London, Canonbury School near Highbury Corner was used as a rest centre with first aid facilities and permanent medical and welfare staff on site. Although houses to the north were destroyed by a V-1 at lunchtime on 27 June 1944, the school itself survived but two teachers from neighbouring Laycock Street School were among the twenty-six fatalities. Local children, caught between the shelter of school or home, were among the eighty-four people seriously injured, or the seventy-one less so. Whittington School on Highgate Hill also escaped being bombed but functioned as a rest centre for local residents who had been bombed out. A quarter of all the V-1s fell on London, but other places also suffered grievously. A V-1, one of the 880 that fell in the county, landed just 25 yards from Tidebrook School in Marks Cross in Sussex. Fortunately, the pupils were out of school, but the buildings were wrecked, never to be rebuilt. Around a further 300 V-1s landed in Surrey: the residential school in Shirley was hit twice; the Lady Edridge Girls' High School had a near miss; and one landed in the grounds of Whitgift Middle School. Although the children had had time to reach the shelters and escaped harm, St John's School in Shirley was destroyed completely in July 1944, its pupils forced to transfer to another school. The heavily targeted Borough of Croydon once more closed its schools, using them to store salvaged furniture from bombed houses. Streatham Hill and Clapham HS for Girls, in Wavertree

Road, was hit, fortunately during the school holidays; it was so badly damaged that it was forced to operate on four separate sites. Only in 1949 could a programme of rebuilding commence, leading to an eventual reopening in 1952. St Clement Danes GS, Hammersmith, was one of those schools that opted to evacuate most of its staff and pupils, in their case, to Oxford, but to retain a working presence in London. During the late summer of 1944 as the Doodlebugs were arriving, rooftop spotters were posted. Their frequent warnings culminated one lunchtime when a V-1 skimmed the roof of the school and landed on the field, destroying the sports pavilion. The hall, functioning as a communal dining area, had been full of pupils, staff, and neighbours, all of whom were shaken by their narrow escape. Highgate School had returned from evacuation to Westward Ho! in Devon in 1943 to reclaim its buildings from the Admiralty. It, too, had a narrow escape when a V-1 landed on its school field the next summer. Brockley Road Elementary School (now Beecroft), hit by a Doodlebug in 1944, was one of sixteen LCC schools that had to be entirely demolished and rebuilt after the war, not to reopen until 1951.

Kent suffered particularly badly from V-1 attacks, with 1,444 making landings and a further 1,000 destroyed over the sea. Primary schools appointed Doodlebug monitors, equipped with steel helmets, to look out for the 'divers'. The county's worst V-1 disaster occurred in June near Edenbridge. The LCC was using a house at Crockham Hill as a nursery for evacuated children but an incendiary attack forced a move to Weald House, a neighbouring property. This was hit by a V-1, causing the death of twenty-two infants under three years old and their eight female carers. The various accounts all differ over the numbers resident in the house and of the victims, but it is likely that only two infants survived. Although it has been suggested, somewhat implausibly, that the V-1 had been aimed at Churchill's country residence, Chartwell, less than a mile away, it had been disabled by AA fire, which deflected it from its intended target in the London area. Instead of crashing harmlessly in the fields as so many did, it caused no less of a tragedy than had it reached its intended destination.

The V-2 attacks

On 11 September, nearly four months after D-Day and when least expected, a new terror was unleashed on Britain. A V-2 rocket landed on Magdalen Laver, near Harlow, damaging buildings including the village school. The next day, one landed on a school field in Dagenham, and the school at Rockland St Mary near Norwich had a near-miss on 4 October. Many of the rockets fortunately fell in open country, but when they did impact built-up areas, they caused significant numbers of casualties. On 16 November, one of the nine V-2 strikes to hit the borough claimed a direct hit on an Islington school in Maryville Road, killing seven people and severely injuring thirteen more. This was just one of the ten schools in the borough damaged in V-2 strikes. On 12 December, Morden Terrace School in Greenwich was struck by a V-2 that killed a sixteen-year-old girl and seriously injured two others. Wallington County (Boys') GS, only opened on that site in 1935, was severely damaged by a V-2 impact that blew out all the windows and collapsed the roof, but the school managed to remain open while repairs were carried out. The City of London Freemen's School in Leatherhead escaped with a near miss in February 1945, as did the Royal Liberty GS in Gidea Park, but Tottenham GS, a few weeks later, suffered a more deadly near miss one lunchtime, which killed two boys outside the school and severely injured a third. Had it hit the school dining room, there would have been carnage. Other targets were not so lucky. At 4:06 p.m. on 4 January 1945, as children from Holy Trinity School were going to change their library books at Dalston Library, the building received a direct hit that entirely obliterated it and caused the deaths of fifteen people, mainly primary school pupils and seriously injured a further twenty-seven. Four days later, a school in Lewisham suffered severe damage from the blast of a rocket that fell in its grounds. On Valentine's Day 1945, a V-2 landed in the school playground of what is now Brook Community School in Sigdon Road, Hackney, causing damage to the school building and demolishing houses. In one of the last strikes of the war, in March 1945, a ten-year-old schoolgirl in Sidcup described the injuries caused to her friends and 'a titch in the infants' when a V-2 rocket landed near her school and the playground quickly filled with police officers, workmen and a nun administering first aid to injured children.

5

The Contributions of Young People to the Home Front

It is important always to keep in mind the fact that approaching 80 per cent of fourteen- to seventeen-year-olds were in employment, and many of them were doing jobs that were greatly benefiting the nation. Beyond training for service in the armed forces, however, or producing munitions, there were many ways in which children and young people could contribute to the war effort. They could provide their labour and trained expertise; produce comforts for service personnel; raise money or recycled materials for war production; or simply carry out activities which raised public morale. As the war dragged on, most youngsters realised that they would be moving on from their current efforts and began to think about the future. Even in the earliest days of the war, some of the older Girl Guides on the movement's HQ staff joined the First Aid Nursing Yeomanry (FANY), a catch-all organisation that provided everyone from staff car and ambulance drivers to radio operators and secret agents. By the end of 1941, the government was planning to enforce youngsters' membership of pre-service organisations by introducing a National Registration Scheme for the sixteen to eighteen age group, trusting that such encouragement would suffice to avoid the imposition of compulsion.

On 2 September 1939, the bill to initiate the call-up to the armed services of all eligible men in the eighteen to forty-one age group, had been presented to a parliament that had enjoyed no prior sight of it. This bill used the provisions of the earlier Military Training Act of April 1939, which had introduced compulsory military training for eligible twenty to twenty-two-year-olds in the reformed Militia but would now add service overseas to the commitment. An attempt was made to encourage, but not require, employers to undertake to reinstate workers in their civilian employment once released from military service. Some members would have preferred conscription to remain at age twenty, based on their experience in the Great War, arguing that untrained eighteen-year-olds were limited in their contribution to the fighting, and that many, even were they to survive physically whole, might be irreparably damaged psychologically by the experience. Speakers felt that young men, who were not as yet citizens, should not be called up before they reached their majority at twenty-one years of age. However, the bill was passed by 340 votes to seven, allowing the government the latitude to decide which cohorts to call up and when. In a subsequent debate, the secretary of state for war undertook to defer the call-up of the eighteen to twenty age group in the hope that it would never become necessary for the country to call on boys of that age. The house settled for the secretary of state's assurance that boys under twenty, in the unlikely event of their being called-up, would not be sent abroad without reference to the house. The clincher to this compromise was the argument that if backs were up against the wall, then all hands were needed to man the pumps, and even the youngest of shoulders must be put to the wheel. In the event, by early 1942 when the country's fortunes were at their lowest ebb, all eighteen-year-olds became liable for conscription, and the undertaking not to send young men under twenty years of age overseas had been rescinded when Churchill expressly requested it in a debate in December 1941, describing the rule as a 'restrictive pledge'. As noted in *Hansard*, December 1941, Column 1031, Churchill argued that in the event of army units being sent abroad at short notice, it would be wrong 'to pull perfectly fit young men of 19 and upwards out of their sections and platoons, and they themselves would be very much offended if they were to be so treated and if they had to see all their comrades going away while they were left, as if they were unfit, on the shore'.

Churchill went on to further justify his argument by pointing out that boys of seventeen, shortly to be lowered to sixteen ('like powder monkeys in Nelson's day'), were serving in the Home Guard, and could find themselves carrying out some of the duties in anti-aircraft and coast defence batteries hitherto performed by regular troops. He also intimated that while the government already had the power to direct young women of eighteen and over into industry, he would shortly be seeking powers to direct them into the auxiliary armed forces as well.

Young People in Industry

The official school-leaving age in 1939 was fourteen and the working week for under-sixteens was fixed in 1937 at forty-four hours, but by 1942, the demands of war production were putting pressure on the Minister of Labour to permit alterations to these regulations. Held in March 1942, parliamentary debates in both houses highlighted problems in respect of youngsters working in, particularly, the manufacturing industries. Responding to a proposal that children should be released to industry immediately on reaching the age of fourteen, R. A. Butler, president of the Board of Education, replied that there was no intention to change the law to allow instant departure from education, suggesting such a change 'would not be in the best interests of education' as noted in *Hansard*, Volume 378, Column

1655. A pointed comment to Butler from John Dugdale MP asked: 'Would the right hon. Gentleman make it clear that we intend to win this war without child labour?'

Questions to Ernest Bevin, Minister of Labour, concerned his approval of an increase in working hours in, specifically, the cotton spinning and pottery industries. Bevin explained that: 'It is extremely difficult to work the differences of hours between 16 and under 16, and sooner or later in subsequent legislation it will have to be straightened out'. Pressed on the question of medical examinations for youngsters being required to work such long hours, he declined to offer a reply, but reiterated his inability to exclude those under sixteen from orders affecting everyone else.

These discussions were taking place in the context of a National Registration Scheme for sixteen- to eighteen-year-olds, designed to facilitate their directed entry into formal youth organisations such as the ACF, SCC, or ATC in preparation for their conscription into the armed forces. However, MPs and local authority officials had begun to voice concerns that long hours worked in the factory or on the land and attendance at compulsory parades for pre-service training might well conflict. Following the publicity attached to such a statement from the chair of a local education committee to the effect that many seventeen-year-olds in Huddersfield could not be recommended for pre-military service training in cadet units as they were already working long hours, a debate in the House of Commons ensued, reported in *Hansard* (19 March 1942, Volume 378, Columns 1746–72). Kenneth Lindsay, MP for Kilmarnock, shared with the house worrying data, which were emerging from the Ministry of Labour's National Registration of sixteen- to eighteen-year-olds. Youngsters in the fourteen to sixteen age group, Lindsay reported, originally working a forty-four-hour week, which had already been extended to forty-eight hours in the spinning industry, were seeing their hours creeping up to fifty-two hours a week in the cotton and fifty-three in the pottery industries; in the sixteen to eighteen age group, hours worked were subject to similar creep, from the base of a forty-eight-hour week to anything from fifty-four to seventy-five hours a week. He went on:

> I have got to be persuaded … that these steps are vital to the war effort and are not resulting in physical and mental disability, and I have got to be persuaded that it is not gravely affecting the future physique of these boys.

He then went on to make the point that the effects of working four or five consecutive ten-hour working days were exacerbated by long journeys to work and that boys as young as fourteen might, in effect, leave home at 7 a.m. and arrive back home at 8 p.m., with consequent deleterious effects on their physical and social development. He added his further concerns about absenteeism from school, and the weakening of apprenticeship structures. He then cited cases of boys being directed to youth organisations such as the ATC but being unable to sustain a commitment owing to the length of the working day; of boys having to give up attendance at evening classes, a condition of their apprenticeship, for the same reason; and of boys dropping out of a secondary education with little expectation of its resumption. He also expressed surprise that Bevin had suggested that a concern for young workers' welfare had been one of the underlying reasons for carrying out the registration exercise in the first place since nowhere was this aspiration explicitly expressed, nor was any attempt made in the process to elicit young workers' opinions on the matter. The debate then moved into matters relating to funfairs and truancy and then, more importantly, to questions regarding the true value that accrued from the employment of the under-sixteens when much of their time appeared to be spent in passing tools to the skilled labourers and making their tea. The general feeling in the house seemed to be that youngsters could better benefit the country by engaging in activities which got them out into the fresh air, improved their health and fitness, and satisfied their need, genuinely, to be helping their country win the war.

Another member, representing a London constituency, next drew attention to the problem of fourteen- and fifteen-year-olds employed in non-essential work, such as hotels and public houses, working up to fourteen hours a day. He suggested that parents had little choice but to acquiesce with this situation as families whose main breadwinners were in the forces, were in desperate need of the income these jobs brought in:

> [But I am] convinced, as I think everybody who has had experience of young people is convinced, that this is most detrimental to their health, their physique, and still more, to what may conveniently be called their psychological and mental outlook. It is stultifying to those children at the present time, and it is having a disastrous effect upon them.
>
> *Hansard*, Volume 378, Column 1757

He then moved on to highlight a situation which was affected by social class, proposing:

> [It would be] disastrous for the future interests of this country that you should have one class of children who are being in some cases exploited, and at any rate, in a great number of cases, worked until they drop, and another class of children who are not liable to those war penalties and consequences, and who grow up in a comparatively sheltered condition till the time when they have to join the Services, whereas their brothers and sisters—mainly their brothers—are exposed to this very onerous tax upon their intelligence and their constitution.

In 1945, the same MP was still asking questions in parliament about legislation restricting the employment of those in the under-sixteens and under-eighteens age groups after 7 p.m. or even all night. It was very clear how important the use of juvenile labour had become in the context of the nation's workforce. The total number of persons employed in the munitions industry in 1939 was a little over 1.25 million. By the end of 1944, this figure had risen to almost 3 million, while at the same time, nearly a million people were employed one way or another in ARP and around 5 million were in uniform.

Memoirs from the period, many of them to be found on the enthralling BBC's WW2 People's War website, describe the circumstances in vivid detail. Terence Crowley returned to Brighton from his evacuation billet in a rural Yorkshire backwater, as a shop lad aged fourteen and a half years in the Southern Railway Locomotive Works building locos and tanks. He worked a forty-eight-hour week including Saturday mornings, fetching and carrying, for 14*s* 2*d* per week (£35.40p). By the time he was sixteen and a locomotive fitter apprentice, he was working a six-day week and attending night school on three evenings a week and his pay had risen to £1.10*s* (£75). In County Durham, Harold Stoves, aged fourteen, became a weighman/ticketer at the Brancepeth Colliery, working 6 a.m. to 2 p.m., five and a half days a week for 12*s* (£30). Despite the dangers of dodging moving coal trucks in the blackout, he survived. One Manchester lad was a messenger in the 1941 Blitz and then, having attained the age of fourteen, went to work in a factory producing diesel engines for generators. He worked a fifty-hour week for 12*s* 6*d* (62.5p or £31.25p). A year later, still only fifteen, he was regularly working night shifts, and another year on, had not yet managed to earn £1 (£50) per week. Jack Coats from Beverley described life as a fourteen-year-old in a small shipyard building light craft for the Royal Navy. Lacking powered cranes, windlasses were all worked by hand, demanding physical strength and stamina. Moreover, apart from masks for the welders and goggles for those working with oxy-acetylene, there was no protective clothing and nowhere to run to in an air raid. Some industries did make changes to accommodate workers' living patterns such as the need for working women to manage family life. The glass industry abolished night shifts but only to enable employees to fulfil their civil defence responsibilities by being available for ARP work or general fire-watching duties.

In 1943, the Public Morality Council (PMC) raised the matter of fourteen- and fifteen-year-old girls being attracted into working for firms manufacturing, testing, and packing contraceptives. What is more, they were being paid £2.5*s* (£2.25p or £112.50p) per week at a time when adult women munitions workers earned £2.16*s* (£2.80p or £140), and Marie Stopes's free clinics were refused supplies while the commercial market operated freely. On the grounds that the girls chose to do this work under no coercion the government refused the PMC's petition to set a minimum age for this work.

Munitions Work

Dozens of Royal Ordnance Factories (ROF) were in operation during the war producing weapons and explosives. Each ROF specialised in a particular activity such as manufacturing rifles, artillery, or tanks; filling shells and bombs; or processing the raw materials that would go into them. Nearly a million women were recruited to work in them, carrying out dangerous tasks in largely unsafe environments. Many died as a result of accidents or from exposure to dangerous substances and materials. Barrier cream provided some protection, but it was quite common for girls' hair to turn strange shades and some of the workers in these plants were young boys and girls of fourteen carrying out tasks ostensibly outside the plant's obvious danger areas. One fifteen-year-old, working in a café in Pontypool, was recruited to serve refreshments to the construction workers building ROF Glascoed. After the plant was up and running, she worked in the new canteen for two years before moving onto the production line in the TNT section, ensuring that all the workers received their glass of milk, drunk as a protection against the toxic substance. She was trained as a member of the air-raid squad, responsible for getting everyone into the shelters and on one occasion, her charges were machine-gunned by an enemy aircraft as she hurried them to safety. Fortunately, no one was hit, and the three landmines dropped all failed to explode, the result, it was understood at the time, of sabotage by those forced to work in the German munitions plants. Following this incident, she was promoted to manage the factory's bakery. At ROF Swynnerton, girls of fifteen were employed in the wages office, not being officially allowed to work with explosives until they were eighteen.

Many other youngsters worked in factories that had switched their production from meeting peacetime needs to munitions. As they were not working directly with explosives, there were no age limitations and they often found themselves facing dangerous working conditions. In Lancashire, while many of the cotton mills met the increasing need for military uniforms and materials such as webbing, others turned to novel production. Many of those working in mills producing gas masks would, over a long period of time, come to develop mesothelioma through exposure to asbestos. The management had recognised the potential danger and forbade workers from taking anything out of the mill for fear of contamination, but this hardly satisfied their need for effective protection. A fourteen-year-old boy, working in a mill producing tentage, described how the wax treatment was so toxic that workers were only allowed in contact with it for half the day as it affected their eyes and caused nosebleeds. Some Lancashire mills utilised the height of their ceilings to suspend large nets and children of twelve and thirteen volunteered to spend their Saturday mornings, on high ladders, threading strips of scrim to assemble camouflage netting.

As well as the dangers of machinery or materials, long hours took their toll on young bodies. One fifteen-year-old worked at Gillette's razor blade factory on the Great West Road in west London, a half-hour cycle ride away from home. Her job as a machine operator entailed making parts for aircraft and she worked an eleven-hour shift, five days a week, plus five hours on a Saturday morning. The night shift which came up every two weeks was thirteen hours. An eighteen-year-old woman working in a factory building Spitfire fighter aircraft recalls working a shift on a Friday starting at 7 a.m., having an hour's break at 6 p.m., and then working straight through until 7 a.m. on the Saturday morning. In the same Castle Bromwich factory, a fourteen-year-old school leaver started in the accounts section working nine to five and earning 10*s* (50p or £25) a week, eventually rising to £5 (£250). Towards the end of the war, women munitions workers could earn £7 (£350) per week, while their male colleagues, often doing the same job, were paid £10 (£500). Alongside the repetitive drudgery of many youngsters' jobs, there were real opportunities for others, and some ended up doing highly challenging or even secret work. Introduced to his father's employers on the strength of some intricate ship models he had made, Geoffrey Pidgeon was offered a job. This turned out to be in the wireless workshops of the Special Communications Unit, the branch of SIS/MI6 that handled the ULTRA material from Bletchley Park. He noted that there were lads as young as fourteen working there and attending day release and night school at Wolverton Technical College. At seventeen and a half, he was put into uniform, ostensibly as a member of the Royal Corps of Signals, despite the fact that Section VIII staff were not paid out of army funds. Also working in the W/T area, Dennis Faulkner, on leaving school in 1942 aged sixteen, went to work at the Gloucester Railway Carriage and Wagon Works, as an unindentured apprentice, fitting No. 19 radio sets into Churchill tanks and field testing them with their army drivers. On the strength of a recommendation by a school friend, he was then accepted for a job with the BBC as a 'Youth-in-Training', at their Chosen Hill transmitting station at Churchdown near Gloucester. This involved monitoring equipment; liaising with a Home Guard unit guarding the transmitter and adjacent reservoirs; and carrying out maintenance tasks, all while serving in the AFS, running a Scout troop and studying for BBC and engineering technology qualifications. Still only seventeen, he was promoted and transferred to Cardiff.

Work in the Coal Mines: The Bevin Boys

These youngsters, named for Ernest Bevin, the Minister of Labour, represented 10 per cent of male conscripts aged eighteen to twenty-four. From December 1943, some 48,000 boys in all were selected by ballot to work in the coal mines in a scheme which ran until 1948. Some lads attempted to pre-empt being conscripted into the mines by volunteering early for the services as, once singled out for the mines, it was impossible to opt for alternatives. Service in the cadets was no protection and many who had joined the ATC in the expectation of joining the RAF found themselves in the mines. Bevin needed a constant workforce of 720,000 miners to keep, primarily, the shipbuilding and munitions industries supplied with their major source of energy. Numbers in the mines had fallen, as although mining was regarded as a reserved occupation, it had been impossible early in the war to prevent many miners volunteering, being conscripted or taking other safer and better paid jobs in the munitions industries. By 1943, when the country's coal reserves had fallen to only a few weeks' supply, the labour shortfall was 36,000, or 5 per cent of the optimum workforce. Given the constant erosion of the workforce through serious long-term illness, disability, enforced retirement, and death in service, there being no continuous replenishment, numbers continued to fall. It has been claimed, reportedly in a piece in the *Daily Express* no less, that a third of all boys starting their working lives as miners would suffer a serious accident or even death in their first year. It was certainly more dangerous than most armed service roles and it comes as no surprise, then, that even the offer of a guaranteed minimum wage failed to attract returners, and the number of 'optants' who favoured work in the mines over joining up in the armed forces, was small. Bevin therefore had little choice but to impose enforced recruitment, starting by compulsorily redeploying 10 per cent of apprentices to the mines. On Tyneside and elsewhere, this policy provoked industrial action among those holding existing apprenticeships (see below). In the event, whether or not as a result of the depth of feeling among the apprentices, it is claimed that no established apprentices were ever conscripted into the mines.

Those Boys who were conscripted received six weeks' training that, from the evidence of a former Boy who, fifty years on, had retained his training notes, could be extremely comprehensive. Classroom days alternated with days in the training pit. Then the work proper commenced. A few Boys were set to filling tubs underground, but the majority, depending on their previous experience, worked in transport, maintenance, or in electrical or engineering roles. The Boys' primary role was to perform tasks that would release experienced and trained miners for work at the coalface so only a small proportion was actually employed in cutting coal. However, the Boys were entitled to some feelings of grievance. Some reported friction between them and those lads, younger than they were, who had gone into the mines straight from school aged fourteen and had already been working underground, either as pony drivers or cutting coal, for upwards of three years. A more justifiable complaint of the Boys was that no uniforms or badges were provided so they could easily be mistaken by the authorities or neighbours for draft dodgers. Moreover, although there was a significant proportion of conscientious objectors who accepted dangerous work in bomb disposal or, to a much lesser extent, as coal miners, most of the general public saw them in a wholly negative light and sometimes failed to differentiate between them and the Bevin Boys. Consequently, this often resulted in Boys suffering verbal or physical abuse. Although Boys might have seen their work as peripheral to the war effort, some would have been in far greater and more constant danger than many of those in uniform and were making a greatly more important contribution. Sadly, even when the scheme was ended in 1948, this achievement was never acknowledged, and the Boys received minimal recognition for their vital and sometimes perilous work. Only in 2008 was belated recognition awarded by Gordon Brown, the then prime minister. Unfortunately, this 'victory' was rather tarnished by the fact that recipients of medals were required to pay for them, so most did not bother. A very full account of the experiences of a Bevin Boy in Stoke-on-Trent between 1943 and 1947 appears on The Workers' War: Home Front Recalled website. Here, Douglas Ayres relates his training, the job, working conditions and lifestyle. As he said, sixty years on: 'no regrets, but I'm not going back'.

The Employment of Apprentices in Heavy Industry

It is often assumed, on the basis of the myths created by the politicians and the media, that the entire population of the UK was single-mindedly dedicated to the success of the war effort to the exclusion of all else. Much of the time this may well have held true, but throughout the war there were instances of established practices over-riding any new wartime circumstances. Entrenched attitudes were particularly prevalent in some mining communities, shipyards, and docks, where the management might very often have been regarded by elements of the workforce as the real enemy rather than the Nazis. The politics engendered by these enmities might only exacerbate the situation, especially when Russia was, initially, the official enemy, soon to become an official ally; members of the Communist Party found it difficult to adjust to changes in the official line. In March 1941, prior to the German invasion of Russia, a by-election was held on the Clyde in the Labour-held seat of Dunbartonshire. This took place during a period of truce for the major political parties, but saw a communist candidate stand, securing 15 per cent of the vote, and enjoying significant support among the shipyard workers. While conditions for all such workers were poor (the John Brown yard had to be personally persuaded by Churchill to provide a canteen for its workers), the apprentices felt particularly hard done by and may have latched onto the communist *zeitgeist*. On the one hand, the employers chose to regard them as learners, under a contractual agreement with their parents and, therefore, denied the right to Union representation. On the other hand, despite the introduction of new techniques that allowed apprentices to become just as productive as older workers, they continued to be paid at much lower rates. A Ministry of Information (MoI) bulletin (No. 24, 19.03.1941) also cited their more specific complaint of being paid less than government trainees but of having to do their work for them as they lacked the necessary skills and knowledge. The trainees were, additionally, reported as being regarded by the apprentices as 'dodging military service'. It may be worth noting here that British and Commonwealth troops often voiced their disgust that they risked their lives for 2*s* 6*d* (£6.25) per day while many of those at home were earning in excess of £1 (£50) and US troops were far more generously paid, earning around 10*s* (£25).

Jeffrey describes the situation where members of the local Young Communists League, impatient with the progress of Union negotiations relating to pay and conditions, formed an unofficial and unrecognised committee. This was described by the MoI as 'a Communist "shadow" organisation' and the employers refused to enter into negotiations with it. Ignoring the Coalition Government's ban on industrial action (Order 1305) as well as the implications of breaking their own indentures, the committee then promoted a series of strikes involving several thousand apprentices in the Clydeside shipyards but unsupported financially by the Union. It would take the intervention of the Ministry of Labour to resolve the situation by forcing through an agreement with the employers, which guaranteed percentages of a journeyman's wage on a sliding scale based on age, collectively negotiated as minimum wages. The Clydeside apprentices returned to work but, by then, the action had spread to parts of Lancashire, especially to Manchester, where it was centred on Metropolitan Vickers/AEI; to Coventry; and to Harland & Wolff's shipyard in Belfast. Some thousands more apprentices came out on strike, only returning to work following reports of threats of immediate conscription into the forces of 1,100 lads of appropriate age. Apprentices were often well-organised and established their own networks. The Tyneside Apprentices Guild had begun in 1942 and was instrumental in organising a strike two years later where the issues remained pay; the proposal to conscript 10 per cent of them into the mines; and training, especially the lack of opportunities for day release. The Tyne-siders gained support for their action from fellow apprentices in Glasgow, Huddersfield, and Teesside and a claimed total of 26,000 joined the strike. A further bone of contention was the shipyard employers' imposition of a new status of 'improver', postponing by two years the time-served apprentice's promotion to journeyman craft-worker and the right to earn full adult pay. Apprentices also participated in the notorious strike at the Vickers Armstrong yard at Barrow-in-Furness in 1943. Unofficial strikes clearly alarmed the establishment and brought forth the following question, posed by an MP in the Commons, who enquired of Bevin:

> ... what policy he proposes to adopt in order to deal with them; and whether he will seek powers to punish those responsible, whether employers, workers, or outsiders, by death or imprisonment for life?
>
> *Hansard*, Volume 393, Columns 1027-9, 14 October, 1943

While recognising the existence of benign and paternalistic employers seeking the best for their apprentices, it is difficult to attribute the delays in paying adult wages to an altruistic employer's stated aim of gradually easing the apprentice into the adult world. Another nuanced element is the matter of the true extent of political involvement in the apprentices' industrial action. Employers both over-emphasised and understated left-wing or communist influence and the apprentices themselves both boasted and repudiated their political affiliations. Apprentice strikes in peacetime had been seen by their employers as causing little economic damage to business, so it was against their wishes that the government justified a court of inquiry into the 1941 Clydeside strike by arguing that 'essential government work was affected by these stoppages'. One of the few issues raised by the apprentices at the inquiry was the continuous deskilling of craft work. This implied an erosion of the future of that very secure skilled employment, which had hitherto constituted the carrot that motivated low-paid apprentices in the first place. The MoI charitably noted that the striking apprentices offered their services in the clearing up operations following the devastating air raids on Clydebank, but Clydeside's strike leaders, where they could be identified, were nevertheless still prosecuted. Two of the young leaders, despite their reserved occupation status, suddenly received their call-up papers and only the threat of a total Clydeside strike reversed this ill-considered decision. Three years later, following the strikes originating on Tyneside, it was members of the Revolutionary Communist Party, or Trotskyists, who, despite the lack of any evidence, would face prosecution, cast by the Cabinet as providers of the apprentices' external support, and held responsible for instigating the strike.

Young People in Agriculture

In 1932, almost half of Norfolk's school-leavers went into agriculture, but they were entering a shrinking and ageing workforce that would decrease by 25 per cent between 1918 and 1939, while the area of land under cultivation would contract by 2.5 million acres (1,000,000 ha) across the country. The total number of people employed in agriculture in Great Britain in 1939 was 607,000, fewer than 4 per cent of the workforce, and earning only two-thirds of the average pay of other working-class groups. In rural areas, it nevertheless remained the norm that children from farming families, who had already become inured to missing school in harvest time, would quit school at fourteen and join their fathers as agricultural labourers. When war broke out in 1939, despite being notionally in reserved occupations, many farmworkers enlisted. In Devon, where over half the agricultural workers were being paid less than the minimum wage, 10,000 labourers were lost, but the War Agricultural Executive Committee (WAEC) still demanded that the acreage under cultivation must be doubled. Northamptonshire's total arable acreage almost trebled during the war, from 112,000 acres (44,800 ha) in 1939 to almost 300,000 acres (120,000 ha) by 1945, a momentous achievement, when the large-scale requisitioning of land for airfields and military training areas is also taken into account. Agriculture was overseen by WAECs, which had, under the provisions of DORA, the power to tell farmers what to grow and where to grow it. Nationally, between 1939 and 1945, the area given over to arable farming increased by over 60 per cent and food production increased extensively: wheat by 240 per cent; potatoes by 6 per cent; meat by 20 per cent; sugar by 75 per cent; eggs by 22 per cent; and bacon by up to 10 per cent. The agricultural workforce, however, grew by only 27 per cent (163,000) between 1939 and 1945, to include nearly 60,000 POWs, 80,000 members of the Women's Land Army and small numbers of conscientious objectors and volunteers. Given that the cohort of children, notionally to be denied to the employment market as a consequence of the proposed raising of the school-leaving age to fifteen, was assessed at just 160,000, most of whom would have gone anywhere but into agriculture, fourteen-year-old school-leavers can have accounted for only a tiny part of the increase in the agricultural workforce. Such was the concern in the spring of 1940 that, in the context of a wider debate on the Board of Education (noted in *Hansard*, 3 May 1940, Col. 243 *et seq.*), it was reported in parliament:

> Plans have been prepared, in consultation with the representatives of headmasters, for encouraging the older boys leaving public and secondary schools to take whole-time employment in agriculture, as a form of national service for the war period or until they are called up for military duty.

Despite the history of the WLA's successes in the Great War, there appears to have been no parallel suggestion aimed at girls' schools whose older leavers were at liberty to join the WLA, but only on their own initiative.

As the farms lost more of their labour to conscription, alternative sources needed to be found. Both the WLA and prisoners of war (POW), particularly Italians but after D-Day more Germans as well, plugged many of the gaps, but it remained necessary to find more hands. The WLA that had operated successfully in the Great War was revived in 1939 with around 1,000 volunteers. Officially, no one under the age of eighteen would be accepted unless she was 'exceptional in physique and mentality'. In practice, as can be found by reading the accounts of Land Girls themselves, many joined as young as sixteen. Even, or maybe especially, after the introduction of conscription, girls continued to join the WLA at seventeen and a half, in order to avoid being directed to munitions factories or unpopular bodies such as the ATS, which was held in general low esteem by the public. However, those girls under eighteen who had managed to join could not officially expect to be paid anything until they attained the official starting age. In some counties, including Essex, underage Land Girls did receive pay, but could be guaranteed only three-quarters of the going rate. Following the introduction of conscription with the National Service Act of 1941, single women and childless widows between the ages of twenty and thirty could opt for service in the WLA, and the lower age limit for these categories was later reduced to nineteen. Eventually, the WLA would number around 80,000 Land Girls who were either billeted in groups of twenty to forty in hostels, or individually on farms. This could cause deep culture shock for young city raised girls who might be living away from home for the first time. Payment, which could be spasmodic, was made by the individual farmer and there were regional differences. Farmers were known to take on the under-eighteens and then sack them when they reached the age when they had to be paid more. Land Girls, although uniformed, enjoyed none of the welfare benefits, such as travel warrants and access to NAAFIs and other clubs for service personnel open to all other sectors. Even some YWCA branches refused to have anything to do with them. One cause of deep-felt resentment for the Land Girls was that while they were often fed notoriously badly, signatories of the Geneva Convention were required to provide POWs with the same level of rations as their armed forces. Land Girls recall watching POWs cooking bacon and brewing coffee while the girls ate their beetroot sandwiches in the rain. In fact, the Land Girls had arguably the worst deal of all the support services, very much at the mercy of farmers. As with evacuees, some placements were with kind, generous, and sympathetic people, who treated their girls as family, but many were not, representing families to which no one would willingly choose to belong. It was all a matter of chance. There are also instances of girls as young as fourteen working as orderlies in WLA hostels in parallel situations to domestic service. Up to 60,000 POWs, a few as young as sixteen, worked on the land, either in large gangs or in twos and threes on individual farms. Many of them were effectively unsupervised but presumably found agricultural work, sustained by military level rations, carried out in generally amenable circumstances, a lesser evil than escape and deployment to the Eastern Front.

Farm Work for Children

One solution to the labour shortage on the land was to put children to work. As early as May 1940, a question was asked in parliament regarding Westmorland County Council's proposal to allow the employment of schoolchildren of any age in agriculture. Gloucestershire's Agricultural Board decided in 1940 that any fit child over ten should work on the land. A clearing house was set up at Berkeley House, Berkeley Street, Gloucester, for farmers to access schoolboy labour. One boy in Tetbury described how he was expected to work on a farm for at least an hour each day after school, and half-days on Saturdays and Sundays. Tasks included milking, feeding animals, and harnessing up wagons. By the time he was twelve, he was driving the farm's new tractor, being scrupulously careful not to stall it as he had discovered the hard way that he lacked the strength to use the starting handle. Evacuee children were also able to contribute. A girl of nine reported getting a card that got her off school to go potato-picking with the promise of an extra cheese ration and clothing coupons as an enticement. A question was asked in parliament in May 1942 regarding the supervision of those under-fourteens volunteering for farm work. The reply referenced a Board of Education publication, which laid out the rules. From the time-honoured way in which parliamentary questions are posed, it might be inferred that these regulations were not universally being rigorously applied. Across Britain, parents, teachers, and school inspectors raised concerns about the balance to be struck between the needs of the nation for food production and the health and educational needs of the children involved. Attempts were made to ensure that the existing legislation was applied but the educational authorities were already committed to a policy of cooperation with the agricultural agencies. The compromise most often agreed was the adjustment of school holidays to dovetail with the needs and demands of the farming year, but this was not always welcomed since it meant that children would miss the benefits of good weather if their 'summer' holiday came in October. In England, LEAs were asked to reschedule school holidays to coincide with harvesting, including a three-week break in October for the potato harvest. In Scotland, unauthorised absences continued and, despite the efforts of safe-guarding groups, the relevant, but effectively unenforceable byelaws, were flagrantly flouted. In England and Wales, legislation was passed limiting the employment of children over twelve in seasonal farm work to thirty-six hours per week and no more than seven hours per day. The Scottish Educational Department (SED) came under pressure from the Department of Agriculture for Scotland (DAS) to eschew such regulations and made increasingly heavy demands on children's labour. By 1943, some 40 per cent of those over eleven were needed for farm work: fruit picking, grain harvesting, and potato lifting, which required the labour of 56,000 children. The Scottish situation had been summed up in 1941 by the DAS as 'The three Rs or Potatoes?' and the spuds would usually prevail. Children in large numbers, often those very children who could least afford to miss out on considerable periods of schooling, continued to be granted exemptions from school attendance.

Schoolchildren and Harvest Camps

Harvest camps developed over time in a piecemeal way as children were mobilised to lend a hand. Some of them were arranged for organised groups such as the Scouts and Guides, or for rurally located boarding schools. Typical of many such efforts, boys from Oundle School began helping on local farms from the autumn of 1939, cycling over after school, and putting in a total of 1,200 hours in October alone. Additionally, the school ran its own farm, growing vegetables and raising livestock. In the summer of 1940, boys stayed on at school during the holidays to work on local farms, some being billeted on the farms themselves. They were paid 6*d* (£1.25p) per hour for long working days. In 1940, Shaftesbury GS cadets attended harvest camp instead of the cancelled cadet camp. During the 1941 summer holidays, Oundle boys worked on a total of forty-five different farms, and a farm camp for thirty boys was set up by the Scouts at Achurch with meals being taken, due to the incessant rain, in the village hall. In the summer term of 1942, boys from Shrewsbury School put in 5,500 hours on Shropshire's farms. Back in Oundle, two three-week-long projects were organised in 1943, involving 250 boys working a total of 100,000 hours. One group of six boys occupied a cottage for a fortnight and were brought meals by local ladies. They were paid for their hedging and ditching efforts but after deductions for bed and board of 14*s* (£35) they were left with just 4*s* (£10) per week, which works out at around £0.20p per hour in 2021 values. Girls from Colston School in Bristol spent their Easter and summer holidays at Slimbridge, planting and picking potatoes. ATC cadets, earmarked for the RAF and awaiting actual call-up, were put to harvesting by the Ministry of Labour. The local authority in Northamptonshire, had found it difficult to absorb the costs of over 8,000 evacuee children in its schools. However, the presence of so much potential teenage labour went some way to offsetting the disadvantages. By 1942, the county's arable acreage had more than doubled, and this extra land which had been brought into use was generally used to increase the production of potatoes and sugar beet. The harvesting of such crops was extremely labour intensive, so evacuees eased the problem to a great extent. However, given the scale of the labour shortfall, this haphazard and undependable provision would still prove inadequate.

One possible solution lay in the systematic establishment of regular, large-scale harvest camps. By 1940, twenty-five camps organised the work of 8,000 children over the summer period. Throughout the war, trade unions, parents, and teachers objected to the compulsory use of schoolchildren for agricultural labour on social and educational grounds, but after the practice had been legalised by Defence Regulations in May 1942, the Board of Education and the Ministry of Agriculture collaborated with the county WAECs to find ways of reconciling the desperate need for food and the needs of children. By 1943, the membership of the WLA represented nearly half the available additional workforce, but it had taken a long time to reach that figure and labour was permanently scarce. In the early years of the war, the workforce was supplemented by volunteers including evacuees in essentially small-scale and local *ad hoc* arrangements, but this effort, however laudable, was still insufficient. Individual schemes included the maximisation of tractor use by training 4,000 senior pupils as drivers. Boys from Winchester, Malvern, Westminster, and Dulwich all benefited from the novel experience of putting in long arduous hours for minimal financial return. For those organising camps on a larger scale, it was an enormous logistical operation to produce tentage, cooking facilities, latrines, and so forth for large numbers of children. Accounts of Roundhay School in Leeds described boys working from early morning until 10 p.m. some days to get the harvest in. Girls from Lewes went to a farm camp during August 1943, those under fifteen being paid 5*d* (£1) per hour and those over-fifteen, 7*d* (£1.40p). Girls' camps were also organised for Girl Guides and the Girls' Training Corps, carrying out such tasks as fruit picking, and like the WLA before them, overcoming farmers' initial scepticism regarding their capabilities. In the peak year of 1943, there was a total of 1,068 camps attended by nearly 70,000 boys and girls, in the ratio of 2:1, providing over 274,000 boy/girl working weeks. Boys from Manchester GS were involved in a whole range of compulsory activities, with whole classes being taken out to a farm for a day's pea or potato-picking and in their summer holidays, they attended camps for fruit-picking and harvesting corn. One boy recorded the competition between the masters and the Land Girls to see who could carry the most stooks, with the Land Girls achieving a decisive victory. Given the conflicting demands for cadets' time, attempts were made from 1941 onwards, to integrate harvest work with military training by organising summer camps which met those dual aims.

Timber was another vital resource that required careful management and harvesting. The Women's Timber Corps was first formed in Scotland in 1941 with 1,000 members. These had to be aged seventeen and a half or over, but girls as young as fourteen managed to enrol. The organisation was extended to England and Wales the following year as a sub-set of the WLA but with the lower age limit of twenty. Members would eventually number around 6,000 'lumber-jills' but could never provide sufficient labour for so enormous a task and alternative, supplementary sources needed to be tapped. Boys from Manchester GS were involved in felling silver birch trees for pit-props. In 1942, fifty Girl Guides from the north-east camped out, most probably in Kielder Forest, where the Ministry of Labour had established hutted camps for unemployed men in the 1930s. The Guides were employed cutting the lower branches off fir trees, a back-breaking activity known as 'brashing', but they achieved their target of one hundred trees a day for two weeks. That same year, boys from Shrewsbury School gave almost 1,000 hours of their summer holidays to forestry work.

Young People and Voluntary Work

Service to the Community

One of the vital activities that youngsters helped with was organising evacuees. Schools in reception areas were usually designated as the processing centres for evacuees and their pupils helped with billeting and settling in. Scouts and Guides helped to organise evacuation, and boys from schools in rural reception areas such as Oundle helped to guide evacuees to local billets. Children of billeting officers helped with administration, messages, etc., and one fifteen-year-old in Bedford was loaned from her school to help with the administration of the evacuation process at the town hall. She was hoping to go for teacher training but as many of the colleges were closing for the duration and as she was only getting half-time teaching since her school had taken in an evacuated school, she accepted the offer of a part-time post with the council. She was soon heavily involved in preparing vacant properties for occupation by evacuees. A Guide in Maidstone helped out at the town hall as evacuees were arriving. She arranged accommodation, set up information centres, and organised the welcome for an evacuated school from south London. Another sixteen-year-old girl, whose father was a billeting officer, helped him by taking on the administrative functions of drawing up the forms and acting as his messenger. Girl Guides had earlier been involved when, from December 1938, following the violence of *Kristallnacht*, the first *Kindertransport* had arrived in Britain bringing unaccompanied Jewish children from Germany and Austria. Within a year, over 10,000 children had arrived. They gathered at reception centres such as Lauriston Road School in Hackney before being despatched to the four corners of Britain to be fostered, with Guides being involved in every aspect of the operation. In

Perthshire, there were problems in finding billets for children evacuated from the slums of Glasgow. A large house was identified and staffed by Guiders who had themselves been evacuated from their hostel for Guides and Brownies in Margate on the vulnerable south coast. Forty children could be accommodated, with more arriving at holiday times, and a strictly maintained Guiding regime was established. When a leader could be found, an Air Scout troop was also started up for the older boys. All the children took part in harvesting and salvage operations, fundraising, processions, and entertainments.

Two particularly noteworthy projects undertaken by the Girl Guides took place in the north. Waddow Hall is a seventeenth-century Grade II listed manor-house near Clitheroe, which was purchased by the Girl Guides Association in 1928 as a Ranger Guiders' training centre. Early in the war, it was converted into an emergency children's isolation hospital for Lancashire County Council. In Scotland, during the first days of the war, the Girl Guides Association set up Northfields House at St Abbs Head as the Trefoil School, its name adopted as a reference to the Girl Guides' badge, for twenty physically disabled children, aged six to sixteen, who would otherwise have had nowhere remotely suitable to go as evacuation plans often failed to include them in their arrangements. The school subsequently moved to other locations near Edinburgh and continued into the 1970s.

There were very many less ambitious, but equally valuable, ways in which youngsters could help their neighbours. The restrictions that the blackout regulations imposed landed all sorts of burdens on the general public. For many, the old, the sick or disabled, just the act of obtaining and installing blackout material was a problem which youngsters, particularly Girl Guides with their dexterity and sewing skills, could solve. In the darkened streets, it could be even more of a problem for everyone who had to travel by vehicle or on foot. On the Home Front, road traffic accidents caused more casualties in the early part of the war than enemy action. Guides helped to ameliorate this by painting trees, gateposts, kerbs, and lampposts with whitewash, while air cadets and Boy Scouts helped to erect sandbag walls to protect hospitals and first aid posts.

Entertainment and hospitality were other areas where the young could help. When the RAF took over a school in Langton Matravers (see Chapter 2), the local Girl Guides teamed up with the RAF personnel to run Christmas parties and to provide presents for village children and evacuees, as well as forming a choir to sing carols. Impromptu shows were put on to entertain communities where people had to organise their own amusements. These activities could be especially valuable during the Blitz when terrified children could be distracted by a singsong. In some areas, clubs were run for evacuees so they could stay in contact with their scattered compatriots, and youngsters themselves were the obvious choice to run these activities. Members of the Boys Brigade and the Girls' Life Brigade would put on displays and band concerts. Work with children in all settings benefited from an increased workforce and Girl Guides were particularly helpful in supplementing the staff of nurseries, many of which were opened to allow mothers to work in munitions factories, or in voluntary groups such as the WVS, founded in 1938 to help with ARP and evacuation services, and one million strong by 1943.

Welfare and Medical Help

The official age for joining first aid organisations such as the Red Cross and the St John Ambulance Brigade was eighteen, but the St Andrew's Ambulance Association, in Scotland, with branches in some parts of northern England, accepted recruits at sixteen. However, youngsters had little trouble in becoming involved with such bodies at much younger ages. Most young people in uniformed organisations were taught first aid and some attended evening classes to learn more. Some, even as young as fifteen, became instructors, passing on their skills to others. The St John Ambulance and the Red Cross assembled teams of girls aged fifteen to eighteen to work in hospitals, first aid posts, and blood transfusion centres. Girls were even trained to help mothers giving birth in shelters during air-raid alerts. Girl Guides working in Maidstone's blood transfusion centre fitted the bungs and tubes into the bottles, ready for the blood to flow into them. As it became increasingly difficult to recruit labour, many of those older Girl Guides working in hospitals found themselves taking on more responsible tasks such as giving injections and handing out medication. First aid training proved of vital importance during air raids when the medical services might easily be overwhelmed by the sheer numbers of the seriously injured. If trained youngsters were present to deal with the minor injuries and walking wounded, then the full-time medical professionals could better devote their attentions to priority cases. Able-bodied Boy Scouts over fourteen could become stretcher-bearers and both Scouts and Guides administered first aid to victims including giving pain-killing injections to those who might be trapped and awaiting rescue. Two of Croydon's Scout Troops provided dozen-strong squads of boys at the Mayday Hospital, Thornton Heath, and other local troops supplied similar support for Croydon General Hospital. The boys, aged from fourteen upwards initially took on general portering tasks, fire-watching, and liaising with patients' families by carrying messages back and forth. They were equipped with steel helmets and heavy-duty gasmasks. As the horrors of the Blitz unfolded, they found themselves carrying patients, including new-born babies, downstairs to relative safety in the cellars; unloading incoming ambulances and assessing casualties; and helping to clean up operating theatres. In January 1944, the town clerk of Sherborne, who was an employee of the boys' school, requested the services of older boys as stretcher-bearers to help when hospital trains arrived at Sherborne railway station to be unloaded *en route* to the nearby US Army military hospital. With the opening of the Second Front on the horizon and an influx of wounded soldiers expected, it was essential to get this important procedure established and rehearsed. Although it was bombing that caused the majority of those casualties attributable to enemy action, Dover also suffered incessant shelling from the enemy's long-range guns between July 1940 and September 1944, causing constant casualties among service personnel and civilians alike, at entirely unpredictable intervals. Girl Guide first-aiders were kept busy caring for seriously injured casualties until specialist medical help might arrive.

Bringing relief to the plight of bombed-out families was another area where Girl Guides could make a difference, collecting and distributing clothes, and generally helping out in the rest centres. Using their trek cart, Guides in Leamington collected clothes, shoes, and toys and delivered them to people bombed out of Coventry and being cared for in Warwick Hospital. They then carted blankets and clothing for distribution in Coventry itself. During the *Baedeker* raids on Canterbury, Girl Guides set up feeding stations and soup kitchens, using their camping and cooking skills to feed large numbers of those taking refuge in the shelters and rest centres. At the height of the various bombing offensives, ARP workers might find themselves on duty for stretches of anything up to seventy-two hours, so it was important to get hot drinks and food to them which could be consumed on the hoof. One Guide Company in Manchester converted a horsebox as a mobile canteen and took it round the country's bombed areas, and girls from Sherborne School set up a mobile canteen after the town had been bombed. In Guildford, senior girls from Tormead School helped WVS members provide refreshments to soldiers fresh from the beaches of Dunkirk, and students of French were encouraged to visit wounded French soldiers in hospital. Guides improvised field kitchens to produce meals in sparsely equipped rest centres. In Nottingham, Rangers and Guiders were responsible for staffing the George Street rest centre and were rostered to sleep in groups there for a week at a time. The government acknowledged that, beyond such emergencies, many Girl Guides had cookery skills that they could put to good use by helping people to make the most of their rations to produce interesting and nutritious dishes, often including as examples, fruit and vegetables, which they had grown on their own Guide Company allotments.

As more women were gathered up into the munitions industry, many of them would be the mothers of young children. Local authorities and individual factories all opened crèches and nurseries for the youngest babies up to school age but found it difficult to staff them. This was another area where Girl Guides helped, gaining their childcare badges in the process. Schoolchildren were also roped in to do clerical work for the local council or the local food office, which had mountains of new ration books awaiting issue, all needing names, addresses and National Insurance numbers written in laboriously, but accurately, by hand.

In London, Sea Rangers were absorbed into the Thames River Emergency Service. This came under the aegis of the Port of London Authority and was intended to evacuate casualties from severely bombed neighbourhoods bordering the Thames. It used requisitioned pleasure steamers, converted into ambulance boats by installing tiers of double bunks. Each steamer carried a doctor, two registered nurses, two volunteer Red Cross nurses, and two Rangers as signallers, whose job it would be to communicate with the fire boats using their semaphore skills. Three such vessels were the *Mapledurham*, the *Cliveden*, and the *Marchioness*. The *Marchioness* had been launched in 1928 for use as a Thames pleasure boat, had been involved in the Dunkirk evacuation and had then been requisitioned and based at Dagenham. She would be sunk in a collision with a dredger in 1989 when fifty-one passengers drowned. The *Cliveden* continued to operate into the 1990s, and the *Mapledurham* remained active well into the twenty-first century.

Some of the boys from the Quakers' Bootham School in York, as pacifists, joined the Friends' Ambulance Unit, and two of their number were killed when the ship they were travelling on was torpedoed. Girl Guides were bluntly informed that if they were subject to a conscientious objection to contributing to the war effort, they had two choices: they could keep their solemn promise to help other people at all times by involving themselves in first aid, civil defence, or other humanitarian activities, or they could resign from the movement.

Home Industry Workshops in Schools

As well as providing agricultural workers, especially during the long summer holidays, many schools turned their practical workshops over to war production. At Oundle, building on a precedent created in the Great War, both wood and metal-working shops were busy meeting Ministry of Supply (MoS) orders. Tens of thousands of fittings and castings were made along with 12,000 wooden boxes for hand grenades. On learning that the local HAA battery never ran short of firing-pins owing to the school workshop providing a regular supply, the MoS placed an order for 30,000 pins for all types of weapons. Boys, especially those with nowhere else to go, were accommodated in the school itself and in local hostels so that work might continue through the school holidays. Boys at Peter Symonds School in Winchester spent their woodwork lessons making wings for Horsa gliders, and boys at Manchester GS used the school's metal-working lathes to manufacture small parts for the aircraft industry. As well as such work in small workshops, schoolchildren could volunteer to do jobs in munitions factories. One boy, whose father was a pacifist minister, had to explain that while he was comfortable growing vegetables for the war effort, he could not make models for aircraft recognition classes.

Fundraising

Throughout the war, the government was desperate to raise funds to meet the crippling daily cost of the war, which was somewhere close to £20 million (£1 billion). Funds were raised in many ways and it was members of the uniformed youth organisations who played a key part in achieving the high targets set. The National Savings Movement had its origins in the Great War as a way of raising war-loans from the small investor and had been largely administered by local committees of volunteers. In 1939, the War Office reinstated the scheme and local savings groups, often based in schools, were formed to raise money for the war effort. As well as collecting funds for unspecified use by the government, separate funds were set up for specific purposes. By the autumn of 1940, over 1,000 appeals had been launched to pay for Spitfire fighter aircraft. The target for a Spitfire was set at a notional £5,000, equal to a significant £250,000 in today's money, as a means of making the raising of such a sum appear attainable. The actual cost of a production Spitfire in 1940 was £6,200 (£310,000) soon rising to just under £9,000 (£450,000), but Nottinghamshire towns such as Mansfield and Retford would take as much pride in meeting their £5,000 target as did Henley-on-Thames or Woolworths. At the end of their news broadcasts, the BBC would announce the names of places or organisations that had successfully reached these targets and certificates and presentation scrolls were produced locally to mark the achievement. It is reckoned that sums exceeding a total of £13 million pounds (£650 million) were raised in this way and Lord Beaverbrook estimated that 1,500 aircraft had been financed through such voluntary contributions. Although, in reality, none of this money was ever earmarked for building Spitfires, this method of raising funds allowed people of modest means to engage with the war effort and to feel they were doing their bit. Later in the war, fundraising efforts would be devoted to a particular focus such as Tank Week and Aircraft Week, providing reinforcement to the tangible and visible results of people's sacrifice. Most of these activities involved processions and other events, which relied heavily on the efforts of the uniformed youth organisations to provide marching bands, display teams, and cheerleaders. Girl Guides were particularly active in assigning themselves apparently impossible targets for specific aims. In May 1940, the designated Guide Gift Week set itself the target of raising £20,000 (£1 million) for the purchase of an Airspeed Oxford flying ambulance for the RAF. In the event, they raised over £46,000 (£2.3 million), which paid for two of the aircraft as well as twenty motor ambulances for the Royal Navy and more besides. Commonweal Lodge School for girls in Purley had opened in 1916, but when its buildings were requisitioned by the military in 1941, it had moved to Okehampton in Devon, making a further move to Gloucestershire in 1944. One of the school's pupils was Pat Moss, sister of the racing driver Stirling, and a future rally driver herself but, perhaps, better known as a star of show-jumping. She proved instrumental in inaugurating Fairford's Horse Show and Gymkhana, all of whose proceeds went to the local cottage hospital.

Salvage Collection

Gather up your salvage, gather up your salvage,
Gather up your salvage and help to win the war.
Gather from your uncles, gather from your aunties,
Gather from your grandmas and help to win the war.

Chorus sung in a school in Co. Durham
Quoted by a contributor to BBC People's War

For a country denied many of its accustomed imports through enemy action at sea, recycling became an extremely important activity that relied on time, enthusiasm, and effort, all attributes available to the young. Nothing would be thrown away and a whole range of materials and objects, previously regarded as junk, would become valued elements in the struggle to survive. While some of the high-profile campaigns to turn pots and pans into Spitfires, and the wanton and needless destruction of ornamental gates and railings, may be regarded in cynical hindsight as little more than attempts to engage the populace in the progress of the war, the vast majority of collected scrap metal was put to good use. In York, as in many other places, a legitimate excuse for disposing of a Great War tank and cannon from the Crimean War will have been welcomed. Paper, rags, bones (mainly animal), bottles, and jam jars could all be recycled. Jam jars were sold back to jam factories such as Moorhouses in Leeds where the proceeds went into the fund to replace the aircraft carrier *Ark Royal*, which the city had adopted. What little food that was not consumed by human agency went into the pig-bins, which sustained private pig clubs.

Foraging could produce a variety of valuable items. Nuts and berries, rich in vitamins and nutrients, could brighten up the often dull fare on offer. Wild fruits would go into pies and preserves. Medicinal herbs went to hospitals and domestic medicine chests alike. Acetone was an important ingredient of explosives and could be sourced from acorns and conkers for supply to the ordnance factories. Wool from hedgerows went to stuff cushions for NAAFI canteens and garments were deconstructed to be recycled into warm clothing for sailors on the Arctic convoys.

The Guides' motto became 'Save All Supplies' as the principles of thrift were more widely adopted. It was now anti-patriotic to waste anything whether it be food, textiles, paper, old iron, tins, or glass. If it could not be recycled, then it could be cleaned and reused for its original purpose. As the little ships brought the BEF back from the beaches of Dunkirk, questions were being asked in parliament about instructions going out to schools to ensure that sacks were made available for the collection of wastepaper. Collection points for salvage were established in every village, town, and suburb by, especially, Scouts and Guides who often toured the streets with hand barrow or horse and cart for people to bring out their offerings. Items, once taken for granted, suddenly became scarce and precious. Jute had to be imported and could be processed by only a small cluster of mills, mainly located in Dundee, so the insatiable demand for sandbags quickly swallowed up the entire supply. This meant, on the one hand, that grain sacks had to be collected and recycled and, on the other, that the use of sandbags was governed by a plethora of bureaucratic procedures.

Other Activities

At Christmas 1943, sixty boys and girls from Guildford's Royal GS and County School for Girls turned out to help sort the Christmas mail. On one day alone, they processed the 105,000 items, which had been posted in the neighbourhood. Knitting comforts and collecting books for soldiers also figured in many children's lives. The recipients of knitwear ranged from Free French and Allied sailors on the Arctic Convoy run, to aircrew in their freezing bombers. Patterns carried catchy slogans such as 'If you can knit, you can do your bit'. At Cropwell Bishop School, fifteen girls were provided with wool for knitting helmets, gloves, socks, mittens, and scarves for the Nottinghamshire Services' Comfort Fund. Elsewhere, generally girls—although some boys were also involved—knitted sea-boot socks for seamen out of heavy, oiled Shetland wool, displaying the indelible blue dye on their hands. Girls and boys as young as seven in Cirencester's schools, deep into sheep land, were knitting scarves, balaclava helmets, socks, blankets, and even hot-water bottle covers for the troops from early in 1940. As well as knitting, they were using a sewing machine to turn tailoring cloth into blankets for use in military hospitals. Soldiers at home on leave visited the schools to convey their appreciation of the children's efforts. Possibly one of the most unusual and widest range of activities carried out by a Girl Guide company would be seen at Whipsnade. When animals and their keepers' families were evacuated from Regent's Park, shortly to be joined by refugee children from Europe, a Girl Guide company became viable. Care and exercise of the animals became a major part of the girls' duties along with training in stalking, tracking, and Morse code. The Guides then undertook the training of the local Home Guard in fieldcraft and Morse. The zoo also had a rifle club, so the girls learned to shoot, winning competitions against the Home Guard and the RAF. They became messengers, guides, and signallers for the Home Guard and turned out with them for defence exercises at night, utilising their local knowledge and youthful energy in helping to outwit the attacking regular troops.

Conclusion

At the end of hostilities in May 1945, the House of Commons debated the burning question of demobilisation. There were apprenticeships and university courses to be resumed and completed; there were sons and daughters needing to return to their families' farms, factories, or shops; there were young men and women desperate to get on with their interrupted lives. At the same time, there were pressing priorities for releasing trades, such as the builders and electricians, plumbers, and plasterers, which needed to begin the task of replenishing the country's shattered housing; the doctors, dentists, nurses, and pharmacists to staff the projected new National Health Service; and all the engineers and technicians needed to reconstruct the nation's infrastructure and to set manufacturing on course to repay the crippling cost of the war by producing exports.

While the Education Act of 1944 had notionally been introduced, there still remained a long way to go in 1945. King George VI's speech to the Lords and

Commons, delivered on 15 August 1945 simply referred to the government's intention to 'bring into practical effect at the earliest possible date the educational reforms which have already been approved'. One point of disagreement in the Commons (noted in *Hansard*, 1945-06-11, Column 1336) was the apparent lack of ambition expressed in the act. It intended that only 15 per cent of children would have access to a secondary (i.e. grammar school) education. This represented no advance on the pre-war level of provision and might even be an overestimate as many MPs were inexplicably of the opinion that the advance of mechanisation in factories diminished the need for technical training. Apart from short-term issues such as the slow de-requisitioning of educational premises, there were major limits to improvement. A quarter of the teaching force consisted of retired teacher returners and married women, and while it was hoped many of them would stay on, the estimated shortfall in the profession stood at 60,000. This meant that the raising of the school leaving age (RoSLA), scheduled originally for 1939, would not now take place until 1947; class sizes would not be reduced for the foreseeable future; and FE colleges would not soon be able to achieve the expansion, necessary to produce the skilled workers vital for the development of the economy. Although, against all the odds, Ellen Wilkinson, Atlee's minister of education, met the planned deadline for RoSLA in January 1947, it would take another twenty years to resolve some of these other problems.

Beyond general expressions of appreciation for the support of the nation on the Home Front from both monarch and prime minister, there was no specific recognition, expressed by either of them, of the sacrifices made by the nation's youth, many of whom had missed their childhood and lost out on opportunities to invest in their futures. As Vera Brittain, despite the loss of close friends and relatives, had put it in respect of the Great War: '... it came to me not as a superlative tragedy, but as an interruption of the most exasperating kind to my personal plans...' She sought to 'rescue something that might be of value ... from the smashing up of my own youth by the war'. Her daughter, Shirley Williams, on the other hand, appears to have grasped the opportunities afforded by the war: spending time in the USA, mixing with national politicians, joining the Labour League of Youth, and, aged seventeen, being sent as a delegate at the end of the war to the youth wing of the German Social Democratic Party, before Oxford and a career in journalism and then politics. For most youngsters, however, life would fall somewhere in between these extremes.

The youth of the nation had given their efforts and, in some cases, their lives to contribute to survival and ultimate victory and one must hope that their achievements had been recognised and appreciated more specifically by the wider population and their descendants if not by the leadership.

APPENDIX I

Percentages of Children Evacuated from Thirty-Six Evacuation Areas

Birkenhead	62%	Middlesbrough	31%
Birmingham	25%	Newcastle	71%
Bootle	68%	Nottingham	22%
Bradford	25%	Portsmouth	30%
Clydebank	38%	Rosyth	36%
Coventry	20%	Rotherham	8%
Croydon	32%	Salford	76%
Derby	27%	Sheffield	15%
Dundee	37%	Smethwick	24%
Edinburgh	28%	Southampton	37%
Gateshead	71%	South Shields	31%
Glasgow	42%	Stretford	52%
Grimsby	12%	Sunderland	33%
Hull	36%	Tynemouth	32%
Leeds	33%	Wallasey	76%
Liverpool	61%	Walsall	18%
London	42%	West Bromwich	26%
Manchester	69%	West Hartlepool	36%

Notes:

1. The total of 827,000 unaccompanied (i.e. without their parents) school-aged children evacuated represented by these comparative percentages takes no account of returners or multiple operations. There were at least three evacuations from London (1939, 1940, and 1944) punctuated by the return of individuals and groups.
2. Manchester is credited with only having 25 per cent of children remaining in the city, which would suggest a significant number of the city's children were evacuated independently of official arrangements: with a parent; to relatives; or to a privately arranged billet.

(Data from Cliff & Smallman-Raynor)

APPENDIX II

London and Glasgow Schools in use by ARP Services

London

Balham, Cavendish Road School: AFS sub-station 86W
Battersea, Cologne Road School: AFS sub-station
Bethnal Green, Virginia Road School: AFS sub-station
Blackwall, Glenister Road Secondary School: AFS sub-station 54(?)
Bow, St Leonards Street, Old Palace Primary School: AFS sub-station
Canning Town, South Hallsville School: rest centre
Catford, St Dunstan's College: first aid post
City, Clerkenwell, Baltic Street School: AFS sub-station 68Z
City, Central Street LCC School: AFS sub-station 68U
City, Chequer Street LCC School: AFS sub-station 68V
Deptford, Stanley Street School: rest centre
Finchley, Hendon Lane, St Mary's School: first aid training centre, 1939
Finchley, Woodhouse School, basement: ARP reporting centre for Middlesex
Finchley, Woodhouse School: bomb disposal squad, 1939–41
Friern Barnet, Holly Park Infants' School: first aid post
Friern Barnet, Oakleigh Road North, Infants' School: first aid post
Friern Barnet, Oakleigh Park, St Andrews School: AFS station
Greenwich, Siebert Road, Invicta Road School: AFS sub-station 54X
Hackney, Cassland Road School: 41 BD Company. detachment base
Hackney, Lauriston Road School: evacuee reception centre
Hackney, Milborne Road School: AFS station 23X
Hampstead, Fleet Road School: first aid training
Harrow, Priestmead School: first aid depot (C.20)
Highbury, Canonbury School: rest centre
Highgate Hill, Whittington School: rest centre

Leytonstone, Trinity Street, Harrow Green School: HQ No. 3 CD Depot
Limehouse, Ricardo Street School: AFS sub-station 24Z
Mile End, St Leonard's Street school: AFS/NFS sub-station
Millwall, Cahir Street, St Cuthbert's School: AFS sub-station 35V
Millwall, Glengall Grove School: heavy rescue depot
Millwall, Harbinger Road School: AFS transport centre
Millwall, Janet Street, Central School: AFS station
Peckham, Denmark Hill, Grove Lane School: AFS sub-station 48Z (2)
Poplar, Saunders Ness Road, Cubitt Town School: AFS sub-station 35U
Southwark, West Square School: rescue service depot
Tooting Bec, Hydethorpe Road, Henry Cavendish PS: AFS sub-station 48Z
Wapping, St Peter's School: reserve shelter and first aid post
West Ham, Abbey Road School: ARP depot, NFS fire control and ambulance station
Woodford Green, St Aubyn's School: bomb disposal transport section
Woolwich, Mulgrave Place School: AFS sub-station 42W

Glasgow Area

Calton, Green Street, St James's School: AFS station SE
Clydebank, Boquhanran School: first aid post
Clydebank, Dalmuir School: first aid post
Clydebank, Hyndland, Notre Dame HS: first aid post
Clydebank, Hyndland School: shelter and rest centre
Clydebank, Janetta Street, Clydebank HS: first aid post and mortuary
Clydebank, North Elgin Street School: first aid post
Clydebank, Whitecrook School: shipyard workers' emergency hostel
Cowcaddens, 6 New City Road, Dundas Vale School: AFS station C4
Croftfoot, Crofthill Road, Croftfoot School: AFS station S4
Dennistoun, Onslow Road, Whitehill School: AFS station E1
Drumoyne, Kenneth Drive, Elder Park School: AFS station SW1
Finnieston, Hyde Park School: AFS station W1
Gilshochill, Kilmun Street, St Mary's School: ARP post
Glasgow Centre, 134 Montrose Street, Allen Glen School: AFS station C4
Glasgow Centre, Bishop Street, St Patrick's School: AFS station C3
Govanhill, Abbotsford Place, Abbotsford School: AFS station C5
Helensburgh, Clyde Street School: rest centre
Jordanhill, Jordanhill Drive, Jordanhill College: AFS station W3
Kelvingrove, Willowbank Crescent, Willowbank School: AFS station C3
Knightswood, Caldwell Avenue, Bankhead School: AFS station (ex 1)
Knightswood, Temple School: rest centre

Partick, St Peters School: AFS station W1
Penilee, Craigmuir School: AFS station SW2
Pollokshaws, Sir John Maxwell School: AFS station S3
Pollokshields PS: rest centre
Riddrie, Smithycroft Road, St Thomas's School: AFS station E1
Ruchill, Avenuepark Street, Eastpark School: rest centre
Springburn, Mollinsburn Street, St Mary's School: AFS station (V43)
Tollcross, Wellshot Road School: AFS station E

APPENDIX III

NW Suburban Relocation Plan for Air Ministry Departments

Harrow County Boys', Gayton Road; Harrow County Girls', Lowlands Road; Eastcote Lane Schools; The Belmont School; Wealdstone Bridge School, Station Road; Hibbert Road School; and Priestmead School, Hartford Avenue, Wealdstone. NB: These establishments, accommodating a total of 1,460 administrative staff, formed part of a complex of government buildings that included the Admiralty Citadel at Oxgate House, 403–5 Edgware Road; the Air Ministry Citadel, Station Z, in Headstone Drive; and the Post Office Research Station at Dollis Hill.

(Data drawn, in part, from Crisp (2006))

APPENDIX IV

Admiralty Shore Establishments using School Premises

Bath, Kingswood School: Admiralty R&D department
Brighton, Roedean School: HMS *Vernon (R)*
Campbeltown GS, Kintyre: HMS *Nimrod*
Devonport, Stoke Damerel School: HMS *Dominion*, HMS *Drake II*
Dover College: HMS *Lynx*
Droxford, Soberton Towers School: HMS *Mercury II*
Eastbourne College: HMS *Marlborough* (elements of HMSs *Collingwood* & *Defiance*)
Eastbourne, St Bede's School: HMS *Mercury II*
Edinburgh, Fettes College: HMS *Vernon*
Eton College: HMS *President II*
Felixstowe, St Margaret's, St Nicholas' & Church Road Schools: HMS *Europa*
Gosport, Bay House: HMS *Porcupine*
Highgate School: HMS *President V*
Hove, Mowden School: Royal Navy Selection Board & HMS *King Alfred III*
Lancing College: HMS *King Alfred II*
Malvern College: HMS *Duke* & TRE
Portsmouth GS: RN accommodation
Weymouth College: HMS *Kredemnon*
Witley, King Edward's School: HMS *Mercury II*, Admiralty Signals Establishment

APPENDIX V

Wartime Employment of Fourteen- to Eighteen-Year-Olds (1943)

According to the Office of National Statistics, specific employment figures for 1939–45 appear not to be generally available, mainly because the census scheduled for 1941 was not carried out. Noted in *Hansard* (Volume 128, para 990, House of Lords debate 4.08.1943), a figure of around 500,000 was claimed for those pupils in secondary education in 1943. This represented 15 per cent of the eleven- to eighteen-year-old cohort, assuming a minimum of 50 per cent of those pupils would leave school aged sixteen after matriculating, the fourteen to eighteen element, would be around 240,000, and the number of those in the fourteen to eighteen cohort in employment would be 1,360,000. The cohort of fourteen-year-old boys affected by the non-implementation of the raising of the school leaving age has been recorded as in the region of 160,000, which would provide a school-leaver total over four years of around 1.3 million, setting the average combined fourteen to eighteen age group, including those remaining in secondary education, at around 1,600,000 for any one year. The application of the immediate post-war breakdown of the industrial workforce showing relative proportions in different occupations as a guide, offers a plausible if rough guestimate:

In full-time secondary education	240,000 (15% of total 14–18 cohort)	240,000
Primary Sector		
Agriculture	26,880 (4%)	
Fishing	60,480 (9%)	
Coal mining	57,120 (8.5%)	144,480
Secondary Sector		
Cotton manufacture	22,175 (3.3%)	
Woollen manufacture	14,785 (2.2%)	
Building & contracting	115,585 (17.2%)	

Chemicals	38,305 (5.7%)	190,850
Metal goods & engineering	329,950 (49.1%)	329,950
Miscellaneous	6,720 (1%)	6,720
	(42% of total 14–18 cohort)	672,000

Tertiary or Service Sector
transport, retail, utilities, finance/clerical, education, health, domestic and hospitality, and also including employment in ARP, VAD, AFS/NFS, WLA and first aid

	(43% of total 14–18 cohort)	688,000
	(100% of total 14–18 cohort)	1,600,000

Note: 1943 saw the highest percentage of the total working population in employment at 76 per cent, but slightly fewer than 50 per cent of those in paid employment were in the primary sector (mining, agriculture, and fisheries) or secondary sector (manufacturing and construction). A quarter of fourteen-year-old school-leaver boys, around 20,000, worked as delivery boys in retail or the GPO. Government figures show that in the same year 7.25 million women, representing 36 per cent of those of working age, were in employment, with 46 per cent of those women aged between fourteen and fifty-nine engaged in National Service or other work contributing to the war effort.

Bibliography

After the Battle 87, *The High Wycombe Air Headquarters* (Stratford: 1995)

Archer, B., *The Internment of Western Civilians under the Japanese, 1941–1945: A Patchwork of Internment* (London: Routledge Curzon, 2004)

Ayres, D., *I was called up for National Service in the autumn of 1943* on The Workers' War: Home Front Recalled, www.unionhistory.info/workers'war

Barrett, D., *When the Germans Came. True stories of life under occupation in the Channel Islands* (London: Simon & Schuster, 2018)

www.bevinboysassociation.co.uk

museum.wales/articles/2008-01-03/Remembering-the-Bevin-Boys-in-the-Second-World-War/

www.bbc.uk/history/ww2peopleswar collected personal reminiscences from all sectors

British Information Service, *Labour & Industry in Britain 1953*

Brittain, V., *Testament of Youth* (London: Virago, 1978 reprint of 1933 edition)

Cliff, A., and Smallman-Raynor, M., *Atlas of Epidemic Britain: A Twentieth Century Picture* (Oxford: OUP, 2012)

Collins, L., *Cadets, the Impact of War on the Cadet Movement* (Oldham: Jade, 2001)

Crisp, G., *Preparation for War* (Thetford: Airfield Review 113, December 2006)

Downes, M., *Oundle's War* (Oundle: The Nene Press, 1995)

Edwards, S., *Youth Movements, Citizenship and the English Countryside, 1930–1960* (unpublished D.Phil. thesis, University of Sussex, 2013)

Gale, A., *A Century of Changes in the Mortality and Incidence of the Principal Infections of Childhood* (London: Medical Office, Ministry of Education, 1945)

Gardiner, J., *The Blitz, the British under attack* (London: Harper Press, 2010)

Gaskin, M., *Blitz, The Story of 29th December 1940* (London: Faber & Faber, 2005)

Gould, J., *The Witley site: What happened before NIO?*, www.oceanswormley.org/uploads/3/4/6/3/34638252/the_witley_site_v3_.pdf

Hampton, J., *How the Girl Guides Won the War* (London: Harper Press, 2010)

Herbert-Davies, A., *Children in the Second World War* (Barnsley: Pen & Sword, 2017)

hovehistory.blogspot.com>2015/11>hms-king-alfred-1939-1945-hove

Hoare, A., *Standing up to Hitler: The Story of Norfolk's Home Guard and Secret Army 1940–1944* (Wymondham: G. Reeve, 1997)

Hodgson, G., *Manchester & its press under the bomb* (unpublished Ph.D. thesis, University of Chester, 2014)

Jeffrey, A., *This Time of Crisis: Glasgow, the West of Scotland and the NW Approaches in the Second World War* (Edinburgh: Mainstream, 1993)
Lampe, D., *The Last Ditch* (London: Cassell, 1968)
Lavery, B., *Hostilities Only: Training the Wartime Royal Navy* (London: National Maritime Museum, 2004)
lesliesguidinghistory.webs.com/guidesatwar.htm
Lloyd, J., *The Scottish School System and the Second World War: a study in central policy and administration* (unpublished Ph.D. thesis, University of Stirling, 1979)
Longden, S., *Blitz Kids, The Children's War Against Hitler* (London: Constable, 2012)
Lowry, B., *The Shropshire Home Guard* (Almeley: Logaston, 2010)
Lowry, B., and Wilks, M., *The Mercian Maquis* (Almeley: Logaston, 2002)
Macleod, J., *River of Fire, the Clydebank Blitz* (Edinburgh: Birlinn, 2011)
Mayall, B., and Morrow, V., *You can help your country: English children's work during the Second World War* (London: Institute of Education, 2011)
Moore-Colyer, R., *Kids in the Corn: Harvest Camps and farm labour supply in England, 1940–50* in Agricultural History Review nd.
O'Flynn, K., *Post-Primary Education in West Ham 1918–39* (unpublished Ph.D. thesis, London Institute of Education, nd)
Ogley, B., *Kent at War 1939–45* (Westerham: Froglets Publications, 1994); *Surrey at War 1939–45* (Westerham: Froglets Publications, 1995)
O'Keefe, P., *The Lads' Army* in Loopholes 7 (Dover: Pillbox Study Group, 1994)
Overy, R., *The Bombing War* (London: Penguin, 2013)
Prescott, E., *Tonbridge At War* and www.blighty-at-war.net/fortress-tonbridge.html
Price, P., *Sayers Croft* Casefile 21 in British Archaeology 144, (York: CBA, 2015)
RCHME, *Pillbox at the Merchant Taylors' School, Rickmansworth, Hertfordshire* (1995)
Roberts, J., *The Significance of Circular 1486: The Service of Youth* (2004): www.infed.org/youthwork/circular1486.htm
Ryan, P., *Apprentice strikes in twentieth century UK engineering and shipbuilding* (London: King's College Management Centre, 2004)
Shaw, F. and J. (eds), *We Remember the Home Guard* (Hinckley: authors, 1990); *We Remember the Blitz* (London: Ebury Press, 2012)
Short, B., *The social impact of state control of agriculture in Britain 1939–1955* (Brighton: University of Sussex, 2009, www.kuleuven.be/icag/files/Brian_Short.pdf)
Smith, L., *Young Voices: British Children Remember the Second World War* (London: Viking & IWM, 2007)
Smith, V., *Anatomy of a Pillbox: Tonbridge School* (Maidstone: Kent County Council, 2018)
Starns, P., *Blitz Families: the children who stayed behind* (Stroud: The History Press, 2012)
Strange, K., *Cardiff Schools and the Age of the Second World War*; resources.hwb.wales.gov.uk/VTC/ngfl/history/Cardiff_schools_and_the_age_of_the_Second_World_War
Subterranea Britannica: www.subbrit.org
Summers, J., *Our Uninvited Guests* (London: Simon & Schuster, 2018)
Taylor, F., *Coventry Thursday 14 November 1940* (London: Bloomsbury, 2015)
Taylor, P., *Women Domestic Servants 1919–1939* (Birmingham: University of Birmingham Centre for Contemporary Studies, 1976)
Tyrer, N., *Stolen Childhoods: The untold story of the children interned by the Japanese in the Second World War* (London: Weidenfeld & Nicolson, 2011)
Westlake, R., *A Register of Territorial Force Cadet Units 1910–1922* (Wembley: Westlake, 1984)
Wilks, M., *Chronicles of the Worcestershire Home Guard* (Almeley: Logaston,2014)
Williamson, A., *East Riding Secret Resistance* (Midhurst: Middleton Press, 2004)
Wood, D., *Attack Warning Red: The Royal Observer Corps and the Defence of Britain 1925–92* (Portsmouth: Carmichael & Sweet, revised edition, 1991)
The Zuckerman Archive, University of East Anglia holds the Hull schoolchildren's essays.

Index

General Index

Schools and *Places*